INNOVATIVE
SALTWATER
FLIES

Yucatan Tarpon by Chet Reneson

INNOVATIVE
SALTWATER
FLIES

Bob Veverka
Color Plates by Michael Radencich

STACKPOLE
BOOKS

Copyright © 1999 by Stackpole Books

Published by
STACKPOLE BOOKS
5067 Ritter Road
Mechanicsburg, PA 17055
www.stackpolebooks.com

Printed in China

First edition

10 9 8 7 6 5 4 5 3 2 1

Cover design by Caroline Stover
Cover photo by Michael Radencich
Drawings by Bill Elliott

Cover photo

1	1 Acrylic Squid by Glen Mikkleson
2	2 Mackerel by Bob Veverka
3	3 Braid Ballyhoo by Bob Veverka
4 6	4 Furnace & Squirrel by Bob Lemay
5	5 Heywood's Ghost Shrimp by Scott Heywood
	6 Marquesa Sunrise Special by Jeffrey Cardenas

Library of Congress Cataloging-in-Publication Data

Veverka, Bob.
    Innovative saltwater flies/Bob Veverka.—1st ed.
        p.   cm.
    ISBN 0-8117-0902-7 (hardcover)
    1. Flies, Artificial.   2. Fly tiers.   3. Fly tying.   4. Saltwater fly fishing.
I. Title
SH451.V48   1998
688.7'9124—DC21   98-18049
                                                                CIP

Contents

*To the person who first thought
of putting feathers and fur
on a hook to catch a fish!*

Foreword

Some years ago Dave McNeese, a fly-shop owner in Salem, Oregon, told me about a prodigious fly-tying talent named Bob Veverka. Veverka, he explained, bought nineteenth-century salmon flies solely for the rare feathers he could salvage from them. Using these materials, he tied full-dressed Atlantic salmon flies historically accurate in every detail. McNeese showed me an example of Veverka's craftsmanship. "I wouldn't take a thousand dollars for the fly," said McNeese.

Veverka's tying skills were so evident that I contacted him at his home in Underhill, Vermont, for some flies to illustrate a book I was writing on steelhead fly fishing. Thus began a long and rewarding friendship. I soon learned that Veverka, unlike many skilled tiers, fly-fished a lot and did so for just about anything with fins. This included saltwater game fish like tarpon and bonefish in the Keys, and tuna and dorado off Mexico's East Cape. After a trip, we often talked over the phone and discussed fly patterns and the way they fished. Always generous with an idea, Veverka began sending me samples of his latest flies, which invariably challenged my conventional thinking.

I packed a handful of Veverka's flies in my tackle bag for a trip off Louisiana, where they accounted for world-record-size speckled trout. I next fished the flies off the coast of Baja California while hosting a trip aboard *Royal Star,* LoPreste-Dunn's San Diego–based long-range boat. One day on this trip we were at anchor off Tosca, and chumming up hordes of skipjack tuna. In spite of the live bait, strikes decreased in frequency until they nearly stopped altogether. Our party of sixteen fly fishers changed flies, tried sinking the flies deep, changed retrieve rates, switched to poppers, but nothing really turned the tuna back on. I then remembered the box of Veverka's flies. Searching through the box, I found a nondescript fly heavily epoxied at the head and carrying a dorsal run of light olive marabou. I tied on the fly and one cast later I was into a skipjack. A companion tied on one of the flies with identical results. The two of us were soon full on the bite again. I've been a big fan of Veverka's saltwater flies ever since.

I was especially enthusiastic when Veverka told me about his plans for a book on saltwater flies. Lately, fly pattern books had been popping up by authors with little saltwater fly-fishing experience. Veverka's book promised to be different. Each tier would be provided a chapter to tell something about his or her experiences, and then to describe the flies, give a rationale for their design, and tell how they were to be fished. Veverka would edit the many parts into an authoritative reference, an anthology of fly fishers and their trick patterns with application to all facets of saltwater fly fishing.

Innovative Saltwater Flies is that and more, a coffee table book as beautiful as it is informative. Veverka's melding of fly-fishing and fly-tying talent promises to expand the sport of saltwater fly fishing as have few other fly-fishing books. I am extremely pleased to be part of this project.

—*Trey Combs*

Editor's Note

Fly tiers tend to be creative types. In building flies to imitate the real thing, tiers want to create patterns that work, that take fish. If the flies happen to be beautiful and original, all the better. Throughout this process, tiers talk and watch, study and borrow. There's a lot of swapping of patterns, techniques, materials, and information, and sometimes even the flies themselves get passed around. Most of this is done in good spirit.

Sometimes, though, a pattern is adapted or modified and the originator does not get credited, or a pattern is changed only slightly and given a new name. Sometimes a fly pattern is blatantly stolen. In the best of worlds this would not happen.

As publishers, when we do a book, such as this one, about some talented tiers who have created some exceptional flies, we work diligently to acknowledge and provide background on the innovators and originators who came before and, in many ways, made it all possible. In their autobiographical sections, you'll hear the tiers in this book credit those who have inspired and helped them. Where flies, pattern styles, and recipes appear, we have been careful to note sources wherever we were able.

We hope we have gotten it right, that no one has been overlooked or slighted or misrepresented, that no one's work has been mislabeled. The ultimate guarantee of originality and authenticity, of course, lies with each tier.

—JMS

Acknowledgments

My basic idea for this book was to show the fly patterns being tied and used today in saltwater fly fishing. I also felt that readers would find the tiers' backgrounds and insights entertaining.

I am indebted to the tiers. Without them this book would have remained just an idea. Many thanks to Steve Abel, Joe Blados, Dan Blanton, Tim Borski, Dick Brown, Jeffrey Cardenas, Bill Catherwood, Trey Combs, Mike Croft, Corbett Davis, Sr., Corbett Davis, Jr., Bill Elliott, Bruce Foster, Jack Gartside, Scott Heywood, Brian Horsley, Bill and Kate Howe, Joe Howell, Tom Kintz, Bob Lemay, Ted Lewis, Glen Mikkleson, Brian O'Keefe, Gail Pucciarelli, Carl Richards, Scott Sanchez, Mark Sedotti, Cam Sigler, Sr., Cam Sigler, Jr., David Skok, Ken and Lori VanDerlaske, Lani Waller, Bob Warren, Mark Waslick, and Chris Windram.

My special thanks to Trey (Mr. Bluewater) Combs for writing the foreword and supplying me with photos from his bluewater excursions. His knowledge of saltwater fly fishing is unsurpassed and his love for this sport is enduring.

A special thanks to Mike Radencich for taking the stunning color photos of the flies.

To Chet Reneson, my Sunday-morning phone buddy, for generously providing his brilliant watercolors.

To Bill Elliott, a fine artist and one who appreciates the art of fly tying, for providing pencil sketches.

To Pamela Bates Richards for providing me with historic photographs and flies from the collection of her late father, Joseph D. Bates, Jr.

To Dave Beshara, Phil Castleman, Alec Jackson, Dave Hall, Susan Locklear, and Woody Sexton for providing me with names and addresses of tiers.

To Paul Betters and Bill Chase of Angler Sport Group for providing hooks by Daiichi.

To Woody Sexton for his insight into early flats fishing in the Florida Keys.

To Derl Stoval for providing materials.

To all the boat captains who took me to fishing grounds where, through time and patience and a little help from the fish, I perfected some of the flies that appear in my chapter.

To my niece Kristyn Forte for her computer knowledge.

A very special thanks to my wife, Diane, for her patience, encouragement, and the many hours of help she gave me in completing this book. The red Saab is in the driveway.

Introduction

I have always been fascinated with fishing flies and the people who tie them. I never thought that saltwater flies could be a thing of beauty, but time has proved me wrong. Not too long ago saltwater flies were very simple, but in the last few years much has changed. Saltwater tiers have begun tying with more complex patterns that match Mother Nature more closely. Not only are these flies pleasing to look at, but they also catch fish. Each one has a well-thought-out idea that makes it unique. With saltwater fly fishers traveling all over the world pursuing their favorite game fish, the need for new and effective patterns has grown. In a word, saltwater fly tying has exploded.

The tiers included in this book are some of the most gifted in the field today. They are dedicated, fanatical, and enthusiastic. They are a bunch of characters. They come from all walks of life, but they have some things in common—they love saltwater fishing and tying, and they are innovative. They fish for every species that swims in the ocean. Some travel widely, while others stay in their backyards. Wherever there is salt water, there is someone fishing it with a fly. I hon-estly believe that if you fish the flies in this book day in and day out, you will catch fish.

It only takes one look at one of the new saltwater pattern books or a visit to one of the many fly-fishing shows to see which way saltwater tying is going. Not too long ago fly tying was a well-kept secret. That has changed. We freely give out information on how to tie flies. Anyone is welcome and can participate in the field of tying.

It is interesting to see how certain tiers look at a specific pattern and then incorporate their own ideas—whatever they feel is important—into the tying of the fly. And those who fish will tie flies that are more apt to catch fish. Fishing helps tiers understand what makes a fly trigger a reaction, and this knowledge can be incorporated into their tying. Sometimes almost anything will work, but there are times when exact imitation are needed. Many tiers study the local prey and develop flies that match it in size, shape, and color to an unbelievable degree—an almost clonelike imitation. Many tie exact patterns to fit certain situations that call for a closer imitation of the real baitfish or crustacean, but always keeping in mind a simple question: Will it catch fish? This principle has been applied with great success to patterns for bonito and false albacore, once thought impossible to catch on a fly. In recent years, tiers have developed patterns—some sparse, some shimmering and translucent—to match specific baitfish that attract these ocean-going speedsters. Here the fish is the final critic and only it can show whether the fly will pass the test or fail. Today there is a friendly competition to come up with the most exacting pattern to represent a specific baitfish or crustacean.

Natural materials, such as hair and feathers, will always be used in saltwater flies, because there are no

---

ALBACORE FLIES

Florida Keys Pilchard
by Michael Schwartz

Bonito Bunny Buster
by Rick Worwood

Silicone fly
by Johnny Glenn

Silicone fly
by Johnny Glenn

Bay Anchovy
by Johnny Glenn

Silicone fly
by Johnny Glenn

Silicone fly
by Johnny Glenn

Sparkling Sand Eel
(Blue) by Chris Windram

Sparkling Bucktail
(Chartreuse)
by Chris Windram

Albacore pin
by Ken VanDerlaske

synthetic substitutes for some fly components, and naturals, I feel, have a superior action to synthetics. Still, synthetics are now widely used; they come in an array of colors that lend themselves to many applications, and they produce a more durable fly. Materials now come from sources we never even thought of before. Everything is game. There seems to be something new each year to incorporate into our flies.

The tiers in this book have brought fly tying to a functional art form. They value their sport to the point that while thousands of fish are caught, most are returned to the water to live for the next encounter.

With the number of talented fly tiers today, plus the wide selection of new materials and ideas, we will see some absolutely amazing patterns come out of the vise. Just when we think an area has been exhausted, something new—be it a material or an idea—sends us off in a new direction.

When we look back on the history of saltwater fly tying, we remember certain names and patterns. Some of the flies created decades ago are still standards. Building on the patterns of our predecessors, we realize that the craft is still in its infancy. Innovative saltwater fly-tying history is being made right now; the following chapter describes how and where it all began.

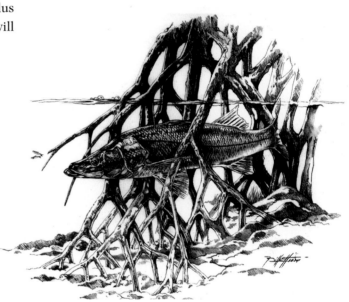

MODERN BAITFISH PATTERNS

Bluefish Bucktail
by David Bell

Bucktail Anchovy
by Bob Veverka

Yak Hair Baitfish
by Richard Murphy

Braid Fly Bunker
by Richard Murphy

Marabou Baitfish
by Umpqua

Silverside
by Bob Veverka

Silicone Baitfish
by Johnny Glenn

Prawn
by Jan Reniers

Silverside
by Tom Kintz

Braided Clouser Sand Eel
(tier unknown)

Bay Anchovy
by Joe Blados

Silicone Baitfish
by Johnny Glenn

Bucktail Sand Eel
by Bob Veverka

Early History

Saltwater fly fishing dates back to the late 1800s. At that time anglers were fishing with large Atlantic salmon flies, because no saltwater flies were available. The earliest saltwater patterns can be traced back to striped bass in the Northeast, bonefish and tarpon in Florida, and Pacific salmon in the Northwest.

Two of the earliest patterns on record are Loving's Bass Fly, tied by Tom Loving in the 1920s especially for striped bass in the Chesapeake Bay, and Bonbright's Tarpon Fly by Howard Bonbright, which was sold by Abercrombie & Fitch in the early 1920s.

An outstanding pioneer saltwater fly caster and early experimenter was Homer Rhode. Rhode tells of taking his first bonefish and permit on regulation fly tackle in 1930. An Everglades naturalist, Rhode roamed the Florida backcountry canals, and boated and waded the shallow waters of Florida Bay often for months without letup. He originated the Homer Rhode Jr. Tarpon Streamer. In his book *Streamers and Bucktails,* Joe Bates states, "This was the first established type of pattern and the forerunner of all tarpon streamers." With long hackles tied in at the hook point it proved less apt to foul, and its palmered hackle caused the fly to land light and sink slow, the hallmarks of a shallow-water tarpon fly. Rhode also experimented with long-shanked hooks. By putting in two 45-degree bends, he found that the hook would fish inverted so it wouldn't snag on the bottom. This is what we know today as the keel fly hook. He also originated the Homer Rhode loop knot.

Harold Gibbs of Rhode Island tied one of the first saltwater flies to actually imitate a specific baitfish. Harold and his brother Frank fished in Canada for Atlantic salmon, but during World War II, gas was so scarce they had to find fishing close to home. Harold tied a bucktail-winged streamer that imitated a silver-sides, a baitfish found on the East Coast. It was an instant success and the fly that we know today as the Gibbs Striper Fly was born. Gibbs promoted the sport of striped bass fishing and personally pioneered fly fishing for this game fish. He also popularized the Magog Smelt as a striped bass fly. Originated by Frier Gulline of Fin, Fur and Feather in Montreal, this fly was used for landlocked salmon in Lake Memphremagog on the Quebec-Vermont border. It represented a smelt, a common baitfish found in Lake Memphremagog.

This is purely speculation on my part, but perhaps here was the idea that gave Gibbs the foundation for his pattern. Gibbs fished in Canada and was familiar with the Magog Smelt, which looks remarkably similar to the Gibbs Striper Fly. Gibbs tied his fly in a few different versions. Some of the similarities to Gulline's fly are three bunches of bucktail in the wing, teal cheeks, and a red throat. When Gibbs fished in the salt, he drew on his vast knowledge of salmon and trout fishing to successfully fly-fish for striped bass. Gibbs originated his fly in the early 1940s, whereas Gulline tied his flies as far back as the 1930s.

Harold's brother Frank also tied flies and originated the Bluefish Bucktail. Also at this time, Edward Materne originated the Pig Tails and Harvey Flint the Palmer Diller.

As far back as 1936 on the West Coast, Letcher Lambuth was experimenting with imitations of specific baitfish for Pacific salmon in Puget Sound. He began to study what fish actually feed upon by viewing baitfish in glass tanks. He noticed that the colors of baitfish were different when held in the hand as opposed to in light. He found herring to have an opalescent quality he could only capture with blended polar bear hair over silver tinsel bodies. It is likely that he was the angler-tier who led the move to more realistic polar bear streamers. He would observe live candlefish and herring in his tanks while he drew streamer flies through it and try to match the baitfish's color. His candlefish and herring patterns became standards and are used widely today.

Saltwater fly casting for Pacific salmon enjoyed perhaps its widest popularity and greatest numbers of practitioners in the mid-1930s. But World War II came along, and when it was over the interest was never quite the same.

After World War II Joe Brooks became a leader in saltwater flies and fishing. Joe started fishing in the salt in the 1920s, but it wasn't until after the war that it really caught on. In *Saltwater Fly Fishing* magazine, Charlie Waterman writes, "Joe Brooks never invented saltwater fly fishing, but he made it move."

In 1946 Joe Brooks, fishing with guide Jimmie Albright, made the first attempt to catch a bonefish on a fly. They succeeded and became instant experts. Albright strongly influenced the development of bonefish flies. According to Joe Brooks, Albright's Frankie Belle "was one of the earliest patterns tied for bonefish," and it remains popular today.

Who actually tied the first bonefish fly is not clear. According to Dick Brown in *Fly Fishing for Bonefish*, not until Captain Bill Smith plucked the hackle off the back end of an Islamorada chicken, tied it to a hook, and took his now famous 1939 bonefish had anyone designed a pattern for bonefish.

Brooks also tied flies, but most of his ideas were incorporated in flies by other tiers. His most popular flies were the Blonde series. The first two Blonde patterns, the Platinum and Honey Blondes, were originated by Joe and Tom Cooney. Another tier who did a lot of work with Joe and tied many of his flies was Bill Gallasch of Skipping Bug fame. Bill was a freshwater tier until he met Joe. In 1948 Brooks caught a West Coast striper weighing 29 pounds, 6 ounces at Coos Bay, Oregon, on a popping bug, a world record at the time.

One of Joe Brooks's favorite bonefish flies was the Pink Shrimp, tied by George Phillips. Phillips varied the amounts of bucktail and dressed the fly on different-size hooks to control the sink rate. Its one drawback was that it snagged on the bottom. Phillips tried to correct this and make it weed-proof by palmering the body with stiff hackle.

This problem wouldn't be corrected until Pete Perinchief, while fishing with Brooks, became so frustrated with his flies snagging on the bottom that he developed a most important feature. Taking an idea from a weedless freshwater fly, he originated the Horror, a fly with the wing on its underside that, when dropped in the water, flips on its back with the hook pointing up. The wing works like a rudder, turning the fly over and also serving as a weed guard. Perinchief's design is now standard on bonefish flies and his original pattern is still a popular fly.

The second most important development in the design of the bonefish fly came with Bob Nauheim's Crazy Charlie, created in the Bahamas in the late 1970s. Drawing from his steelhead fly-tying experience, Nauheim tied a pair of metal bead-chain eyes on a hook, which enabled the fly to sink to the bottom fast. The eyes also helped flip the fly so the hook rode point up, making it snag-proof, and added an up-and-down action, making it sink naturally and quickly to the fish's level. The Crazy Charlie was the prototype for many variations of bead-chain-eyed bonefish flies tied today.

Nat Ragland contributed to the development of bonefish flies when he created the Puff, using chenille in the head and body to cushion its landing so it's less likely to spook fish. This was one of the first patterns tied for permit.

These features—sink rate, action, snag-proofing, and a quiet landing—are all key attributes of what we now know as a bonefish fly.

Joe Brooks's articles in fishing magazines had an enormous effect on saltwater fly fishing. He influenced two other early saltwater fly fishers and tiers, Lefty Kreh and Stu Apte. Lefty Kreh, an avid smallmouth bass fisherman from Maryland, recalls that one of his

Pink Shrimp by Jimmie Albright	Frankie Belle by Jimmie Albright
Magog Smelt by Mike Martinek	
Bluefish Fly by Peter Sang	Gibb's Striper Fly by Mike Martinek
Silverside by Don Brown	Sand Eel by Don Brown
	Horror by S.L. (Pete) Perinchief

most important moments was when he met Joe Brooks in the late 1950s. When Lefty began fishing in the salt water around the Chesapeake Bay in the 1950s, he wanted a fly that was shaped like a baitfish, swam well, and cast with little wind resistance. In the early 1960s, he originated the Lefty's Deceiver, probably the most popular saltwater fly ever designed.

Stu Apte was another who fished with Joe Brooks and looked to him as a mentor. During high school and college, Stu tied simple bucktails and, to earn money for fishing gear, sold them under the name of bonefish flies. He started guiding in the Florida Keys in the late 1950s, just as the modern era of saltwater fly fishing was beginning. Apte has fished widely and holds many records. He changed the design of Keys-style flies, tying them less than 3 inches long. His Stu Apte Tarpon Fly, originated in 1969, was considered one of the best at that time and is still widely used. Tied with red and yellow, it resembles the tarpon's favorite food, the palolo worm.

Woody Sexton guided in the Florida Keys from 1959 to 1988. He and Jim Adams headed out of California for Florida in the late 1950s with a small aluminum boat filled with fishing gear. When they arrived they saw hundreds of schools of tarpon. Flies were very primitive at the time. They used simple bucktails, and because almost anything worked, there was no need to develop more elaborate patterns. The tackle back then was also rather crude, and the tarpon were very docile, not the spooky, skitterish creatures they have become. According to Woody, one of the best tarpon flies at that time was the High Tie, originated by Bart Foth. It cast well, landed lightly, and had a very seductive action.

During the early 1960s, Dr. Webster Robinson and his wife, Helen, guided by Lefty Reagan, aimed to perfect the method for taking a billfish on a fly. Robinson wasn't successful until 1962 in Piñas Bay, Panama, where he landed the first Pacific sailfish on a fly. It weighed 74$\frac{1}{2}$ pounds. Robinson used a homemade Styrofoam combination popper-streamer built around a #7/0 hook with white saddle hackles about 4 inches long and a white Styrofoam head about 1 inch long, chopped off square to ensure popping action. This type of fly is widely used today. Others who successfully incorporated Robinson's method for teasing billfish include Stu Apte and Billy Pate. In 1964 off Islamorada, Florida, Lee Cuddy landed the first Atlantic sailfish on a fly. It weighed forty-seven pounds.

During the early 1960s, many tiers started tying saltwater flies. One pioneer was Bill Catherwood of Tewksbury, Massachusetts, the originator of the Giant Killer series. Catherwood's flies initiated the shift from attracters to imitaters. He used spun deer hair heads to give his baitfish patterns a three-dimensional shape. He studied colors of baitfish and used dyed materials to achieve the realistic look of squid, shrimp, and crabs.

Another originator of the 1960s, Dan Blanton, created the Whistler series in 1964 for striped bass in the San Francisco Bay area. He incorporated bead-chain eyes to give the fly a bucktail jig action.

Hal Janssen, a brilliant tier and an artist when it comes to saltwater flies, originated the Janssen Striper Fly and the Halfbeak, which imitates a balao. Bob Edgely and Dan Blanton originated the Sea-Arrow Squid. Larry Green, a leading angler and writer, originated the Bonito Bandit and beer-belly-fashioned flies for bonito off the California coast. Another pioneer, Harry Kime, created the Tutti-Frutti, a squid pattern used to tease billfish, and numerous patterns for Costa Rican tarpon and offshore fish in Baja. Bob Nauheim modeled his West Coast striper flies the Bay Tern and Sea Tern after the Gibbs Striper Fly. Winston Moore's Winston's Billfish Fly has taken numerous marlin and sailfish. Moore says in Deke Meyer's *Saltwater Flies*, "It is not a work of art but it certainly is effective." Moore also developed the Agent Orange, which he claims is one of his best bonefish flies. In 1966, Russell Chatham broke the world record for striped bass with a 36-pound, 6-ounce fish from San Francisco Bay caught while using an 8-inch black streamer. Ned Gray developed the Streaker, the first fly to incorporate a pair of pea-

---

Early epoxy fly*

Cockroach
by Lefty Kreh

Janssen's Halfbeak
by Hal Janssen

White Deceiver
by Lefty Kreh

Janssen's Striper Fly
by Hal Janssen

---

* Ken Vanderlaske found this beautiful old fly at an antique tackle show and speculated that it may be the first epoxy fly. It is well-tied, with a small married tail of red and yellow. The body, held on by wraps of tinsel, appears to be clear epoxy or plastic and is molded to the shape of the hook. Perhaps some reader will recognize the fly and provide us with its history.

cock sword feathers for the wing, for fishing in Baja, Mexico, where he caught a fifty-pound roosterfish on it. East Coast tiers of this era include Al Brewster, one of Harold Gibbs's fishing cronies; Paul Kukonen, who fished early shrimp patterns in Narragansett Bay, Rhode Island, for weakfish; Joe Bates, who fished extensively, promoted spin casting when it was first introduced, and authored many books on all types of fishing; and Elmwood "Cap" Colvin, who operated a tackle shop along the New Jersey coast, encouraged many to try saltwater fly fishing, and developed the Kaboomboom poppers, named after the sound they make.

Frank Woolner was the editor of *Salt Water Sportsman* magazine and very knowledgeable about northeastern fly fishing. Fishing mostly on Cape Cod, he originated the Woolner's Sand Eel, which features neck hackles with the tips removed and inserted into mylar piping as a tail. Many tiers now incorporate this feature in their baitfish patterns. One of Woolner's fishing partners, Hal Lyman, another editor of *Salt Water Sportsman,* originated the Lyman's Terror.

In 1970, George X. Sand published *Salt-water Fly Fishing,* one of the first books to deal strictly with saltwater fly fishing. Two years later, Kenneth E. Bay's *Salt Water Flies* became the first to deal strictly with saltwater flies and how to tie them.

During the 1970s, Peter B. Sang of Percy Tackle Company of Portland, Maine, also developed a sand eel pattern, the Percy Sand Eel, while Don Brown of Massachusetts originated his Silversides and Sand Eel.

Around the same time, George "Chappie" Chapman enlarged his smallmouth bass poppers, added pearlescent tape, and began using them for striped bass. The first time he saw mylar piping, he knew exactly how he was going to use it. Chapman's Mylar Covered Poppers have taken numerous offshore and inshore species.

Another true saltwater-fly innovator is Bob Popovics, who started tying saltwater flies in 1971. Striving to make a fly durable enough for toothy bluefish, he originated a style of flies with the heads and bodies covered with epoxy. Not only did the epoxy make the fly more durable, but it also allowed tiers to set the shape of any baitfish they wished to duplicate. Popovics originated the Surf Candies, Bob's Bangers, and, his most recent, the Spread Flies, which have the silhouettes of large-bodied baitfish. He is truly a saltwater fly innovator, and his style has sent many in a new direction.

Another tier to experiment with epoxy is Harry Spear, a flats guide in the Florida Keys. His Mother of Epoxy was the first epoxy fly to draw the attention of bonefish anglers. During the late 1980s, saltwater tying innovation really took off. In his 1987 *Book of Fly Patterns,* Eric Leiser writes, "The salt water category of flies is still a wide open area with many new opportunities for pioneering." Some of the true innovators of this time were Matt Vinciguerra, who developed the Salty Beady Eye, and Larry Dahlberg, whose revolutionary Dahlberg Diver dives, swims, and resurfaces like a spinning lure. Dahlberg learned much about fly design by studying the attracting and triggering attributes of artificial lures.

During the late 1980s and early 1990s many western trout-fly tiers took off to fish the bonefish flats in the winter. Mike Wolverton created his Flats Master, and Craig Mathews developed new patterns while chasing bonefish and permit in Belize and the Bahamas, including Pop's Bonefish Bitters and the Turneffe Crab.

Many tiers tried to devise crab patterns to catch the elusive permit. Dave Whitlock developed the clipped Deer-Hair Crab. George Anderson, with the help of John Barr and Jim Brungardt, designed one of the first flies to take permit consistently, the McCrab. Del Brown used rug yarn for the body of his Merkin. It isn't a realistic pattern, but it looks enough like a crab and is effective because of the way it dives to the bottom. Many Florida Keys guides use it, and Del's permit count certainly confirms that it works. Tied in small sizes it is also a good bonefish fly.

Other successful crab patterns include Phil Chapman's Hair-Ball and Infuraytor. Tied with rabbit fur, they hang suspended in the water with lots of action. Bill Catherwood has a truly unique pattern. Tied articulated, it takes on a defensive stance when at rest on the bottom. Another novel crab pattern is the Krohel's Permit Krab by Ken Krohel, which he creates using hot glue, shaped cork, rubber bands, a diving fin, and an outer shell of leather. Tim Borski ties his Chernobyl Crab with long, soft, tan hackle much like a Spey fly. He likes the action of the long hackle and uses it in many of his patterns. Carl Richards has taken crab patterns to the extreme. These truly artistic flies look as if they could crawl off the tying bench.

In 1992 Randall Kaufmann published *Bonefishing with a Fly*. Having fished from Venezuela to Christmas Island, Kaufmann claims to have studied, collected, dissected, designed, redesigned, ordered, sold, explained, demonstrated, and dreamed flies for thirty years, a mania that has led to better and more efficient fishing and tying. His patterns include the Pink Sands and Marabou Shrimp.

Other bonefish patterns include Jim McVay's Gotcha, a standard on Bahama bonefish flats; Jim Orthwein's Jim's Golden Eye Shrimp, which accounted for three bonefish fly records; and Barry and Cathy Beck's Sili Legs.

One of the most versatile, popular, and effective saltwater patterns used today is the Clouser Minnow, developed by Bob Clouser for smallmouth bass. According to Bob, "An effective smallmouth bass fly should have a darting motion and must sink as the fly is dead drifted or between strips." The Clouser Minnow mimics this fleeing trait—the fly never stops.

Steve Abel

I was born in Oceanside, California, near San Diego, and as a child began fishing off the local piers and jetties. My family moved to Camarillo, about seventy-five miles north of Los Angeles, when I was twelve.

I was always interested in cars and mechanical things. Following high school, I worked in a number of different machine shops performing various chores until I knew all aspects of high-tech machining and metalwork. As a young adult I moved to New Orleans, where I became a professional deep-sea diver, using both my deep-sea diving and machinist skills to remove sunken ships from the Suez Canal.

I returned to the machinist trade in Camarillo in 1976, and in 1977 I opened my own super-high-tech shop specializing in military and aerospace parts as well as the usual job shop projects. Some of my work is in virtually every Boeing jet. I also produced parts for both military and civilian satellites. As the aerospace industry changed, I began producing more components for the medical and computer industries—some as small as $1/16$ inch in diameter.

During this time I became interested in fly fishing, honing my skills on Hot Creek, the Owens River, and various other Sierra waters.

As is the case with many machine shop owners, I always wanted to produce my own product, not be at the whim of other manufacturers or economic conditions. I began experimenting with designs for a precision fly reel in the mid-1980s and took every quality big-game fly reel apart to study features, both good and bad. I determined the needs of anglers with cold hands, sweaty palms, and all the conditions anglers encounter. The result is the Abel Reel, introduced in March 1988 and an instant success. The Abel Reel was presented the Kudo Award for product excellence by *Fly Rod & Reel* magazine.

Soon I was designing and manufacturing tackle bags, wader bags, duffel bags, and other specialty luggage. About a year after the introduction of the Abel Big Game Reels, I began experimenting with a new lightweight trout and steelhead reel. Some three years in design and testing, the Abel TR/Series of three reels was introduced in March 1992. In 1993, I introduced the TR/Light.

I set and hold four International Game Fish Association world records for two sharks, a skipjack tuna, and a sixty-seven-pound wahoo on a fly rod. The sharks are a 140-pound blue and a 72-pound, 8-ounce mako. Both fish were taken off Anacapa Island in the Santa Barbara Channel on 16-pound-test tippets. I took the black skipjack and wahoo in Mexican waters on a bluewater trip.

In October 1991, I chartered the 113-foot *Royal Polaris* out of San Diego for the first-ever big-game bluewater fly-fishing trip. Anglers caught world-record yellowfin and skipjack tuna as well as dorado, wahoo, and yellowtails. In November 1992, I accompanied sports show promoter Ed Rice on a similar bluewater trip. Ed said, "This opens a new era of big-game fly fishing. In other places there are flats for saltwater anglers seeking tarpon, bonefish, or permit. The West Coast is not blessed with flats, but we do have tremendous potential for big-game fly rod excitement during week-long trips to Mexican waters."

My wife, Gina, who is the company's sales director, is also an active fly fisher and frequently accompanies me to Alaska, Canada, Florida, and Belize. She set one world record for a trevally, which has subsequently been broken.

I began designing what we now call the Abel Anchovy in 1985 or 1986 while fishing for sharks. I had previously used standard-pattern saltwater flies with little success. The process I used was to chum sharks to my boat, then toss the circling sharks frozen anchovies.

When they began looking for frozen 'chovies, I'd cast a fly. For the most part, the sharks would ignore the artificial. Then one day I noticed something: As the frozen anchovies hit the water, there was a spray of scales. On countless trips for sharks, tuna, stripers, salmon, wahoo, and other bluewater game, I had observed both singles and schools of feeders slashing through anchovies, mackerel, and menhaden. Often the bait would be crippled in the water . . . easy prey for later consumption. Characteristically, the scales on injured fish would become dislodged, floating off in a sort of halo effect. So I imitated the flash of scales by using strands of silver and pearl Flashabou. And—maybe the most important—I added big eyes and a head made with a hot glue gun instead of epoxy. The oversize eyes are critical.

The results were impressive. To date, I have taken world-record blue and mako sharks, world-record wahoo and skipjack tuna. The fly in various configurations has caught everything from a world-record peacock bass in Venezuela to dorado in Mexico, Alaska salmon, Pacific bonito, skipjacks, barracudas, yellowtails, tarpon, sailfish, and virtually every other game fish.

5	Abel Anchovy
Hook	#4/0, 3/0, 2/0, or 1/0
Thread	Black or chartreuse, size A
Body	Silver or pearl Diamond Braid
Collar	White bucktail, FisHair, or Polar Hair
Beard	Red Flashabou, Crystal Hair, or Krystal Flash
Wing	Bucktail, FisHair, or Polar Hair: blue on top of green over white
Topping	Peacock herl over silver and pearl Flashabou
Head	Hot glue (Thermogrip glue gun)
Eyes	5- or 6-millimeter paper or doll eyes, white with black dot

1. First, take a moment to sharpen the hook.

2. For the body, wind Diamond Braid forward to a point one-third of the shank length from the eye.

3. Turn the hook over in your vise and select a large bunch of white bucktail, FisHair, or Polar Hair. Tie the bunch in right where the Diamond Braid stops. Wind tightly to the eye of the hook. Tie in a beard 1/2 to 3/4 inch long.

4. Turn the hook back over and tie in a second bunch of white hair exactly as you did the first. Next, tie in a bunch of green hair; then, on top of the green, tie in a bunch of blue hair. Important: The hair should be as long as the anchovies you will be using as chum—3 to 5 inches. The four clumps of hair should be approximately the same size; that is, use 25 percent of each color.

5. Tie in fifteen to twenty strands of silver tinsel Flashabou, then fifteen to twenty strands of pearl Flashabou on top. Top off with ten to fifteen peacock herls over the Flashabou. The topping should be the same length as the collar and wing. Whip-finish in the center of the head.

6. With a Thermogrip glue gun, apply a coating of glue completely around the head. (It helps to have a vise with a rotating head.) Rotate the fly to keep the glue from dripping and to give the head the shape you want. As the glue cools, you may stop rotating the vise. Don't let the glue cool too much. Before it gets completely hard, stick a doll eye on each side of the head. Moisten your fingers with water or saliva and shape the head. After the glue cools, dip the head in Jolly Glaze or brush clear nail polish on the head and eyes. This helps the eyes stay on.

With a little practice, you can do wonders with a glue gun. Variations on the Abel Anchovy include versions tied for wahoo and for tarpon.

1	Abel Anchovy—Tarpon Fly

This is the same pattern as the Abel Anchovy, but tied Florida Keys tarpon style, with all materials to the rear of the hook. Chartreuse tying thread is wound over the shank of the hook and hot glue applied over it. The eye is placed just over the hook barb and point.

2	Abel Sardine
Hook	Mustad 34007, #6/0
Thread	Chartreuse, size A
Body	Pearl Diamond Braid
Collar	White FisHair
Wing	White FisHair; green and silver holographic Flashabou
Topping	Peacock herl
Beard	Red Flashabou
Sides	Long lime green grizzly hackles
Eyes	5- or 6-millimeter paper or doll eyes, black on white

1
2
3
4
5

3	**Abel Holy Mackerel**
Hook	Mustad 34007, #8/0
Thread	Chartreuse, size A
Body	Peacock ice chenille
Collar	Pearl Krystal Flash; white FisHair
Wing	White FisHair
Topping	Silver holographic Flashabou; blue Flashabou twist; peacock herl
Sides	Four teal blue grizzly hackles on each side
Beard	Red Flashabou, Crystal Hair, or Krystal Flash
Eyes	5- or 6-millimeter paper or doll eyes, black on white
Head	Hot glue (Thermogrip glue gun); Jolly Glaze or clear nail polish

4	**Abel Anchovy—Wahoo Fly**
Hook	Mustad 34011, #3/0 to 5/0
Thread	Chartreuse, size A
Body	Mylar tubing over Krystal Flash
Tail	Krystal Flash: pearl, chartreuse, olive, blue, black; mylar tubing strands
Beard	Red Flashabou, Crystal Hair, or Krystal Flash
Eyes	Large doll eyes, black on white
Head	Hot glue (Thermogrip glue gun); Jolly Glaze or clear nail polish

AUTHOR'S NOTE: Steve uses many synthetic materials to build the flies he uses. In the very harsh environment of offshore saltwater fly fishing, it doesn't hurt to have a durable fly when some of your target species are sharks and wahoo. Steve also adds natural materials for special effects, like the saddle hackles on his Big Mac and Sardine, and the use of peacock herl to top off his patterns—hard to beat as a material to match the iridescent coloring atop baitfish. A nice blend of synthetic and natural materials.

Capt. Joe Blados

What the hell is a Crease Fly?" a spin rodder yelled as I released another bass. The score was fifteen to nothing in the last innings before the light. Not a great night, but one that was typical of my early fly-fishing years. I didn't get much help from anyone then because there just weren't many local people fly-fishing out here at the time, or at least not any I knew. I live on the north fork of Long Island and fish from Mattituck to Orient. I concentrate my fishing on this area because I feel that to get good results, you need to know a certain area well. I come from a background of commercial fishermen and I fly-fish for striped bass, big blues, weakfish, and—my favorite—albacore.

I made lures for other types of saltwater fishing so it was only natural that I tie my own flies. I did things back then by trial and error, with lots of error. I look at my early flies and laugh. Must have been drinking when I tied that. I didn't catch many fish in those early days, and that in itself was the challenge that kept me at the sport. I like to draw and I am a stickler for detail. I used to paint pictures on Harleys and thought about doing tattoos. So I stuck it out, met some mighty fine people, sold my Harley and bought a Maverick Flats Skiff. As far as learning the sport of fly fishing? Well, I'm getting better.

In my early days of fly tying, I would hollow out popper cylinders with a Dremel tool, then squeeze and glue them to get a tall but thin profile, like the bait I was trying to imitate. These flies worked well; the problem was that to construct them I made a lot of foam dust. My loving wife, whom I really credit this fly to, was not a happy foam-dust cleaner. With a little innovation, I found I could get the same body form and no dust if I used sheet foam. What evolved was the Crease Fly. I can honestly say that the Crease Fly is mine in origin—but that doesn't mean a hoot if it doesn't catch fish. I devised Crease Fly poppers to meet a specific need—when game fish are geared to topwater action. What sold me on this fly style over conventional patterns and sliders was its realistic action and look in the water. And the smaller versions were easy to cast. They work with any style of fly line, and best of all, the fish eat the heck out of them day and night.

One of the things that makes this fly possible are cyanoacrylate glues. They come in various thicknesses. The thin CAs have the consistency of water and are the least desirable. Thick or gap-filling glues and gels allow more control. All can be sprayed with accelerant to make an instant bond. Being a welder by trade has probably helped me in understanding and using glues, as did model airplane construction in my younger days. Glues, adhesives, and epoxies have created possibilities in fly tying that could not be done otherwise.

It is not difficult to tie a Crease Fly, but there are critical steps that make this fly work. The first is to cover the hook shank with a lot of thread. This is the foundation for the glue and foam. Foam does not stick well to a bare hook.

When cutting the body, fold the foam sheet. By doing this you cut both sides at the same time. Keep the front of the fly straight. If you slope or slant the front, it has a tendency to spin. Position the hook as low on the body as possible. It acts like a keel and holds the fly in the upright position. Note that if the fly lies on its side, it will still catch fish.

As with any fly, hook size determines final fly size. I like the longer-shanked hooks, such as Mustad 34011, 34039SS, and 90233S. On flies that have a body of over 4 inches, the fly may lie on its side at rest, but stand up on a retrieve. Longer flies require wire in place of long-shanked hooks. I have fished flies with bodies of over 8 inches without much effort to cast.

Most baitfish, whether juvenile or adult, have silver bodies or highlights, which I try to imitate in this pattern. In the past I would use sticky-backed chrome tapes, but the adhesives are poor and don't stick unless the fly is covered with epoxy. I do not like to add weight to a fly unless it is called for.

The next experiment involves a model airplane wing covering called Monokote. This is a mylar sheet with a heat-activated glue on one side. It's available in all colors of the rainbow, including chrome. Monokote is lightweight, and it does not have to have epoxy over it to be durable. Nevertheless, I still use CA glue in lieu of heat to attach the Monokote to the foam sheet.

Charlie Benjamin, a fishing partner, introduced me to Jones Tones Foil, a product used in hobby crafts. It also has a heat-activated glue; on a foam sheet, however, it's best to spread a thin layer of Flex Coat or CA glue. Then stack some books on the top of the foil. Let it dry at least overnight, then peel off the film that covers this product. This stuff works great.

There are many types of bait that can be imitated using folding sheet foam. They include crabs, shrimp, squid, and baitfish.

In general, all of these flies will float. I do add lead wire to the crab and squid flies only. The baitfish Crease Fly, depending on body size, can be fished subsurface with sinking fly lines. When I'm in my boat I like to use an intermediate fly line. The fly will start out on the surface and gain depth as it nears the boat. Fish don't seem to spook so easily as the fly approaches the boat.

Lately I've added glass rattles to some of my flies. Shrimp or krill have been known to make sounds audible over hydrophones, even on submarines busy with noise. Whether they help these flies is yet to be proved. There are a lot of people who use rattles and swear by them. This is my first year to try, and they fit nicely in the throat of the poppers. We'll see.

Spring fishing in the Northeast is not normally associated with popper-type flies. In cold water, it's thought, the fish are not aggressive enough to chase poppers. My best fishing last spring was in some of the entrances of creeks. If you let the tide do most of the work and fish Crease Fly poppers slow with a small occasional *pop,* the fish will eat the heck out of them.

A couple of years ago I was night fishing with two friends, one of whom was Nick Curcione, at a place on Long Island Sound called Petty's Bite. This is the only spot in the sound on the north fork that has abundant eelgrass beds. This grass will reach four feet in height in August. In turn, sand gets trapped up, similar to snow in front of a snow fence.

There will be a row of eelgrass, then a sandbar, then another row of grass running parallel to the beach, an ideal habitat for holding bait. The downside is abundant grass, meaning abundant bioluminescence at night. All of those little buggers that make your fly line look like Halley's Comet like to live on the grass.

We knew there were fish around because you could hear them. After an hour of no hits with assorted flies, I put on the biggest Crease Fly in my box, water-hauled it in the same spot a couple of times, then just let it sit. *Smack!* It was one of those Dobermans with fins, a bluefish.

It seemed like every time I used this technique, I'd get at least a hit, if not the fish. Nick was cursing about his stripping basket coming apart and the other guy wasn't doing a thing. But hell, I was having a good time.

After that episode, I now use Crease Flies a lot for night fishing with great success, mostly for stripers. Again, they must be fished slow.

Ask any two salty fly fishermen a question about gear or favorite flies and you will likely get two different answers. The one thing they might agree on is that there's nothing more exciting than a surface strike.

Luck, skill, and downright determination can make you stand above others on the beach. Crease Flies have given me that extra edge when all else fails.

Crease Squid
Crease Slider
Crease Slider
Crease Shrimp
Crease Crab

Crease Flies

Hook	Tiemco 511S popper hook, #2/0
Tail	Various colors of bucktail to match the body color of the baitfish you wish to duplicate; Flashabou to accent the tail color
Body	Foam sheeting cut to shape, folded or creased, glued at the bottom, and held onto the hook shank
Eyes	Witchcraft stick-ons
Body Color	Added to the fly with various colored marking pens to match the baitfish you wish to duplicate

1. Tie in the tail. Use bucktail or synthetic fibers and add a bit of flash to suit the pattern. (I've found that starting my thread just behind the hook and wrapping all the way back makes the gluing operation in step 5 easier.)

2. Cut a rectangle of sheet foam to match the size of your hook, fold it over, and cut the open ends on a slight curve to taper the body from head to tail. Fold the foam and cut both open ends at the same time. This creates a uniform belly profile. (My wife, Lorraine, named the Crease Fly when she saw me doing this on pattern after pattern.)

3. Snip the top of the tail at an angle toward the head to provide an opening for the tail fibers and to further enhance the body profile.

4. Test-fit the foam body on the hook and trim if necessary.

5. Run a bead of instant glue along the length of the thread. Superglues don't set until they come into contact with two surfaces, so you have a little bit of working time. (The thread wrap absorbs the tine glue, distributes it around the shank, and prevents it from dripping.) Crease the foam into shape, align the bottom edges with the hook shank, hold everything in place, and run your fingers along the sides. The glue will bond as soon as the foam is squeezed against the hook. (Be careful not to glue your fingers to the Crease Fly. It makes the pattern very difficult to cast.)

6. Glue the back closed and push down on the top to create a tunnel-shaped opening up front. Add a few drops of superglue to the front to secure this shape. Use a superglue accelerant spray for an instant setup. Make sure your glue lines are tight, and you're done. Note that the front of the popper is open and the leading edges are straight. I learned that cutting the face of the popper on a slant invites the pattern to spin, disrupting your presentation and twisting your line.

The hook acts as a keel and the pattern will sit and swim more naturally than conventional poppers, which must carry the hook either in the center or in the lower one-third of the body.

The key element is sheet foam, which is available in fly shops as Live Body or in craft stores. It is a flat sheet of pliable foam about $1/16$ inch thick that comes in a variety of colors. Still, I use white 99 percent of the time and color the foam with marking pens to simulate a variety of baitfish colors. It is easy and the only trick is to blend the inks with your fingers before they dry. Add stick-on eyes and seal the body with a light coat of a finish such as Gloss Coat, Hard As Nails, or thinned epoxy. Test to make sure your choice of finish coat doesn't lift the ink.

I also came up with a variation—the Chrome Crease Fly popper—to stand out amid hordes of baby bunker. There are three ways to create chrome-sided patterns. The first is a model airplane wing covering called Monokote, the second is a silver-leaf T-shirt decorative material that Charlie Benjamin discovered in a craft shop, and the third is an adhesive-backed mylar tape. The first two have heat-activated glues and must be ironed onto the foam before you start. Mylar tape is easier, but I prefer the first two materials.

CREASE FLY POPPERS

Dan Blanton

I am from San Jose, California, and am an angling instructor, lecturer, author, photographer, and travel and tackle consultant. I have fished for most freshwater and saltwater species along the Atlantic and Pacific coasts of North and Central America. I spearheaded fly fishing for giant tarpon in Costa Rica in the early 1970s and have fly-fished extensively for tarpon, bonefish, and snook in the Florida Keys and for billfish in Panama, Costa Rica, and Mexico.

In the early days of saltwater fly fishing, the flies used to take marine game fish were rather simple. By and large it's still the same today. Some old-timers will remember taking tarpon on popping bugs all along the Florida Keys, but today a large, noisy bug will scare the hell out of most tarpon in the same water.

As more and more anglers turn to the salt for their fly-rodding fun, fish, in turn, are getting wiser and harder to take. Some saltwater game fish are more particular about what they eat than others, and since many saltwater species are highly selective about their food, saltwater fly casters often become frustrated.

While I agree that simple dressings often produce tremendous saltwater-fly catches, that they have a place in your selection of marine flies, and that they may make up the majority of the total volume, these days you had better include a few more realistic patterns, too, to entice the reluctant ones into striking.

Superior baitfish simulations and lifelike animation are what I am referring to when I speak of sophisticated saltwater flies. The time-proven Joe Brooks's Blondes have taken hundreds of fish of infinite variety, yet they will fail miserably with certain species. A more carefully thought-out and realistic fly such as the Lefty's Deceiver takes fish the Blonde cannot.

One of the first great fly tiers to think in terms of realistic saltwater dressing is Bill Catherwood, the

master fly tier from Tewksbury, Massachusetts. The Catherwood originals are specialized patterns. Some are floaters, others sinkers; all are phenomenal creations! Using hair and feathers bound to steel, Catherwood fabricates exact, lifelike imitations of marine baitfish and squid.

I admire Catherwood and over the years have tried to coin saltwater flies that simulate—through silhouette, color, and animation—marine baitfish in the most realistic manner possible, without having to exactly imitate individual species of baitfish, crustaceans, and squid. Realistic simulation is, in my opinion, the key to a productive saltwater fly.

When freshwater fly fishermen make the transition to salt water, one of the first things they ask is, Which fly patterns are successful? They need to know and fish patterns simply to eliminate the uncertainty of fishing with an unsuccessful fly.

Only four important types of food are of concern to saltwater fish and fishermen. These are the baitfish, including eels; crustaceans such as the shrimp and crabs; the mollusks, including many varieties of shellfish; and cephalopods, including octopi and squid. Of these categories, only the baitfish have enough separate species to require exact imitations for game fish that have become selective.

In the early years of saltwater fly fishing, flies were tied to simulate baitfish in general without much emphasis on exact imitations. Today many dressings are designed to simulate a particular species of baitfish.

If there are certain components that make a fly better, unquestionably two are action (animation) and optics (large, conspicuous eyes), particularly optics that promote dipping and diving action. To me, these easily outweigh all others.

A lead-head jig derives its dipping and diving action from the mass of lead formed at the front of the hook. This motion triggers the strike instinct of predator game fish by parodying the antics of an injured baitfish trying to get the hell out of town. Healthy baitfish can swim with game fish for hours without being molested. Let them show signs of weakness, injury, or fear, however, and they instantly become fish fodder. Build this type of action into a fly and you will have at least one of the two prime ingredients that make a highly successful pattern.

Last and most important, my watchword for selecting flies—that they be time tested. Any fly that finds a permanent place in my box has had numerous encounters with fish lips. And when it comes to baitfish simulation and subsurface patterns, these flies must fall into the oceanic category: They must fish well anywhere on the globe!

4 Blanton's SPS (Shad-Perch Simulator) Flashtail Whistler

Hook	Tiemco 800S, Eagle Claw 254, or Trey Combs Big Game Fly Hook, #3/0 to 4/0
Thread	Red
Underbody	Ten wraps of .030-inch lead wire
Body/Collar	Medium red chenille
Optics	Silver bead-chain eyes, large to extra large
Tail/Wing	White, crinkly bucktail
Tail/Wing Topping	Purple bucktail over hot pink bucktail; purple Krystal Flash
Shoulder	Large grizzly neck hackle
Flashtail	Silver and pearl Flashabou, mixed
Side Flash	Rainbow Krystal Flash
Shoulder Flash	Hot pink Krystal Flash
Hackle Collar	Two or three white saddle hackles faced with one grizzly

1. Wind a layer of thread from the hook eye to the hook point, no farther; the fly is tied using only this portion of the hook shank. Cement.

2. Place the bead eyes against the hook eye and tie them on using crossing wraps. Cement.

3. Wrap ten turns of lead wire onto the shank. The wire should stop against the bead eyes. Overwrap with thread and cement.

4. Tie in a first bunch of white bucktail directly on top of the hook shank. At the hook point position, taper the stubs and wrap them completely down. The stubs should taper all the way to the bead eyes. Do not form a wall by cutting the stubs off square. Cement.

5. Now cut forty to fifty strands each of silver and pearl Flashabou and tie directly on top of the bucktail. Wetting the Flashabou helps you control it. Leave the flashtail long; you'll cut it to size once the fly is completed.

6. Next tie on the hot pink bucktail (or another bunch of white, if needed for more profile), followed by a lesser amount of purple bucktail, to form the two-tone topping. Taper the stubs, wrap them completely down, and cement.

7. Cut about ten strands of dark purple Krystal Flash and tie those on top of the purple bucktail. Now tie in the shoulder flash—about ten strands of hot pink Krystal Flash, angled upward and lying alongside the hot pink bucktail.

8. Now tie one large grizzly neck hackle, curved side against the tail/wing, on each side of the tail/wing. Be sure these lie flat.

9. Next comes the body/collar. Tie in two turns only of medium red chenille exactly where the bucktail is tied on. This collar simulates gills; it's not to be a body. Take one turn of chenille in front of the first and tie off, leaving a 3/8- to 1/2-inch gap between the collar and the bead eyes. Cement.

10. Now tie in two to three large webby white saddle hackles, butt first, curve toward the bend. Place the first one against the chenille collar, opposite yourself; place the next slightly forward, on the same side as yourself; the third goes on top, slightly forward of the second hackle. Spiral-wrap the hackles, one at a time, starting with the one closest to the eyes, to form a broad hackle collar. Face the white hackle collar with a single, large grizzly neck or saddle hackle. Pick out matted barbs.

11. Fold the hackle collar back out of the way with your fingers and finish the head with many wraps, both behind and in front of the eyes.

I originated this fly to take striped bass from the San Francisco Bay and its river delta system in 1964. This pattern, a worldwide standard, has accounted for thousands of striped bass of trophy proportions and hundreds of other species, from snook to tarpon in salt water and from largemouth bass to pike and peacock bass in fresh water—to name a few of the species that find favor with the fly. Engineered to work like a lead-headed bucktail jug, the Whistler will take any species a lead-head will.

1   Sea-Arrow Squid

Hook	Mustad 79573, 3X long, 3X strong, #2/0 to 3/0, or equivalent
Thread	White
Tip	Gold mylar piping wound like tinsel from the halfway point of the hook bend to the end of the shank
Butt	Several turns of large white chenille in a ball—enough to make the hackles splay out
Tail	As a wing, eight white saddle hackles about 3 inches long, splaying in all directions. Also, centered on each side, a white saddle hackle about 5 inches long, to simulate tentacles
Optics	4- to 9-millimeter, yellow, post-type, post removed, glued on
Topping/ Throat	Fill the gaps between the eyes, both above and below, with hackle fluff or marabou tufts of the same color as the finish hackles
Weight	Wrap lead wire around the hook shank (optional)
Body	Pad the body with cotton or floss, tapered from the eyes to the head. Wrap on a body of medium to large chenille, leaving about a 1/8-inch gap between the body and the hook eye
Head	Acrylic fiber yarn comes in a three-wrap strand. Cut two strands 1½ inches long and bind one strand on each side of the hook by its middle. Secure tightly. Taking one side at a time, pull strands out tightly at a 90-degree angle to the hook shank, binding them at the base of the fibers by figure-eights around both sides. A whip completes the tying on of materials
Variations	White, natural, and hot pink

This pattern was developed in 1964 by myself and Bob Edgley and, like the Sar-Mul-Mac, originally had glass eyes instead of the solid plastic ones used today. This is another forerunner of a lot of recent-era squid flies that are very similar in appearance but don't work nearly as well. The pattern is tied in both sinking and floating versions. Squid are an oceanic bait that game fish relish the world over, and the Sea-Arrow is a squid pattern that rarely fails to take a fish, accounting for a huge variety of species, from king salmon to billfish.

2   Sar-Mul-Mac (Sardine-Mullet-Mackerel Simulator)

Hook	Tiemco 811S or Mustad 34007 or 3407
Thread	White Danville flat waxed
Optics	4- to 9-millimeter, yellow, post-type, post removed, glued on
Underbody	Eight to ten wraps of lead wire
Body Collar	Medium red chenille, two turns
Underwing/ Tail	Medium bunch of white bucktail
Overwing	Three long white saddle hackles on each side, curved-sides inward
Throat	Medium bunch of white bucktail
Side Flash	Silver Flashabou
Topping, Wing/ Head	Royal blue bucktail; royal blue Krystal Flash; peacock or multicolored Krystal Flash
Variations	Blue/Green Anchovy, Sardine, Green Mackerel

I originated this pattern in 1971 to simulate a variety of elongated marine baitfish species. It is the forefather of all the eyed, anchovy-style patterns used today; and with the exception of the addition of modern flash materials and the changing from glass eyes to glued-on plastic versions, the fly has remained unchanged since its inception. It is an oceanic pattern, meaning it will work both nearshore and offshore, worldwide, for a tremendous variety of game species. It is also a tremendous producer of big freshwater fish, from largemouth bass to pike and double-digit trout.

3   Bay-Delta Eelet

Hook	Mustad 34007 stainless steel, #2/0 to 4/0
Thread	Black Nymo, size A
Optics	1/8-inch silver bead-chain eyes
Materials	Long black horse mane or dyed nylon hair (optional); twelve long black saddle hackles and two grizzly saddle hackles; medium black chenille

I originated this pattern in 1970 for both fresh and salt water—wherever eels are found. Use it for river fishing during striped bass spawning runs. It has been a hell of a fly.

1
2
3
4
5

5	Blanton's Punch
Hook	Eagle Claw 254, #2/0 to 3/0
Thread	Radiant green monocord or equivalent, size A
Optics	1/8-inch silver bead-chain eyes
Tail	Radiant-green-dyed bucktail
Flashtail	Green Flashabou
Body	Green mylar piping or green Crystal Hair
Hackle	Radiant green, saddle hackle, long, barbed, and webby
Underwing	Light green Crystal Hair
Overwing	Peacock Crystal Hair
Topping	Peacock herl
Wing	Radiant green paired grizzly neck or saddle hackles
Head	Radiant green medium chenille
Head	
Topping	Peacock herl
Variations	Tropical Punch, Sabalo Punch

This pattern is a brighter, smaller variation of the Sar-Mul-Mac and was developed in the mid-1970s to take flats mutton snappers, jacks, kelp bass, snook, tarpon, and many other tropical species that were attracted to small, bright, but more realistically proportioned flies. These patterns work well on the flats, in brackish rivers, and in estuaries, as well as nearshore and offshore, particularly around structure.

Tim Borski

One nine-pound bonefish is responsible for my being hurled into a life of warm salt waters, tide tables, fly fishing, and near poverty.

The evening of April 19, dateline early 1980s, found me staring into a large green Dumpster behind a 7-11 on Kendall Drive in South Miami. I had just shredded my plane ticket home to Middle America and was wondering if things had gone a bit too far. The day, my first attempt at bonefishing, had been a success. After a long, uneasy minute I walked around front, purchased an ice-cold six-pack of Bud longnecks, and placed a very brief long-distance call. "Don't wait up."

There have been a few experiences in my life that have been impossible to shake. One is watching bright blue dishwashing detergent gliding silently and syruplike into an electrical outlet—which resulted in startlingly similar bright blue circles superimposing themselves on my two closed eyelids. (To this day, I go out of my way to buy the yellow detergent.) And there was the semifinals game of Monster Whiffleball waged one late-summer afternoon on the rooftop of McDill Elementary School. I went deep for a long fly ball and ran out of building. Supper was cold by the time I got around to eating that night.

Strong through the test of time is my first bonefish on a fly. The events (or nonevents) leading to the capture could be loosely termed a struggle, but more accurately described as an entirely foreign and, for the most part, cluelessly waged campaign. Only blind determination made it work in the end. The memory of that single, hard-won fish, all olive bars and lavender sides, solid as a summer melon, a bit cool to the touch and weighty in the hands, is still exactly as it should be . . . cleanly focused and readily accessible whenever I choose to relive it. I've forgotten more recent fish. I know this to be true because above my drawing table is a framed eight-by-ten of me cradling what is obvi-ously a much larger one. I don't recall when that catch occurred or even who leaned on the shutter. It's one of those photos that simply materialize every fifteen or so rolls of film. I guess my point is this: A bona fide milestone in one's life is damned tough to forget.

Somewhere in the beginning, a friend of mine walked me through a very basic hairwing Bend Back. It was my first legitimate fly-tying encounter and I would venture to guess that thousands of the pests have rolled off my vise since then, but I still have that very fly and it's never been wet, never will be.

Through the years, a considerable amount of water has slid by the skiff and I've decided, contrary to popular opinion, that the fish in my neck of the woods are not all that particular in what they choose to put in their mouths. A solid, no-nonsense, working pattern chosen for sink rate and silhouette matched to conditions—water depth, current flow, and speed of target—will, more times than not, get the grab. I'm of the opinion that if the angler does the job correctly with the proper tool, he or she is more than likely going to stay busy.

I'm embarrassed to say how long it took me to build the confidence I need to toss an unproven pattern at fish during lean times, but once I got over this stumbling block, the fundamentals of controlled experimentation took over and I've never looked back. I got to the point where once I'd used a particular fly to dupe a few fish, I retired it to make way for a new scheme. Although I will still dust off a particularly consistent fly when I need a certain fish for a painting reference, photos, or a good friend's first, day in and day out I'm usually throwing something new.

Focusing on the properties of a brand-new fly snugged tight in my vise, still wet and smelling of a Sally Hanson product, and knowing it will work on the edge of a certain shallow bank at first light tomorrow is still the reward. I don't see that changing anytime soon.

In closing, I'd like to thank Frank Oblak for that first fly, Arthur E. Knox for *Autumns on the Spey*, and MC 5 for "Kicking Out the Jams." It's been a fine ride.

9   Chernobyl Crab

1. Place the hook upside down in the vise (point up). Tie in a clump of calf tail and top it with six strands of Krystal Flash. Tie in two grizzly hackles, one on each side, for the tail.

2. Secure a clump of deer hair on the shank just in front of the tail, allowing it to flare outward but not spinning it. Tie in wide, webby grizzly, cree, or badger hackle in front of the deer hair. This hackle will later be palmered forward, but leave it as it is for now.

3. Add more deer hair and spin it forward along the shank, forming a thick body to a point just behind the eye of the hook.

4. Use a double-edged razor blade to trim the deer hair flat on the top and bottom, taking care not to cut the grizzly hackle. Then trim the deer hair to form a crab shape.

5. Attach the lead eyes behind the hook eye, positioned so that the hook rides point up. Palmer the grizzly hackle forward through the deer-hair body and tie it off behind the eyes. Trim away excess material. Trim the hackle flat on the bottom. Paint the eyes yellow with black pupils.

6. If you choose to add a weed guard, use 15- or 20-pound test hard mono.

1   Indestructo Clouser

Hook	Mustad 34007, #2
Tail	Light tan craft fur and pearlescent Krystal Flash
Body	Silver mylar tinsel
Eyes	Lead dumbbells, painted yellow with black pupils
Body	Epoxy

2   Purple Dredge Fly

Hook	Mustad 34007, #2
Tail	4- to 5-inch strip of purple rabbit fur
Body	Very long, soft brown hackle palmered heavily forward over the body
Eyes	Lead dumbbells tied under the hook, painted yellow with black pupils

3   Sand Eel Deceiver

Hook	Tiemco 811S, #1/0
Tail	Four long white saddle hackles, flanked on each side by black saddle hackles barred with an olive waterproof marker
Body	Light tan marabou, also barred with an olive waterproof marker
Topping	Long dark brown Icelandic goat hair
Head	Black with a yellow eye and black pupils

4   Deer Hair Shrimp

Hook	Tiemco 811S, #1
Tail	Tan craft fur
Legs	Long tan hackles
Body	Natural deer body hair, spun and clipped
Eyes	Burned monofilament
Underside	Clipped deer hair body barred with an olive waterproof marking pen

5   Bonefish Short, Tan

Hook	Mustad 34007, #6
Tail	Orange Krystal Flash over light tan calf tail
Skirt	Grizzly hackle, long and webby
Wing	Two short grizzly hackle tips, tied flat and delta-wing-style
Eyes	Glass beads, strung on stiff monofilament and positioned at the midpoint of the hook shank
Head	Wrap gold mylar tinsel on the front half of the hook shank. From the eyes forward, form a flat, triangular-shaped head with epoxy

AUTHOR'S NOTE: Tim created this fly in the late 1980s, and says that this is the most effective bonefish fly he uses.

1
2
3

6	**Bonefish Slider**
Hook	Mustad 34007, #4
Wing	Pearlescent Krystal Flash over clear craft fur hair barred with an olive waterproof marking pen
Hackle	Long, soft grizzly, palmered over the rear half of the hook and trimmed on the bottom
Eyes	Lead, yellow with black pupils
Collar	Dark deer body hair, on top only
Head	Natural dark and light deer body hair, spun and trimmed flat. The finished head should look mottled; coloration can be added with a marking pen

7	**Kraft Fur Shrimp**
Hook	Mustad 34007, Tiemco 811S, #4 to 1/0
Tail	Tan Craft Fur #1872; Pantone marker #147-M; hot orange Krystal Flash
Body	White thread
Body Hackle	Wide grizzly or badger, palmered and clipped on top
Eyes	Lead, painted black on yellow
Weed Guard	15- or 20-pound Mason hard mono

8	**Bonefish Critter**
Hook	Mustad 34007, #1 to 4
Tail	Burned-monofilament eye stalks
Body	Hot orange Crystal Chenille; tan wool; Pantone marker #147-M
Eyes	Lead, varied
Weed Guard	15- or 20-pound Mason hard mono

AUTHOR'S NOTE: Tim lives in the Florida Keys, where he fishes for the big three of the flats: tarpon, bonefish, and permit. When not out on the flats fishing he spends his time painting fish and spinning up flies to pursue them.

His flies are well thought out and honed to the Keys' extremely smart bonefish and permit. His use of materials is unique among flats flies. His tails are colored with alternating bars, the body hackles are long and Spey-like in appearance, the bodies are of spun deer hair for a full look and a soft landing. His patterns always have eyes, whether hand-painted on dumbbells or made of burned mono. When at rest, they look like some type of shrimp or crab burrowing into the bottom to get away from a bonefish or permit—real fishing flies.

Tim's flies give the impression of underwater life—with an artistic touch.

4	5
6	7
8	9

Dick Brown

From the beginning, my fly tying has been driven more by catching fish than by constructing good-looking flies. It's not that I made a conscious decision about it. I just got bitten by the bonefish bug in the mid-1970s when there were few choices in flats flies . . . and even fewer places to buy them.

The first fly I tied was a Crazy Charlie. Bill Sullivan, a friend who worked for the little Orvis shop just outside Boston, showed me how to put it together. I'd never had any lessons or read anything about tying. I just wanted to fill my box with flies and go bonefishing.

My first Charlies were horrible. I wound the V-Rib onto the shank as an underbody, covered it with a hundred wraps of Flashabou, then spiraled the V-Rib down the shank a second time as an overbody. It looked like a plastic marshmallow with cocked eyes. The thing was so fat it smacked the water like a hammer and spooked fish on flats three miles away. But I stayed with tying and took some lessons. Eventually I managed to teach myself enough by trial and error, mostly error. After a while, I even began to catch fish with my own flies, and it was a real kick. But the biggest reward was having more control over how my flies performed . . . and in bonefishing that's critical.

Bonefish flies have to accomplish more than flies tied for other game fish. They have to land softly to avoid spooking quarry, and they must sink fast to reach cruising schools before they change direction. They also have to cut wind, avoid snagging the bottom, and emit just the right amount of flash to attract but not spook fish. And they should animate well even when at rest. That's a lot to ask of a single fly!

But by learning to construct my own flies, I discovered that there were ways to control all these variables, and, even more important, I could emphasize one element over another for different situations. For exam-

ple, I could tie Tom McGuane's Sea Flea with reflective materials like Swannundaze and Krystal Flash for cloudy days and murky waters. Then I could make the same fly with a dull dubbed body for bright days. I could tie shrimp patterns like Winston Moore's Green Puff with a thin body and a heavy eye weights for deep waters and construct a second version with a fluffy body and no weight for thin, spooky conditions.

It was exciting to add these weapons to my flats-fishing arsenal, and tying became an important part of my fishing. Lately, as I've begun studying flats prey and identifying what bonefish eat, I've experimented—as have many others before me in freshwater fishing—with the body shapes, colors, and actions of different crabs, shrimp, urchins, worms, mantises, gobies, toadfish, and even clams. Tying has enriched my angling far beyond the simple catching of fish. It has pushed me to think about the *why* more than the *what* of fishing. And it has led me to a new understanding of bonefish and prey.

I'm an eclectic. And I'm a rough tier, not a fine artisan. I build flies to seduce fish. Usually I tie only a few at a time, and I'm almost always in a hurry. Although I've tied with master salmon fly tiers such as Poul Jorgensen, Ron Alcott, and Bill Wilbur, I'll never have their delicate talents. I marvel at their exquisite artistry and adapt it to my fishing-fly needs, but that's as far as I go.

I also admire the ingenious techniques of such talented innovators as Jack Gartside, Craig Mathews, and Dick Talleur. And I'm struck by the work of creative tiers Carl Richards, Tim Borski, Will Myers, and Bill Catherwood.

Most of all, I love to study flies from guys who live on fly fishing's edge—those who spend a lot of time where the fish are and think about what they're doing. People like Harry Spear, Rick Ruoff, Warren Brewster, Winston Moore, Del Brown, Lefty Kreh, and Tom McGuane.

I tie trout flies, salmon flies, and striper flies. For the most part, I tie what others have designed for these species. If there is anything special about my tying, it's in the bonefish patterns I tie. I'm fascinated with this species and its prey. And I'm obsessed with the functional requirements of sight fishing for a moving target. It's in this area that I've done most of my own tinkering.

Big prey such as crabs, mantises, and toadfish fascinate me as shapes to imitate, especially when the flies have to be cast through the wind, land quietly, and sink fast. Flies like Harry Spear's MOE, Jim Orthwein's Golden Eye, and my own Beady Crab and Slinky are good examples, combining hard and soft, heavy and aerodynamic properties while also delivering the proper suggestion of shape and color.

Chenille and wool in their many forms produce a meaty shape and they both land quietly and absorb water so they sink well. Small-faceted reflective materials suggest the sparkle of light reflecting off moving appendages and carapace plates, yet avoid the megaflashes that put fish down. Rubber tails and legs wiggle appetizingly, yet hold up to chewing and to the abuses of casting.

The fish I chase, other than the Atlantic salmon, hit flies out of the simple need to put food in their bellies. What triggers them to think that a hook with feathers or plastic is prey and not predator can vary with the fish and the habitat. Blue sharks hit flies that look like chum,

stripers eat baitfish and eel patterns, and bonefish gobble flies that look like the crabs, shrimp, toadfish, and worms they see banging around on the flat's floor.

If I had to pick the most important invention in bonefish-fly design in the last twenty years, it would be Bob Nauheim's metal eyes on his original Charlie. This archetypal design got the fly down in front of the fish, inverted it to make it weedless, and bounced it up and down on the bottom so it made puffy little mud clouds. That's what made the Charlie drive bonefish crazy and gave it a place in every flats-bound fly box.

The only time I know when you can aggravate bonefish into hitting a fly is when they're swarming in spawning schools. They'll porpoise and roll on or near the surface in huge packs, and even a fly landing on the back of one won't scare them off. I've thrown big noisy flies at these fish, casting beyond them, and had strong takes when I pulled the fly toward the fish, making it look as if it was going to attack.

In my kind of fishing, if it looks like food, moves like food, and looks easy to kill, it'll get the attention of the fish. But then a fly also has to be designed so you can get it down in front of fish fast without scaring them. It must animate well when retrieved, without snagging on grass or coral, and it's a real plus if it's durable and easy to tie. If a fly can do all these things, it should do the job.

My favorite place is the Bahamas. The fish aren't always as big as those in Florida, but they're big enough. And the Bahamas are like the Keys were thirty years ago. I can fish all day and never see another boat or angler.

There are plenty of other great flats-fishing places, too—like Mexico's east coast, Venezuela's atoll at Los Roques, and the Pacific's Christmas Island. But for me the Bahamas are closer, the fish are bigger, and the variety of habitat is limitless. I'll fish there as long as I can walk.

6   Beady Crab

Hook	Mustad 34007, #2, 4, or 6
Thread	Chartreuse Danville flat waxed nylon, #3/0
Underbody/	
Weight	Two strands of 3/32-inch bead chain, each four beads long
Claws	Pair of cree hackle tips
Legs	Four strands of Sili Legs
Body	Olive or beige Danville Speckled Crystal Chenille, size 0 (or XS)
Weed	
Guard	12-pound Mason (optional)

1. At its midpoint, figure-eight one four-bead strand of bead chain to the spine at the hook bend. Figure-eight the second strand parallel to the first, just behind the hook eye. Bind both strands tightly—the way you would normally attach a standard two-bead segment for eyes—by winding figure-eight fashion and then tightening up with horizontal doughnut wraps underneath the bead chain.

2. Bind the two outermost beads of the two strands (those on the side closest to you) together, pulling them almost into a V, then angle your bobbin 90 degrees and make additional wraps perpendicular to the first wraps to form a bow tie in the center. This tightens the bead chain into a frame and forms a thread platform for the claws and legs.

3. Attach the two hackle claws, shiny-side down. (They will be inverted in the fly's final orientation.) Lay their butts along the hook's spine and between the two strands of bead chain; bind the stubs to the thread platform and shank.

4. Pull the hackle claws into their approximate position—at a 90-degree angle from the shank and lying along the two strands of bead chain. Gently lock them into this orientation by taking a couple of wraps in the corners at their base.

5. Cut four 1½-inch segments of Sili Legs and fold them over your tying thread. Pull them along the thread down onto the thread platform and bind them down, splaying them toward the hook point side. This will help invert the fly when it sinks.

6. Tie in the chenille, and move the thread to the hook eye. Wind the chenille in large figure-eight wraps, separating the legs and filling in the body.

7. Invert the fly. Then angle the chenille 90 degrees and wrap two or three perpendicular turns so the chenille lies between the claws and eyes. This finishes filling the body profile and binds it together. Tie off and trim the legs.

1   Bonefish Crab

Winston Moore

Hook	Mustad 34007, #2, 4, or 6
Thread	Chartreuse Danville flat waxed nylon, #3/0
Claws/	
Antennae	Furnace hackle tips, creamy white marabou, then two strands Krystal Flash, all 1½ shank lengths long
Body	Strands of cream wool or wool tufts from a hide, figure-eighted to the shank then brushed out, flattened, and glued with contact cement (not superglue) into a stiff carapace
Legs	White round rubber "hackles" tied in when the wool strands are applied, before gluing
Weight	3/32-inch (1/100 ounce) lead barbells; vary for hook size and water depth
Variations	The fly can also be tied in pink, brown, or tan

2   Jim's Golden Eye Shrimp

Jim Orthwein

Hook	Mustad 9674 or 38941, #2 or 4
Thread	Beige monocord, #3/0
Antennae	Peccary hair (or moose mane)
Eyes	Medium (1/8-inch) gold bead-chain eyes
Head/Face	Nugget gold synthetic hair ends (FisHair No. 15-B, 70 denier) over gold mylar tubing ends, brushed out
Body	Slip a section of mylar tubing over the shank so the hook goes inside the tubing (core removed); tie down the tubing and overwrap with clear Swannundaze or V-Rib
Legs	Brown saddle hackle, palmered into the spiraled crevices of the V-Rib and clipped on the back and sides
Carapace/	
Tail	Nugget gold FisHair twisted into a rope and pulled over the back, then doubled back alongside itself and lashed to one side as an off-center tail or telson. Coat the back heavily with Hard As Nails

The bronze hook must be humped by bending it down at both ends when you're finished, making the back adhere tightly to the body.

Jim says he often finds it best to continue a steady retrieve after the fish has seen the fly, a strategy that clearly works very well for him. Jim has taken three of his four IGFA world-record bonefish on this fly, as well as many double-digit fish.

1	2
3	4
6	5
	7

3	**Gotcha**
	Jim McVay
Hook	Mustad 34007, #2 or 4
Thread	Fluorescent or Gotcha pink Danville flat waxed nylon
Eyes	1/8-inch bead-chain eyes on #4, 5/32-inch bead-chain eyes on #2, or 1/50-ounce (5/32-inch) lead barbells for a fast sink
Tail	Pearl mylar tubing
Body	Pearl Diamond Braid
Wing	Yellow Krystal Flash over blond craft fur

The tail is as long as, or longer than, the body; the wing length reaches past the tail. McVay also ties the fly with an orange wing for dark flats (Fish Fuzz No. 13, goldfish orange).

Tied with 1/8-inch or 3/16-inch bead chain, this is a good medium-depth shrimp pattern; with lead eyes it is often effective in deeper water. It is very productive in low light and surprisingly also in bright light. Apparently, small-faceted materials make this bright fly less prone to bright-light spooking than shinier Charlies. The Gotcha is especially effective in Andros, Abaco, and the Berry Islands.

This fly was named by Rupert Leadon of Andros Island because every time someone would throw the fly and a fish would hit it, we would say "Gotcha."

4	**MOE (Mother of Epoxy) Shrimp**
	Harry Spear
Hook	Mustad 34007, #2 or 4
Thread	Chartreuse monocord or flat waxed nylon, #3/0
Tail/Claws/ Legs	White marabou fibers (one side of a marabou blood feather pulled from the quill), then tan marabou fibers (same amount), then a pair of furnace neck or saddle hackles flanking the marabou and flared out. Next, pull one wrap of thread under and behind the entire tail to kick it up from the shank. Resume normal wraps
Eyes	Burned 60- or 80-pound, prestretched monofilament, figure-eighted to the shank
Body	Fasco Fas-Stick epoxy glue No. 110 or a similar tub epoxy mixed in exactly equal parts and mixed thoroughly for one full minute (or it comes out tacky and won't harden). Do not let the mix begin to set before applying or it will develop memory and will not retain shaping. Applying with a toothpick or dental tool, form the flat diamond shape over the edges of the cross into crescent-shaped, concave curves between each point on the body's outline. Keep the body thin; fish don't seem to like fat bodies

Weed Guard	Pair of clear monofilament spikes, 15-pound hard Mason for #2 hook, and 12-pound for #4 hook. Prepare by passing the butt ends near a flame to slightly fatten. When they're hard, sink anchors into the epoxy body
Finishing	Place in fishing orientation (body up, hook down) into an oven preheated to 140 degrees then turned off. Leave in the oven to remove moisture and set epoxy

Prepare the eyes by cutting a 3/4-inch piece of mono. Then, holding it in a forceps, put its end into a sooty candle flame, melt and blacken it, and invert it to the vertical to allow a round eye to form as a droplet. Repeat for the other side. You should have an eye shaft about 7/16 to 9/16 inch long when you are finished. Another version uses olive over white marabou, flanked by splayed grizzly tips.

For the Florida Keys I tie this in #2; for the Bahamas, #4.

5	**Sili Legs Bonefish Fly**
	Barry and Cathy Beck
Hook	Orvis SW, #2, 4, or 6
Thread	White monocord, #3/0
Eyes	Clouser lead eyes, 1/24 to 1/32 ounce, midshank
Tail	Chartreuse calf tail and pearl Krystal Flash
Legs	Chartreuse Sili Legs material
Body	Kreinik 1/8-inch Tyers' Ribbon
Throat	Krystal Flash over chartreuse calf tail

This pattern was designed to fish flats in relatively low water on both incoming and outgoing tides. Stripping action should start slowly and increase when the bonefish show interest. The pattern can be used in all situations—mudding, cruising, and tailing.

7	**Jim's Rubber Band Worm**
	Jim Orthwein
Hook	Mustad 34007 or 3407, #4 or 6
Thread	Beige monocord, #3/0
Eyes	Medium (1/8-inch) gold bead-chain eyes
Tail	Walgreen, CVS, or similar beige rubber band (1/8-inch wide), trimmed to a point at the end
Body	Gold-colored rug wool or yarn; the color should closely match the nugget gold FisHair (No. 15-B) in the Jim's Golden Eye

Capt. Jeffrey Cardenas

I am a South Florida native. I guided for ten years in the Key West area and am now the owner of The Saltwater Angler, a fly-fishing specialty store that also books guides and provides guest house accommodations.

As a writer and photographer, my specialty is salt-water-related subjects. I have worked on assignment for numerous magazines and newspapers, including *The New York Times, Sports Illustrated, Time,* and *Outside* magazine. *Marquesa: A Time & Place with Fish,* a natural history book about the Marquesas Keys near Key West, was published by Meadow Run Press in 1995. A limited edition of this book was also produced featuring a portfolio of unique black-and-white underwater landscapes of the area.

The Grand Slam is every flats fisherman's Holy Grail. While it would be nice to say that the fly selection below will provide the key to this goal, the reality of catching a tarpon, bonefish, and (especially) permit on a fly is that it's better to be lucky than good. Still, if I could reduce my fly patterns to just three flies that would give me the best shot at catching a Grand Slam, these are the flies I would use.

2, 3, 4, 5 Bonefish Bunny

Hook	Mustad 34007, #6
Weight	Varies with sink rate, from bead chain to dumbbells
Tail	Rabbit fur; two strands of Krystal Flash. Use gray for mottled bottoms and dark brown for turtle grass
Body	Aunt Lydia's Rug Yarn, to match rabbit fur

The Bunny Bone patterns are so simple that, as one wag puts it, you can tie them using your teeth as a vise. The basic concept is that these patterns can be presented very close to bonefish, enticing them with natural movement and minimal stripping. Each fly blends into its surroundings. Camouflage is the only hope bonefish prey has to survive on a tropical saltwater flat. The prey doesn't dart around, as some stripping techniques might indicate. It hides in its camouflage but, unlike a piece of grass or debris, the prey is alive. Bonefish are looking for subtle indications of life amid the camouflage. The rabbit fur tied into the Bunny Bone patterns brings these flies to life in the most natural manner.

Use a small hook. A #6 Mustad 34007 is appropriate. Color and weight vary with water depth and bottom pattern. I like gray over mottled, hard-marl bottoms. Dark brown is ideal for turtle grass and coral. Light tan and white are best when there is a predominance of sand. I use anywhere from a $1/50$-ounce dumbbell eye for deep-cruising fish to a weightless mono eye for ultra-shallow tailing fish. The body is either wrapped (if you're tying it in your teeth) or dubbed in Aunt Lydia's Rug Yarn in a color to match the rabbit fur. Tie two long strands of Krystal Flash into the tail and that's it.

1   Marquesa Sunrise Special

Hook	Eagle Claw D67 Billy Pate Tarpon Hook, #2/0
Tail	Puff of orange marabou; two pairs of orange-dyed grizzly (the width, shape, and length of a child's finger) tied Keys-style, curved outward; eight or ten strands of copper Krystal Flash
Collar	Puff of tan marabou one-third of the length of the tail; palmered orange-dyed grizzly half the length of the marabou
Head	Fluorescent orange thread two-thirds of the hook shank; paint one eye and epoxy

1. The recipe begins, as always, with the hook. I like a #2/0 hook with strong carbon-steel tensile strength, a short point, and minimal barb. The Eagle Claw D67 Billy Pate Tarpon Hook is perfectly designed for Key West tarpon. I don't sharpen it before I tie it; I prefer to file a double-sided edge on the fly the day I'm going to fish it. In the corrosive environment of Key West I don't count on any steel staying sharp over a period of time.

2. Next, I tie in a puff of orange marabou at the top of the bend of the hook. High-quality marabou is an essential ingredient in tarpon flies. The tarpon of Key West are primarily shrimp eaters, and shrimplike marabou is rarely motionless. It should be noted that the marabou in the tail will also keep the tail feathers from fouling.

3. I use the best saltwater hackle I can find for the tail feathers. For the Marquesa Sunrise Special it is orange-dyed grizzly that is the width, length, and shape of a child's finger. It should be webby and well rounded at the tip. I tie in two pairs Keys-style—the natural bend turns outward so that the tail feathers are splayed. It is impor-

tant that the feathers stay aligned. Tie them in lightly at first. Align, straighten, pull, and tweak them until they are perfect. Then cinch them down and lock them in with a touch of head cement.

4. Tie in eight or ten strands of copper Krystal Flash, evenly spread on each side of the tail feathers.

5. The collar is a simple laid-back puff of tan marabou. Use the most delicate tip ends of the marabou, and use plenty of them. Marabou has a tendency to disappear when it becomes wet. The collar should extend one-third of the length of the tail feathers.

6. In front of the marabou make a couple of palmered turns of orange-dyed grizzly and tie these in so that they lie back against half the length of the marabou. This palmered hackle will help streamline the collar.

7. I wrap the head with fluorescent orange thread two-thirds of the way to the eye. This allows a clean surface of hook shank on which to snell a shock-tippet leader.

8. Finally, I coat the head with epoxy and paint in an eye. What the heck, the eye's more for me than the fish—but if we can't allow ourselves a little artistic expression in our fly fishing we might as well be data processors in our spare time.

Gary Borger looked at my tarpon fly selection once and noted wryly that the selection of colors, even fluorescent colors, might be well suited for steelhead and salmon. The brightest of these tarpon patterns is the Marquesa Sunrise Special. It is also the most effective.

This fly has the silhouette and contrast that pull the appetite trigger on early-morning tarpon. What the tarpon think about the bright orange color is something Gary Borger would be more qualified to answer.

6   Palmered Crab

Hook	Mustad 34007, #1
Weight	Heaviest dumbbell eyes you feel comfortable casting
Tail	Puff of marabou; two grizzly hackles splayed Keys-style; two strands of Krystal Flash
Body	Palmer three grizzly hackles, tied full. Trim the bottom of the hackle

I tied my first Palmered Crabs the glorious summer I spent alone in the Marquesas on my houseboat, the *Huck Finn*. There was plenty of time to experiment with new patterns and plenty of permit to test those patterns out on. The first field tests were actually made on the savvy gray snappers that lived among the mangrove roots. The biggest fish, four- and five-pounders, regularly scoffed at Clousers, Deceivers, and Charlies. These snappers were true predators with great eyes. Something about the Palmered Crab, however, appealed to their greedy nature. The big snappers would bully their way out of the mangroves and tear into the

Palmered Crab with their sharp, rattlesnakelike fangs. Of course, the predatory cycle did not end there. I felt no guilt laying one or two of those fat snappers on the barbecue grill at the end of the day.

The Palmered Crab was clearly a huge success on snappers; it was also the most effective pattern I used on the Marquesas permit. (And no, the permit did not end up on the grill with the snappers at the end of the day.) The atoll west of Key West is, by most accounts, the richest permit area in the world. Here the fish, often over forty pounds, come into the flats off the wreck and reefs to scour the shallow water for crabs. They will also eat shrimp and a glass minnow called a *majuga*. I've even found snails and a full-size squid in the stomach of a Marquesas permit that was chopped in half by a shark. But the food they want most is a live crab, and for anglers wanting to succeed at taking a permit on a fly the fly

	1	
2		3
4		5
	6	

doesn't so much have to look like a crab as it has to move like one.

Color variations should be chosen with regard to the indigenous species of crab and the bottom conditions that will be fished. I use a grizzly crab over turtle grass bottoms, a white-and-gray crab over sand, and an orange crab in poor visibility, muds, and marls.

Hooks of #1 are ideal. Go down a size for small tailing fish. Go up a size if the fish are twenty-five pounds or larger. I use Mustad 34007 stainless hooks because this is a difficult tie and I don't want the hooks to rust in my fly box.

Start with a puff of marabou tied in at the tail. Marabou, like rabbit, is always moving in the water. This is important for a fly that will be worked with minimal stripping. Next, add two opposing dry-fly-quality grizzly feathers to the tail. Go ahead and break down and buy a grade-1 Metz neck. Catching a permit on a fly is worth any price. Add two strands of Krystal Flash.

Tie in the heaviest dumbbell eyes you feel you can throw. A live crab darts for the bottom and so should your Palmered Crab. Superglue the eyes after they are tied in so that they don't move.

The palmering can be done with three feathers simultaneously if you are careful. Leave some of the fluff at the base of the feather; it will add density to the body. Make sure the hackle is wide enough to provide leg length. If the body is not full enough, compress the feathers toward the bend of the hook and palmer in another set. Heavy palmered hackle is essential to this pattern. Bring the feathers flush to the dumbbell eyes.

Trim the fly carefully and close along the hook shank opposite the bend. Leave the hackle untrimmed on the side of the fly and in the bend. This will add buoyancy to allow the hook to ride upright. It will also provide a natural weed guard for the fly.

Cast close, read the fish, twitch-strip as necessary . . . and hang on.

Bill Catherwood

Every now and then over the years someone asks, "What inspired you to design and tie imitations of saltwater baitfish?" This question used to come as a surprise to me, because I have always believed in matching the available fodder.

I began tying flies professionally in my late teens and raised my own chickens to meet my demands. Through years of breeding I was able to produce chickens with long hackles for my saltwater patterns. I wing my flies with natural materials because I am convinced that their action is superior to any synthetic.

I began fly-rodding in fresh water but switched to conventional surf casting when I went to the ocean waters. Occasionally while at the beach I would think, "Wow! Wouldn't that fish have been great to take on a fly rod?" I began to take my fly rod to the ocean, but I couldn't find any good fly patterns that imitated the baitfish the game fish were feeding on.

So I began to develop patterns to fish with. These were the early days of saltwater fly fishing, before many fly fishermen ventured to the ocean with fly rods, let alone tied flies to match the local baitfish. First I developed my Herring and Tinker Mackerel patterns. These two patterns went through stages of evolution until they became fixed and remained unchanged for thirty years.

Originally these streamers were 2½ to 3 inches in length. It occurred to me that these lengths in no way approached the proportions of the naturals and so, like Topsy, "they just grew." Along the way I also developed a style of tying that gave my patterns realistic outlines and truly three-dimensional appearances.

I believe that the most effective fly patterns are those that imitate specific prey. Game fish are visual predators and they have their favorite foods just like me and you. It makes sense to offer them something that resembles what they are feeding on—especially if

they are feeding selectively. Each of my imitations is developed with a purpose. My Giant Killer series numbers almost forty patterns, with baitfish, squid, shrimp, and crabs. I love to fish but even more I like studying saltwater baitfish and crustaceans and designing patterns to imitate them.

I remember that in the earlier years, total strangers sometimes took valuable time from their fishing to patiently try to explain to me the reasons why I couldn't use my fly-fishing tackle in the sea. During the late 1950s and early 1960s I caught my first fly-rod bluefish on Plum Island, Massachusetts. A local bait-shop owner informed me later that a customer came in saying, "There's some guy trying to catch a bluefish on a fly rod." Ten minutes later another customer came in and said, "Hey, some guy just caught a bluefish on a fly rod."

As my flies grew, my rod and fly line seemed to shrink. Leon Martuche of Scientific Anglers was pioneering saltwater tapered lines up to 10-weights, and he graciously sent some to me. At the same time Helen Desteffano, a great Boston rod builder, acquired an experimental black Harnel blank and she built a great rod for me. The rod was an arm breaker but it moved my big hair-headed streamers. Not knowing better, I really enjoyed it. At that time I worked for my dad driving a truck and picking up milk at the area farms. I lifted forty-quart milk jugs that, when full, weighed a bit over a hundred pounds. It took a spell of fishing before it dawned on me why my arm was aching. I kick myself for selling that rod to a customer who insisted that he had to have it then, after his girlfriend slammed a car door on it, offered to sell it back to me six inches shorter.

Fly fishermen may not be aware that for many years my wife, Grace, and I made a comfortable living producing tackle for saltwater fishermen who "had to catch fish." We catered to commercial fishermen, charter skippers, and sport fishermen. I designed and produced harpoons for giant tuna and trolling hand lines for charter skippers. I never claimed to be the originator of umbrella rigs, though I'm widely credited with this distinction. Somewhere in my cellar I have an umbrella rig that is over one hundred years old.

As time went on I became aware that I had developed a real fish-calling style with my deer body hair heads with their bullet-shaped noses and their slightly more than neutral buoyancy. My years spent working with aircraft stood me in good stead as I designed many three-dimensional streamers with aerodynamics that screamed, "Here I am!" I first became aware of this when I noticed that small baitfish would erupt from the water two or three feet ahead of my hair-headed streamers. My aircraft years also influenced my making hair heads so very durable. Fly fishermen may believe that a hair head cannot be tied that can withstand the onslaught of toothed fish. Not so! When Orvis's Pip Winslow handed back one of my hair-headed American eel patterns, I asked, "Pip, what's wrong with it?" He replied, "Nothing is wrong with it, I took over fifty toothed fish with it and I thought that you might like to have it." I guess that Pip thought that I might frame it. Wrong! I took it fishing.

In the last few years I have had many requests to give tying seminars. I usually begin one of my seminars with a narrated slide presentation that is both informative and, I hope, entertaining. The Giant Killers—which feature a three-dimensional style of tying using only four bunches of hair instead of the expected twenty or more—is a common request, along with patterns for tinker mackerel, squid, smelt, herring, crabs, and needlefish. My seminars usually zero in on salt water but my big streamers have also done a great job with pike.

It has been many years and I have developed many patterns in imitation of the naturals, but I still want to do more. I can't get old while feeling this compulsion. I'm too set in my ways to change but I realize that tiers don't have to follow my style exactly. Good tiers can temper my rules and do great things with their own variations.

Come what may, it has been a very interesting experience for me.

1	Hair-Head White Perch
Hook	Mustad 94151, #7/0
Tail	White, green, gray, and blue Icelandic goat hair
Overwing	Four badger hackles
Sides	Pink marabou and gold Icelandic goat hair, 3/4 the length of the wing
Head	Olive-green clipped deer hair, with collar at the back of the head
Eyes	Glass taxidermist eyes, brown with black pupil

2, 3	Catherwood's Pogy
Hook	Mustad 94151, #7/0
Thread	Heavy blue cotton-wrapped polyester
Wing	Scottish blackface (sheep) hair. Each bunch should be about 1/4 inch in diameter when loose. The first bunch should be white and about 3 inches long. The next bunch, tied on top of the first, is also white and should be about 4 inches. Next is a bunch dyed silvery blue dun, about 4 1/2 inches long. A bunch of pink, the same length as the last, is tied to encircle the wing. Next is another bunch of blue dun (but not tied to encircle the wing). Then tie a bunch of yellow to veil or encircle the wing to give the fly its yellowish cast. Next, tie a bunch of blue (blackface hair dyed with Rit Evening Blue) prominently over the back
Head	Deer body hair bunched and trimmed to shape; two bunches of white (the first rather long and flowing back over the wing), one small bunch of yellow, another small bunch of white, and a bunch of blue at the nose
Eyes	Glass, 1/4 inch for the largest flies, attached figure-eight-style after the yellow deer body hair

1	2
4	3
5	6
7	8

4	Catherwood's Raging Squid
Hook	Mustad 94151, #7/0
Thread	Heavy pink cotton-wrapped polyester
Marabou	Pink
Wing	Eight long ginger hackles over purple Scottish blackface hair
Tentacles	Eight short ginger hackles tied just behind the eye of the hook to encircle the shank. The hackles will splay when the fly is retrieved
Eyes	Glass, 1/4 inch in diameter

5	Pink Squid
Hook	Mustad 94151, #7/0
Thread	Heavy pink cotton-wrapped polyester
Marabou	Pink
Wing	Eight long pink hackles over black Scottish blackface hair
Tentacles	Eight short pink hackles tied just behind the eye of the hook to encircle the shank. The hackles will splay when the fly is retrieved
Eyes	Glass, 1/4 inch in diameter

6	Articulated Crab
Hook	Mustad 94151, #6/0
Hook Dressing	Sand cemented to a base of built-up thread and wire
Connection	Wire loops connect the hook to a cross-shaped wire frame on which the fly is constructed
Eyes	Melted monofilament black beads
Claws	Two brown-and-black mottled body feathers with heavy curved stems, cemented into shape with the barbs all pulled forward
Legs	Ginger variant hackles secured to the base of the claws, four per side
Back	Speckled brown hen body feather
Underbelly	Speckled brown hen body feather

AUTHOR'S NOTE: Bill designed this fly to imitate a crab with its claws raised in a defensive position. The sand camouflages the hook and blends in with sandy bottoms. There are many crab imitations, but Catherwood's design is surely unique.

7	Hair-Head Tinker Mackerel
Hook	Mustad 94151, #7/0
Thread	Heavy blue cotton-wrapped polyester
Marabou	White for the belly, one or two feathers tied concave-side up on top of the shank at the bend of the hook and over the barb. Over this is a silvery blue dun feather, also concave-side up. Over the dun, fasten a pink feather—with the end section cut out to form a V—concave-side down. Over this, fasten a green feather and then a blue, both concave-side down
Wing	Four or eight long saddle hackles—equal numbers of blue and green—tied in alternately (blue, green, blue, green). On each side of this, tie a long grizzly saddle hackle. The wing numbers six to ten feathers total
Head	Deer body hair. First, fasten two thick bunches of blue and one thick bunch of green hair. The first bunch of hair should be exceptionally long and flare out over the wing. Then secure the eyes, fasten a single bunch of blue hair in front of them, and tie off. Trim the head to shape
Eyes	Glass, 1/4 inch in diameter for the largest flies, fastened to the shank using figure-eight wraps after the first two bunches of deer hair have been secured. The Tinker Mackerel can also be tied without a hair head. To do this, fasten the eyes before you begin to tie the pattern, and secure the marabou farther forward on the shank, laying the stems between the glass eyes

AUTHOR'S NOTE: Bill was awarded the Lifetime Achievement Award in 1995 by the Federation of Fly Fishers for being the originator of the Giant Killers and a true pioneer in saltwater fly tying.

8	Hair-Head Herring
Hook	Mustad 94151, #7/0
Underwing	White, light pink, light blue, and white marabou feathers attached in this order, bottom to top. You want to choose plumes with fairly rigid stems; these will help support the wing and keep it from wrapping around the hook
Wing	On each side a set of two light blue hackles, outside of which are two pearl gray hackles, tied in so the base fluff is showing
Sides	Pink, light blue, and dark blue Krystal Flash
Head	White and light blue deer body hair, spun and trimmed
Eyes	Solid glass

AUTHOR'S NOTE: This is Bill's original design for the Hair-Head Herring, except that the sides, once made of emu plumes, are now made of Krystal Flash. Bill was the first tier I know of to use a clipped deer hair head on a saltwater fly.

Trey Combs

As I write this I've just returned from hosting a long-range fly-fishing trip to Mexico's Revillagigedo Islands. The *Royal Star* had motored south from Baja's Cabo San Lucas with twenty anglers and a three-person film crew to explore and find adventure in an area never before visited by fly fishers. We soon found yellowfin tuna and wahoo out of control, in water that bordered on the epical. Against the strongest rods and most powerful reels yellowfin in the one-hundred- to two-hundred-pound range made initial runs that we came to describe in terms of miles. Wahoo ran in packs more concentrated than I'd ever experienced. Many of our party who were hardly aware of this game fish before the trip now took them regularly on flies. Large sharks ate our flies or catches and generally added a sense of danger. Jacks and trevally ran to over thirty pounds and kept the fishing percolating when the pelagics were taking the middle of the day off.

An angler who experiences this kind of fly fishing develops a prejudice for flies of his or her own invention. After all, they worked so dramatically. Never mind the myriad variables: What were the fish feeding on? Was live or dead chum used to attract? What diameter and type of leader material was used? Time of day? Was the fly deep running or right at the surface? Was the fly tied on with a loop knot? And often most important—was the fly head heavy enough to dive on the drop?

Much of my offshore fly fishing takes place aboard the *Royal Star,* a ninety-two-foot San Diego–based long-range fishing boat. In 1996 I hosted five trips spanning a total of fifty days at sea. With at least a dozen anglers on board, this twenty-four-hour-a-day fishing provides the best possible side-by-side comparison of flies. I've seen flies highly touted by their inventors prove all but worthless. Other newly created flies were a revelation. In this laboratory anglers can experiment and immediately see

how the marriage of new materials and new baitfish designs attracts the game fish. If ego doesn't trample common sense, these trips prove to be great learning experiences. With each trip, nearly everyone discards a few beliefs and gains an equal number of insights.

These experiences have led to some opinions. When tuna (sometimes joined by dorado) are in a bonkers-style feeding frenzy, anything white and stripped back fast will be hit. Commercial fishermen, who once stood in the racks and poled tuna, tie a white chicken feather on a hook and slap the fly on the water to get bites. But when tuna, especially large tuna, are cruising and feeding through, and have time for a second look, they are far more discriminating. If they're being chummed with chunks of fish rather than live bait, they laze into the chum line and casually pick up a fly that's soaking and looking like a baitfish gone bad. A billfish behaves much the same whether it's out of its mind over a teaser, eating live chum and looking for something that swims and resembles what it's eating, or looking for something that sinks and resembles a dead baitfish or piece of fish.

I've tried to tie and fish my Sea Habit Bucktails for these circumstances. I want a fly to look like a baitfish, and do so without fouling. Game fish almost never take a fouled fly. I want a fly to be supple, and for me that means using natural materials more often than not. I want a fly to carry pearlescent flash from within. To accomplish this, I use pearl Flashabou to build the interior of the fly. This material does not hold water, keeps water flowing through the fly, and provides life-suggesting flash to my baitfish patterns. I cover the heads of my flies with mylar piping and coat the head twice with epoxy. The result is a head-heavy fly that has a real baitfish look. Except when fishing for billfish, I always tie the fly on with a loop knot. When some slack is given to the swimming fly, it will tip over and dive nearly straight down. Large tuna and wahoo that refuse a fly on the strip often find a fly in this more casual attitude to be irresistible. I often add a few turns of lead wire just behind the eye to accentuate this action.

On those Sea Habit Bucktails I tie for billfish, I epoxy on large prismatic eyes. These eyes carry air and will keep the fly floating head-up on the surface. Before fishing the fly, I remember to puncture the eyes, force water into each, and soak the fly in water so that it swims correctly when it first hits the water. If I'm fishing for billfish that are actively feeding, often the case on the long-range trips, I fish only a single-hook fly. If I'm casting to a billfish that is coming off a tease, I may fish a tandem-hook fly, especially if the boat slides along after the captain has taken it out of gear. If I tie the fly with a stinger hook, I tie in an artificial hair such as FisHair on the stinger hook to obtain the length I want, and use only bucktail on the lead hook. This helps prevent the artificial hair from catching on the barb of the stinger hook and forming a huge mess. I rarely use sliding popper heads in front of the fly. If I do, I never, ever put eyes on the sliding head. Billfish are headhunters with relatively small mouths, and I want the hook point and the head of the fly as close together as possible. I hosted billfish camps in Costa Rica for six seasons and repeatedly watched Pacific sailfish take a client's big-eyed popper head and race away with the fly dangling outside its mouth. I've also seen marlin so distracted by the dangling popper head that they stopped in their panic to try and bat it away with their bill. This quickly abraded the class tippet and the billfish was lost. I now use only a thin wafer of foam set directly in front of the fly if I want to fish a sliding head. The foam still provides the *pop* to get attention without getting between the fly and the billfish.

Over the years I've experienced a lot of frustration with the hooks available for offshore fly tying, hooks that were designed essentially for trolling. In the larger sizes, #5/0 and larger, the hooks were too massive, with points too long and barbs too large for fly fishing. A massive point, razor sharp, still must cut and penetrate into dense tissue with a fly rod and with tippets testing no more than 10 kilograms (about 22 pounds), and often a lot less. Eventually I took refuge in the Gamakatsu Octopus bait hook. Though it had an upturned eye and was offset, it possessed many properties I valued: a very thin rolled beak-style point that gave incredible penetration, a tiny barb, and wire with a small diameter that had great strength. My hookup ratio on billfish changed dramatically; a sailfish or marlin that tossed the fly now became the rare exception. However, I still wanted a fly hook, not a bait hook. With the blessings and assistance of Gamakatsu, and using the Octopus as a starting point, I came up with a new style of big-game fly-fishing hook that Gamakatsu put into production in 1996 and marketed as the Trey Combs Big Game Fly. All my Sea Habit Bucktails are now tied on this hook.

Any Sea Habit Bucktail can, of course, be tied as a tube fly. I can't, without a lot of silly additions, tie on the fly with a loop and get the dramatic, jiglike drop I find so desirable. To help prevent the fly from fouling, I use a short-shanked hook and a tube as short as possible. This keeps the point of the hook close to the eye of the fly, and results in better hookups. The tube can also be made so long that the hook extends beyond the bucktail. The fly can't foul and swims well when being trolled.

My Sea Habit Bucktail, regardless of the size, is basically an all-white fly that suggests a baitfish. Dorsal color is added to the fly—more a veiling around the white rather than a stacking of one color over another—to more closely suggest a specific baitfish. These flies, however, never exactly imitate. I would be content with three to four basic patterns: Anchovy Blue, Flying Fish, Herring, and Clarion Pink Lady. I suggest you read through my approach to tying the all-white Sea Habit as a starting point for any of my other patterns.

1
2
5 3
4

1   Anchovy Blue

Hook	Trey Combs Big Game Fly hook, #1/0 to 7/0
Tail	White bucktail and pearl Flashabou
Underwing	Pearl Flashabou and white bucktail
Overwing	Above the midline tie in lime green and olive Krystal Flash, and tie over a very small bunch of lime green bucktail. This should look like a flush of lime green rather than a topping. Top with pearl blue Krystal Flash. Tie over a small bunch of turquoise blue bucktail. Top with peacock herl
Shoulder	Pearl Flashabou and a few strands of silver Flashabou. If you're tying for wahoo, shoulder heavily with both pearl and silver Flashabou. Keep the fly slim
Head	After an initial coat of five-minute epoxy has been applied to the head, attach the eyes. Coat the dorsal head with Scribbles in the color Glittering Night Star. Apply a final coat of epoxy to give the head its final contour and to completely secure the eyes

I have found the Anchovy Blue to be an effective all-purpose pattern for a great variety of game fish in sizes from 1/0 to 7/0.

2   Clarion Pink Lady

Hook	Trey Combs Big Game Fly hook, #1/0 to 7/0
Tail	White bucktail and pearl Flashabou
Underwing	Pearl Flashabou and white bucktail
Overwing	Above the midline tie in a bunch of pink Reflections on each side. Top with a bunch of pink bucktail. Between the pink bucktail, tie in a bunch of purple-green Reflections. Cover with a small bunch of purple bucktail. Top with peacock herl
Shoulder	Pearl and silver Flashabou in equal amounts
Head	Complete as for Anchovy Blue, but using Scribbles Glittering Violet Flash

This attractor pattern works well on most species of inshore and offshore game fish. I think it's especially effective on wahoo.

3   Sand Lance

Hook	Trey Combs Big Game Fly hook, #1/0 to 6/0
Tail	White bucktail and pearl Flashabou
Underwing	Pearl Flashabou and white bucktail
Overwing	Above the midline tie in olive and lime green Krystal Flash, followed by a few hairs of lime green bucktail. Top with pearl blue Krystal Flash and a few hairs of olive bucktail. Top with a small bunch of moss FisHair
Shoulder	A heavy bunch of pearl Flashabou and a few strands of silver Flashabou
Head	Complete as for Anchovy Blue

This simple-looking fly often fishes extremely well for school tuna and Pacific salmon.

5   Sea Habit Bucktail

Hook	Trey Combs Big Game Fly hook by Gamakatsu, #2/0 to 10/0
Tail	White bucktail; pearl Flashabou
Shoulder	Pearl Flashabou
Underbody	Pearl Flashabou
Overbody	White bucktail; pearl Reflections

1. Choose a hook in #2/0 to 4/0 for school tuna and dorado; #4/0 to 6/0 for wahoo, Atlantic sailfish, white marlin, and small black marlin; #6/0 for large Pacific sailfish; #7/0 for striped marlin and small blue marlin; and #8/0 to 10/0 for large black marlin and blue marlin.

2. For the tail, tie in a small bunch of white bucktail, as long as possible. Top with pearl Flashabou. Repeat as needed to produce one full half of a baitfish profile. If you're tying for billfish, repeat the steps using those artificial materials available that are longer than bucktail; in this manner you can make the tail 8 or 9 inches long. I still like to wrap this material in bucktail to help prevent it from fouling the hook.

3. Shoulder with a heavy, short bunch of pearl Flashabou on each side. If I'm tying the fly for wahoo, I shoulder again with a dozen strands of silver Flashabou on each side.

4. The construction of the tail creates a bump. Just forward of this point I tie in short bunches of pearl Flashabou in a complete circle. I don't tie in much under the fly, because I want the gap to be as wide as possible. The bump gives the Flashabou some necessary flare. On smaller flies, I repeat the process once with mostly a dorsal application. With billfish flies, I go forward and repeat with pearl Flashabou again. At this point, if I wet the fly and stroke it toward the tail, a general baitfish profile results.

5. For the overbody, starting under the fly, I tie in a thin bunch of bucktail that extends no farther than the bend of the hook. As I work up the sides of the fly, I increase the length of the bucktail. Before tying in the longest white bucktail on top, I like to trap in some long strands of pearl Reflections.

6. When all the bucktail has been tied in, the basic fly is complete. The various patterns result by veiling small amounts of reflective material and colored bucktail on the dorsal length of the fly. Feel free to substitute other reflective materials with like colors.

4   Flying Fish

Hook	Trey Combs Big Game Fly hook, #1/0 to 7/0
Tail	White bucktail and pearl Flashabou
Underwing	Pearl Flashabou and white bucktail
Overwing	Above the midline tie in a bunch of pearl blue Krystal Flash and cover with a very thin bunch of blue bucktail. Top with a few strands of royal blue Krystal Flash topped with a few hairs of black bucktail
Shoulder	An equal mix of pearl and silver Krystal Flash
Head	Complete as for Anchovy Blue, but using Scribbles Glittering Pacific Blue for the dorsal color

This pattern has worked well for me on dorado and other game fish when they're feeding on flying fish.

Mike Croft

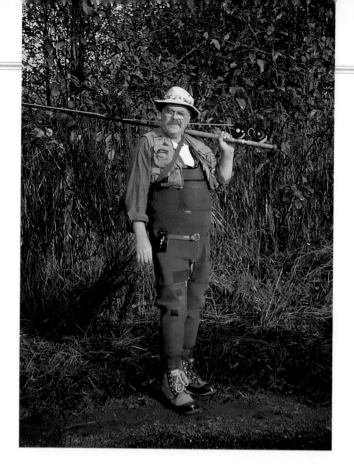

I am the design director for Fly Pros, a company that imports fishing flies from its factory in Kenya. Several times a year I do training programs and give instruction on patterns in Africa, which provides challenges I never thought I would have to face in fly fishing, like learning Swahili. I purchase materials related to each pattern and try to anticipate trends and suggest directions so the company can better position itself in the marketplace. One of the most enjoyable aspects of my work is evaluating new materials for their potential use in new patterns.

I also do design work for Roaring Fork Graphics, where my paintings and cartoons are marketed on T-shirts. My cartoons appeared in *American Angler* during the late 1980s and early 1990s when Dick Stewart edited the magazine, but my dark sense of humor and disregard for the politically correct make my work difficult to market. I do a small business in watercolor portraits, painting trophy fish mounted with the fly that caught them.

During and shortly after college I worked with my father as a commercial fisherman out of the Coos Bay region on our boats, *Finder* and *Gypsy*. These were trollers and, because we ran many rigs simultaneously, this was my first laboratory for field testing color as it relates to depth.

I started tying flies at age fourteen when a shattered kneecap took me forever from the football field and put me on the water. I didn't look back even once. Within a year I was tying all the striped bass flies for Hal's Tackle Shop in Coos Bay, famous in those days for its stripers. Harold Grey was the man who taught me to tie flies and his little store in Coos Bay was the closest thing to a fly shop at the time. By sixteen I was tying for stores as far away as Eugene. My first order for 150

dozen was also the beginning of the end of my production fly tying. To this day I have a hard time tying more than two dozen of a size and pattern.

Through college I lived close to the McKenzie River and fished between classes and after work. My wife and I moved to Washington so that I could go to graduate school and we have been here ever since. Because we live very close to the salt water and have a resident year-round population of silver salmon, I now concentrate on this fishery.

I prefer the lightest-wire stainless-steel hooks I can find. Eagle Claw has a Carpenter's Stainless No. 54, very similar to Mustad's famous 34007. Daiichi 2546 is also a great hook. These hooks all have a fine wire and a short shank. The smaller the wire, the easier the hook penetrates, but because stainless is not tempered like high carbon it can also straighten out easier. These hooks have a common standard-length shank. I believe the angle of penetration reaches perfection in a standard-length hook. The angle of penetration in longer-shanked hooks is too shallow and in extra-short hooks, too steep. When I fish, barbless and extra-short hooks pull out too easily, and long-shanked hooks open too large a hole as the fish changes direction. The added length acts like the handle on a crowbar, increasing the leverage being transferred from the line down to the point. This also allows for the hook to lose its footing and the slightest slack results in losing the fish. That is not to say I don't use long-shanked hooks, because I do, but all things being equal I prefer to fish with a standard-length hook. Most novice saltwater fishermen who come to the sport with a trout-fishing background are overly concerned with short strikes. So in their eyes, a bucktail tied on a long-shanked hook has better proportion than one tied on a short-shanked hook. Most ocean species are not timid about nipping on the tail of a fly, and design prejudices need to be tempered. My last reason for preferring stainless is the length of time an unused fly will stay in pristine shape before rusting. I never use tippets whose breaking strength exceeds 50 percent of the breaking strength of my backing, for obvious reasons. I don't need hooks that are incredibly strong. If they won't straighten out with thirty pounds of pressure, then I can catch fish with them.

I have a preference for natural tying materials. Someone is going to have to develop some pretty spectacular materials to replace the bucktail. Its one drawback is length. It is almost impossible to tie flies of over 6 inches, and then casting one of that length is not much fun anyway. For longer flies I use synthetic fibers; most fibers that length, however, don't have the taper that helps produce nice fish shapes.

When it comes to sparkle, old-timers used to use a lot of polar bear, but here is where synthetic fibers have come into their own. Krystal Flash, Flashabou, Fire Fly, and the new holographic tinsels have made new and important contributions to modern fly tying. Bucktail with a few synthetic strands can give the glitter associated with polar bear. In general warm-water species prefer more flash; cold-water fish such as the salmon can be put off by too much flash. I tie many patterns both ways so I can take advantage of those days when the fish are being difficult.

Matching the hatch is not as important as giving the illusion of life. A saltwater fly rodder has the advantage of being able to make a uniform retrieve, something that's very difficult to do with a spinning rod. Regrabbing the line with each strip produces an erratic retrieve. Watching underwater nature shows, you'll see footage of baitfish swimming among predators, but when they start to act erratically they get hit. Patterns that call attention to themselves or don't totally match the hatch are the ones that give the greatest success. Many patterns can be more effective when tied upside down. Most patterns have white or light-colored bellies and dark backs, but I've found that when this color scheme is reversed, the pattern is more visible from under the water. It still acts alive though in distress and is the perfect target for an easy meal.

My favorite tying thread is not a thread at all but a fine, 2-pound-test monofilament. Epoxy over the mono and it disappears, leaving the color of the bucktail or whatever you are using coming through. Never epoxy over head cement, because water will cause the head to cloud and crack. You can epoxy over superglues with fine results.

Eyes are an important element, because they seem to be the target most predator fish use to key their strikes. Witness how many tropical fish use false eyes on their tail sections as a way of confusing the predators. Eyes are more important than gills. How many reef fish have a red slash that incorporates gills in their protective coloration? I can't think of one. Red Krystal Flash is very popular for gills but I prefer red floss. I'm not so sure the red represents gills; it may resemble a wound. The Krystal Flash gills are too flashy and always remind me of a hooker with too much makeup.

```
        1
        2
        3
    4   5
```

2, 8   Duster (aka TUMS—Triple Unbraided Mylar Streamer)

Front Hook	Mustad 34007
Stinger	
Hook	Mustad 92553S
Thread	Clear fine monofilament
Stinger	
Harness	30-pound braided monofilament; 25-pound or higher monofilament
Lower Wing	Three strands of braided mylar
Upper Wing	Icelandic sheep
Gills	Red rabbit or red hackle (optional)
Eyes	Stick-ons
Head	
Cement	Five-minute epoxy (Z-Poxy is my favorite)
Other	
Goodies	Fast superglue; superglue accelerant

1. Thread the 25-pound mono down the inside of the braided mono. This is only difficult the first couple of times. After you get the knack, it only takes about ten seconds to do. Notice that the mono will have a natural bend from being on a spool.

2. Place the stinger hook in the vise. Note that this hook has a turned-up eye. Insert the braided mono (with mono core) through the eye of the hook.

3. For a stinger with an upturned eye, make sure the natural bend is down. Take care to align the bend with the plane of the hook; don't cant the mono to the right or the left. Tie down to the shank of the stinger with mono tying thread, up and back about three times, keeping the wraps tight and close together. Note that there is no knot holding the stinger hook, so don't fudge on the tying thread. (I have never had one fail, however.) Trim any excess from behind the bend of the hook. Remove the stinger and braided mono from the vise.

4. Place the lead hook in the vise and lay down a wrap of tying thread the length of the shank. Place the braided mono on top of the shank and make just a couple of wraps. While it is still loose, align the stinger so that it is in an exact plane with the lead hook. Tie down with the same care you did the stinger hook. In larger sizes, run the front of the braided mono through the eye of the hook and back down on the underside of the shank; tie down, then trim. Pull the stinger out straight and run superglue from the stinger up the braided mono to the eye of your main hook. Spray with accelerant. When you have done this there will no longer be a bend in the braided mono and the stinger

and main hook will be in a perfect plane. There is a slight offset to the 92553S, but you can just ignore it; it won't affect the performance.

5. Next, take three strands of braided mylar. Tie one on each side and one underneath. Don't unravel yet.

6. Tie the Icelandic sheep on top and the red gill underneath. Carefully place one drop of superglue on the nose of the fly. This will anchor the head to the shank so that the fly won't rotate or slide down the shank of the hook. Two or more drops would migrate into the wing and ruin the fly. Be careful here!

7. Place stick-on eyes on each side of the head. If you have a slow superglue then place a drop in the space between the eyes and hit with accelerant. This will prevent them from becoming dislodged in the epoxy. When you are happy with the eyes, coat in a thick layer of five-minute epoxy and rotate for five minutes. Let stand for an hour before handling. When the epoxy has cured, unravel the braided mylar.

In the fall of 1992 I was fishing sea-run cutthroats with Chuck Springer, an already accomplished fisherman but a novice fly tier. Chuck was using a popular pattern from the late 1980s, a Zonker. Since Chuck hadn't mastered the whip finish, the wrappings on his Zonker came undone and the braided tinsel tube started to unravel. Chuck told me that it seemed the more his fly unraveled, the better it seemed to work. My ears, of course, perked right up.

Later, at my vise, I tried out a fly whose body was made solely of unraveled mylar tubing, with just enough wing material to give it some color. It was an instant fish-catching success.

Pulling the unraveled mylar through the water is much like stretching a Slinky across the floor. It will stretch and stretch and then at some point spring back. Each strand of mylar does this individually in the water, giving an amazing action to the fly. Mylar tubing comes in long ropelike coils, so there is no upper size limit to the flies you can tie.

Icelandic sheep is a very fine fiber that can come in lengths of up to 12 inches. When this fiber is wet it produces a translucent effect. I believe the move to translucent flies will be big in the future, especially for midday fishing. Opaque flies like the Deceiver will continue to be important when the sun is low and the light is penetrating the water at a sharper angle.

In billfish sizes you may want to use up to fifteen strands of mylar in this pattern. It makes for an expensive fly but will give spectacular results.

6
7
8
9   10

1	Pacific Streaker
Tail Hook	Mustad 92553S, #1/0
Front Hook	Mustad 34007, #6/0
Tail-Hook	
Dressing	Yellow bucktail; pearl Fire Fly; yellow saddle hackles; blue and green Krystal Flash
Wing	Kelly green goat hair; pearl Krystal Flash; blue Krystal Flash; two long peacock sword feathers
Belly	Yellow bucktail
Cheeks	Red Floss

The original Streaker was tied by Ned Grey of California. The version I've tied here is a baby dorado tied with a tandem hook, sailfish-style. The new adhesives available to the fly tier better allow sculpting of feathers, so in this case I can tie and cement the forehead of the dorado and ensure it will keep its shape.

3, 4, 5	Chuggers
Tail Hook	Mustad 92553, #2
Front Hook	Mustad 34007, #6/0
Thread	White
Wing	White bucktail; pearl Fire Fly; grizzly saddle hackles; root beer and green Flashabou
Cheek	Grizzly hackles, curving outward
Head	Edgewater popper head, painted in mackerel colors

Popper heads are made by Edgewater and can be purchased in fly shops. The finish can be achieved with the purchase of a Flex Coat iridescent finish kit, also available in a lot of fly shops. By carefully laying a grizzly hackle on the first coat of wet epoxy and brushing out the feathers, then applying a second coat of epoxy, you can give these chugger heads wonderful finishes. The fly itself will pull into the soft head a bit and lock into place until a fish hits. The most important feature in any fly for sailfish is glitter or sparkle—so don't spare the mylar or tinsel or whatever reflective material you use. Also for sailfish, attach an upturned stinger hook to try for the soft spot in the upper mouth.

6	Croft's Articulated Candlefish
Hook	Mustad 34007, #6
Body	A series of 3/8- to 1 1/2-inch-length pearlescent tubes and glass beads
Wing	Light green FisHair with dark green FisHair over
Gills	Red floss
Eyes	Black on silver
Head	Epoxy tinted on top to match the color of the wing
Variations	Dark green and olive; chartreuse, black, and pink; purple and pink

I worked on this for about a year and it is a nice system because the components are interchangeable. For example, if you find you're fishing over smaller baitfish, segments of the fly can be dropped to reach the right length. Heads can be tied in many different colors and changed to match your needs, and, with a quick trim of the FisHair, will match the body length.

The tubes are small ones found on spray solvents with tubular mylar epoxied over the top. Left long at both ends and unraveled, this tube helps hide the hook. The remainder of the tube should be cut in 3/8- to 1/2-inch lengths, with two beads to act as ball bearings, allowing each segment to rotate.

Most salmon hit then turn and run away from the boat, carrying the fly in their mouths like a dog carries a bone. I'm not really sure what they are running from, or even if they know there is a boat; they may just be going in the opposite direction of the original course of the fly. In large sizes tube flies are thus less effective, because as the fish turns away and you set the hook, which is outside the fish's mouth, it will swing in an arc, clearing the nose and missing the fish altogether.

The vast majority of my saltwater fishing is for salmon. On three out of four days they will show themselves but on the one day they are not showing you can be casting over a lot of empty water. The absolute best way to find the stretch of water where the fish are holding is to troll the Articulated Candlefish behind a Cortland Atlantic salmon trolling line with a sequin or flutter disk in front. In the old days you could add more action to a damselfly nymph by slipping a sequin up the tippet in front of the fly. Well, some clever fellows expanded this idea, making the devices in a variety of sizes that suited saltwater flies and selling them under the name of Flutters. I haven't seen these on the shelf at the fly shop for the last year or so; perhaps the company is out of business. The purists shudder, but they do make the candlefish swim like the real thing.

7	**Croft's Glo Squid**
Hook	Mustad 34007, #2 to 3/0
Body	⅛-inch tubing overwrapped with clear ice chenille
Hook lock	Soft plastic tubing
Thread	Fine mono tying thread
Tentacles	White and tan ostrich
Head	White Arctic fox
Underbody	Clear ice chenille, Near Hair
Eyes	Doll eyes

Determine the length squid you want to create and then cut the tubing ½ inch longer than half the length of the fly. Slip 1 inch of soft plastic tubing over this as a hook lock, to prevent the fly from rotating and snarling the arms of the fly.

Tie in about 8 strands of white ostrich over the spot where the two tubes overlap. Tie in an equal number of tan ostrich over the white. Strip the fibers from two white hackles, except for the last ½ inch, and tie these on either side of the ostrich to form two tentacles. Ring the base of the tentacles with Arctic fox.

Wrap clear ice chenille from the tentacles to about ¾ inch from the end of the tube. Tie a sparse clump of Near Hair just forward of the ice chenille, top and bottom, and work it together to shape the body.

To make the fins (optional), take a 4-inch clump of Near Hair, tie it in the middle and soak it with head cement. When it feels tacky, press it into two fins. Let these dry overnight, then cut them apart at the center, tie a fin on each side of the body, and trim them to shape.

Tie in a clump of Near Hair, top and bottom, to form the shape of the squid and to hide the tie-in point of the fins.

Paint the body with tan florist's spray paint (the kind used for tinting dry flowers). Protect the tentacles while spraying by placing them in an old magazine held shut with clothespins. When the paint is dry, add dots and shading with a permanent marker. Use acrylic glow-in-the-dark paint to add spots along the back and tentacles. After again covering the tentacles, spray the body with an acrylic sealer.

9	**Croft's Internally Ballasted Crab**
Hook	Mustad 34011, #2
Legs	Rubber bands
Body	Clipped deer hair
Ballast	Lead Zonker strips
Eyes	Burned monofilament
Color	
Variations	Waterproof marking pens

The beauty of this little number is that it is tied mostly from stuff you throw away. A ½-inch-wide rubber band will make the legs. The coarse hair from the base of a bucktail—you can spin this, but it flares too much for tying streamers—makes up the body. Lead Zonker strips form the ballast. Because the carapace goes all the way around, it looks as much like a crab from underneath.

10	**Croft's Marabou Candlefish**
Hook	Mustad 3407, #6
Thread	White
Tail	White marabou, with olive marabou on top
Sides	Pearl Saltwater Flashabou
Eyes	Black on silver
Head	Epoxied and colored on top with a Pantone marker to match the wing color
Variations	Green, olive, and white; kelly green and white; kelly green, yellow, and white; chartreuse and white; purple, pink, and white

This one was so obvious that I searched the books in my meager library for the name of the pattern and couldn't find it. Dry, these patterns look ridiculous, but wet one and hold it in your hand and it is the closest pattern to a sand lance or candlefish you can find. Fished with a moderate retrieve it even acts a little like a candlefish. This pattern has two drawbacks. One, it can't be tied longer than the length of the marabou. Two, if you make a bad cast the marabou will wrap around the bend of the hook. I've tried to address this by adding cheeks of Saltwater Flashabou for extra support. The cheeks used to be quite long, but as the fly went through the air it would have a dull flutter that sounded obscene. It used to drive my partners crazy so I cut it back and at least it's more quiet. I thought the fly would be delicate but it holds up surprisingly well. I tie these in all the colors I fish. In the early season olive, forest green, and chartreuse are the three most useful colors.

Cheap, easy to tie, and effective are the three most important factors in a good fishing fly and this one has all three.

Corbett Davis, Sr.

I was introduced to fly fishing and fly tying about fifteen years ago by Pres Gallagher, a close friend of forty-seven years, who has fly-fished for over fifty years.

Retiring at fifty years of age and being accustomed to using my hands in making and repairing jewelry, I found I continued to need to use my hands and mind. Fly tying was a perfect outlet. I read many books and tied and discarded many flies; I found I could make my fingers perform okay but I could not satisfy my desire for perfection. There always was and still is that little something that I should have done on each fly. I found myself looking for new or different patterns to challenge my tying, but I think I always had tying classic Atlantic salmon flies in the back of my mind. Then at the Federation of Fly Fishers Southeastern Council Conclave in Haines City, Florida, in June 1993, I met Bob Veverka. Bob was more than courteous and generous with his time and materials as I watched and questioned him for hours at his tying station. I returned home with a list of requirements. I located and ordered the books he'd recommended and started ordering and looking for the feathers and materials he'd suggested, and others he hadn't. After accumulating a ton of useless feathers I finally had enough to work with. I am now in my third year of tying Atlantic salmon flies and have learned enough to know there is no such thing as a perfectly tied fly. At least I know I'll never be able to tie the perfect fly, though I'll continue to try.

Of my inventions and innovations, my most successful flies are for salt water: the Crustacean A.D., Curve and Dive, Calamari Deluxe, Catch A Dandy, and a new source of eyes I call Tri Eyes.

In developing new patterns or tying existing ones, I think the vibrations built into the fly will determine how successful it will be. I live on Pensacola Bay, next door to my son, Corbett, Jr., who keeps a high-intensity light burning all night, every night, on the end of his 250-foot pier. Though I am too cheap to leave one burning on the end of my pier all night, this gives me a perfect place to test my new patterns. It's like fishing in a large aquarium where I can watch the fish and their reactions. The light attracts a variety of bait, which in turn attracts the larger fish—redfish, speckled trout, white trout, and on occasion other species. After many hours observing the bait, including shrimp, squid, minnows, and crabs, I try to determine what makes the predator strike.

The previously mentioned flies were designed to mimic the vibrations of the bait, each in its own distinct way. When a predator flushes a shrimp, the shrimp will snap (jump or flick) away and then swim either up to the surface or down to the bottom, depending on whether the fish is under or over the shrimp when it is flushed. When a shrimp swims in this manner, it swims with a stick-straight body, using its swimming legs. When it reaches the bottom, it walks there using its five walking legs. The only time a shrimp curves its body is to jump out of the way the instant a predator tries to eat it (or maybe when you boil the shrimp to eat it), sometimes even coming several inches out of the water. When the shrimp is on the bottom, it tries to find cover to hide in, walking under rocks, burrowing in mud, or, if nothing is available, standing straight with antennae up and vibrating, trying to frighten the predator away.

The Crustacean A.D. with its antennae flattened on the tips vibrates when being retrieved. The motions transmitted by the soft hackle and stiff hackle represent the swimming legs and the walking legs of the shrimp. The tail undulates and simulates the moving tail of the shrimp as it expands and contracts.

The Curve and Dive does exactly what its name implies: It curves as it dives. With its lead eyes, it goes down fast. It is fished in small jerks along the bottom. The curving simulates a wounded minnow, and bouncing off the bottom represents the vibration of burrowing in the sand as bait tries to escape.

The Calamari Deluxe has a unique method of expelling water, similar to a squid's fleeing from danger with its jet system. The fingertip of a latex glove tied on as a mantle (body) expels water from within when retrieved and takes in water on the pause. The feathers represent the vibrations of the tentacles and arms. When dressed all black, it also is a great largemouth bass fly.

The Catch A Dandy was designed specifically for little tunny (locally called bonito, and known to some as little tuna, false albacore, albies, and alberts) feeding on glass minnows. Most flies made to imitate any type of fry have to be retrieved so fast that I was not comfortable with them. The Catch A Dandy represents a wounded minnow, not a swimming or fleeing one. It has up-tied splayed wings and a lead underbody, and as it falls on the pause, the wings spring up and out. On the retrieve they fold in. This up-and-down of the fly plus the in-and-out of the wings send out vibrations of a wounded minnow that little tunny cannot resist. Sometimes they take the fly with no retrieve.

Tri Eyes, in my opinion, are the best eyes for certain patterns. I find them unexcelled for night fishing under a light. Tri Eyes cannot be purchased in fly shops at present but can be made with beads called Tri Beads found in craft stores.

6	Catch A Dandy

Hook	Mustad 31007 stainless steel, #4
Thread	Pink and red (depth ray nylon), or substitute red
Tail	Light pink hackle feather tips (very thin)
Weight	Lead solder, $1/16$ inch in diameter
Body	Mylar tubing, a little less than $1/8$ inch in diameter
Beard	Hot pink marabou
Head	Head cement and thinned head cement
Eyes	White and black lacquer or fingernail polish

1. Debarb and sharpen the hook. Wrap pink thread from $1/8$ inch behind the hook eye to a point over the barb of the hook. Tie two red hackle tips, one on each side of the hook, extending beyond the hook approximately $5/8$ inch (the length of the hook shank); separate a little. Touch the thread with thinned head cement.

2. Cut a piece of lead solder on a slant $1/2$ inch long. Tie on top of the hook shank $1/16$ inch behind the hook eye. Bind down thoroughly, return the thread to above the hook's barb, and touch the thread with thinned head cement.

3. Cut the mylar tubing $5/8$ to $3/4$ inch long. Remove the cord filler from the center of the tubing. Slide over the eye of the hook and tie down on the butt of the tail feathers. Make a small, neat binding. Whip-finish and cut the thread off. Touch with thinned head cement. Tie on red thread behind the hook eye and tie the tubing down. Touch with thinned head cement.

4. Tie one light pink hackle tip approximately $1^1/4$ inches long on each side of the hook, extending up and out. Tie in a small clump of hot pink marabou as a beard. It should be long enough to cover the hook barb. Whip-finish and cut the thread off. Coat the head with head cement and let dry. Paint on large white eyes with black pupils. Let dry; coat with head cement.

The Catch A Dandy bonito fly was developed to catch bonito with a retrieve suitable for fly fishing. After years of catching and trying to catch bonito on spinning tackle, I found that a lightning-fast retrieve is necessary. I also learned that bonito seem to prefer pink and small lures. After trying some of the standard small minnow imitations with my 8-weight fly line I discovered that I could not retrieve my line fast enough to interest the bonito. I decided that if I could not impart the speed to the fly I would have to make the fly look like a glass minnow (which bonito feed on) and give it movement simulating speed or injury—thus the silver body, large eyes, extra weight, and exaggerated, splayed wings.

The way I fish this fly in the Gulf of Mexico is to locate the feeding bonito. The best way to do this is to search the skies for feeding birds or for the frothed-up water created by the frantic feeding of the bonito. Once the fish are located, move your boat to a position approximately two hundred feet in front of the moving fish, and idle the boat into a position of favorable wind. When bonito are almost in casting range put the boat in neutral and cast your fly approximately six feet in front of the lead boils of water. Let it sink for a second or two as you take slack out of the line, then retrieve in $1^1/2$- to 2-foot smooth, even strips. If there's no take, pick up and cast into boils of feeding fish. Repeat until the school moves beyond reach, then relocate your boat as before. The bonito is a difficult fish to catch on a fly but using the Catch A Dandy as described above should catch you at least one. There is only a negligible chance of losing a bonito on a debarbed hook, and it will be easier to release the fish unharmed if you use one.

1	Glass Minnow
Hook	Mustad 34007, #6
Body	Oval silver tinsel
Wing	Sparse white calf tail, sparse green (chartreuse) bucktail, and a few strands of black bucktail
Sides	Medium flat silver tinsel tied in with an outward curve, so they pulsate when retrieved
Head	White with a black eye

2	Curve and Dive Streamer
Hook	Mustad 34007, #4
Thread	Light tan or white
Tag	Red thread
Body	Mylar tubing (gold)
Eyes	CAD eyes or lead eyes
Wing	Dyed-yellow, twisted pheasant shoulder feather that has been trimmed (look between the cape as it curves around the shoulder; if there is a twist in the feather, that is the one you want)
Veil	Pheasant blood feathers from the area of the cape or below
Gills	Red thread

Wind red thread from $\frac{1}{8}$ inch behind the eye of the hook to a point above the barb. Touch with thinned head cement.

Cut a piece of gold tubing to $\frac{5}{8}$ inch and remove its center cord. Slip over the eye of the hook and secure with red thread at the barb. Whip-finish and remove the thread; touch with thin head cement.

Tie in tan or white thread behind the eye of the hook and secure the tubing $\frac{5}{32}$ inch behind the hook eye.

Tie in CAD eyes with figure-eight wraps and a few wraps around each eye stem. Touch with head cement.

Tie in the curved feather on top of and between the eyes. Tie in at a 45-degree angle. (This should run from the top, down the right side, to curve across the back of the hook to the left side.) Tie in one or two blood feathers, make the head, whip-finish, and remove the thread.

Attach red thread between the hook and the right CAD eye. Wind the eye stem until almost flush with the eye. Form several half hitches on the whip finish and remove the thread. Repeat this procedure for the left eye.

Paint the eyes white and put a black dot on each. Let dry then recoat the head, eyes, and tag with thick clean lacquer.

3, 4	Calamari Deluxe
Hook	Mustad 34011, #1
Tag	Gold or silver oval tinsel (the tag goes all the way to the center of the hook bend)
Butt	White chenille, #00, to form a ball $\frac{3}{16}$ inch in diameter
Arms	Eight saddle hackles, extending $2\frac{1}{2}$ inches beyond the hook, tied splayed around the hook shank
Tentacles	Two wider hackles, 3 to $3\frac{1}{2}$ inches beyond the hook, one on each side
Veins	A small amount of magenta, red, or purple bucktail fibers on each side
Skirt	One wide soft hackle with marabou left on; wind on the tip first as a skirt
Eyes	Tri Eyes (or glass eyes), red with black pupils, tied $\frac{1}{8}$ inch in front of the hackle
Underbody	Medium white chenille behind, around, and in front of the eyes, built up to the hook eye
Body (Mantle)	Fingertip (approximately $\frac{3}{4}$ inch) from a small latex glove tied on inverted, behind the hook eye; then remove the thread and push the latex over the underbody

5	Crustacean A.D.
Hook	Mustad 34011, #2 bent to modified keel shape
Thread	#2/0 flat nylon, or #3/0 waxed monocord
Weight	Round lead wire, $\frac{1}{16}$ inch in diameter
Tail	Fox squirrel tail, or FisHair and Flashabou
Ribbing	White nylon thread, #2/0 or 3/0
Hackle	Extra-long saddle hackle ($4\frac{1}{2}$ to 5 inches long after the webby part is removed)
Overbody	Glimmer Flash Chenille
Body	Extra-small chenille (#00)
Eyes	50-pound-test monofilament, $1\frac{1}{2}$ inches long, bent to a V shape and melted to form balls so that the finished stems are $\frac{3}{8}$ inch long
Shell	Pearlescent tubing, $\frac{3}{16}$ inch in diameter
Antennae	30-pound-test extra-stiff black monofilament, crimped and bent to form a V with each side $1\frac{1}{4}$ inches long. Flatten $\frac{1}{16}$ inch on each tip

```
1   2
    3
    4
    5
    6
```

Corbett Davis, Jr.

Ten years ago, when I was thirty-five, my father was kind enough to introduce me to the sport of fly fishing. For Christmas that year he gave me an 8-weight Lamiglas rod with a Pflueger Medalist reel. At the time I thought an 8-weight rod and reel was sufficient for all types of fishing. I quickly realized how wrong I was.

Until that Christmas I was a meat fisherman, what Howell Raines refers to as "a redneck fisherman." And I have the photos to prove it. Looking back at those fish baking in the sun, I feel embarrassed, almost ashamed, but I do have many good memories in those old pictures.

With the exception of an occasional bottom-fishing trip for fresh snappers or groupers, I release my catch and now mostly fly-fish. And I now know why I love fishing so much. It isn't killing the fish that I enjoy, or standing at the cleaning table for hours after each trip. It isn't even the taste of the fresh fried fillets. The reasons I love to fish, and always have, are the adventure, the companionship, and the challenge. Looking back at each trip, I remember the place, the time, and the people. I remember the clarity of the water over the grassy flats and marl bottom of the Marquesas as my father and I stalked my first tarpon on a fly. I recall those long days that our guide, Jeffrey Cardenas, patiently poled and instructed us on those gorgeous flats. I remember my father when I caught my first tarpon on fly, and I do remember that fish. I have caught larger tarpon since, but there will never be another one like the first. I framed the photo, along with the Marquesa Sunrise tarpon fly my dad had tied.

But what I remember and value the most is the friendship that Jeffrey and I have developed.

I don't remember how good my first fly-caught cobia tasted, but I do remember the taste of the salt air as Captain Fuzzy Davis ran us up the river near Hilton Head Island. I also remember the fly I used to catch the twenty-one-pounder. It was a bright yellow-and-chartreuse Whistler that I had tied earlier. I can't remember how long my cast was, how I stripped in the fly, or how I set the hook, but I do remember Fuzzy. The Fuzz Head lives in Hilton Head, South Carolina, and I live in Gulf Breeze, Florida, almost six hundred miles away. Ever since that twenty-one-pound cobia, Fuzzy and I have been best of friends. We talk at least once a week, every week. In the eight years since we met on that trip, we have fished together in Costa Rica, the Bahamas, the Keys, and Alaska. That's fishing. That's friendship!

The fishing, not the catching, is what my memories are about. Wading alongside my father in knee-deep water on the Gulf side of Boca Grande. Watching his green-and-white Clouser bounce up and down in the sand seconds before a nice snook swallowed it. The straw hat, the smell of sunscreen, and the happy look as he held up his first snook.

Good fishing memories of a trip I made to Costa Rica. Before the trip I tied nearly fifty flies—tube flies, tandem-hook flies, and every type of billfish fly I could come up with. The first day, before we fished, I thought I'd impress the captain and pulled out my box of flies all on perfectly tied leaders and showed them to him.

"None of those will work," he said.

I wanted to throw him overboard, but I listened. He and all the other captains used the same fly, a large pink tube fly with a white cork head and tandem #6/0 standard steel hooks. On that once-in-a-lifetime trip it is not only the two ninety-pound sails I caught on flies that stick in my mind. What left an impression were the friendly people of Costa Rica, the bus ride through the rain forest, the waterfall, the monkeys and birds, the natural hot springs at the base of an active volcano, and the acres of dolphins and yellowfin tuna churning the surface of the Pacific Ocean as we snorkeled among them.

I remember sharing stories, fishing, and a motel room with a good friend from back home, Jimbo Meador. The only feeling that can top catching fish with friends and family is catching those fish on a fly that you tied yourself.

In my family when someone calls out the name Corbett, three of us look up—my father, Corbett Davis, Sr.; myself, Corbett, Jr.; and my son, Corbett III. One hot August day when the Gulf of Mexico was like a sheet of glass and the temperature was near a hundred, the three Corbetts decided to try out Sr.'s new bonito fly. It was a good day.

I tie simple flies that are quick and easy. My father ties beautiful flies that should be considered art. Since I fish more than he does, I often run out of my own flies, so I sneak into his tying area and grab handfuls of whatever I need. He never misses them. He has patience while tying and I have patience while fishing.

Just like the people and places, I remember the flies I use. The biggest bonefish I ever caught was on Corbett Sr.'s pink-and-white Crustacean A.D. I hooked it right at dusk near Key West, Florida.

The only fly I've ever designed myself is a crab imitation. I tie it in small sizes for bonefish, larger sizes for redfish and permit, and very large sizes for tarpon and cobia. Since my father has taught me all I know about fishing, conservation, and fly tying, I named the fly after him, the Crabmudgeon. It's still a new fly; I've only caught redfish with it so far.

3	Crabmudgeon
Hooks	Two stainless-steel hooks, #2
Thread	Brown
Claws	Red Testors model paint or red fingernail polish (optional)
Body	Two narrow grizzley hackles; small clump of tan kip tail; two brown or tan webby hackles
Shell	Dark brown Furry Foam
Legs	Light tan Aunt Lydia's Rug Yarn
Eyes	Lead dumbbells

1. With your vise turned 45 degrees, clamp two hooks together with brown thread. Start at the hook eyes and wrap back to the bends. Coat the threads with head cement.

2. If you wish, paint the hook ends and barbs red to the center of the hook bend, to serve as crab claws. If you are planning to tie up a few flies at once, paint a bunch of hooks ahead of time.

3. Tie on two narrow grizzly hackles at the hook bend, flared out away from each other.

4. Tie in a small clump of tan kip tail between the feathers on the tops of the hook shanks.

5. At the rear of the hook, tie in two brown or tan webby hackles, palmer 1/8 inch forward, and tie off. Tie back toward the hook. Bend Keys-style.

6. Cut a square piece of dark brown Furry Foam 1/2 inch by 1/2 inch and tie on where the palmered hackles end. Let the piece of foam stand up out of the way for now, and bring the thread slightly forward.

7. Turn the fly upside down and tie in three strands of Aunt Lydia's Rug Yarn; separate slightly. This represents legs and the bottom of the shell.

8. Next, tie in lead dumbbell eyes on the bottom, next to the yarn.

9. Turn the fly back over, pull Furry Foam (shell) down, and secure. At the hook eye, whip-finish and coat the thread with head cement.

1   Cock-Eyed Deceiver

Hook   Mustad 34007, #2/0
Thread   Brown
Tail   Gray saddle hackles, white bucktail, red bucktail
Throat   White bucktail
Wing   White and blue bucktail
Shoulders   Jungle cock body feather
Cheeks   Jungle cock

2   Cobia Whistler

Hook   Mustad 34007, #1
Thread   Orange
Weight   Bead-chain eyes
Tail   Yellow bucktail, yellow saddle hackle, orange-dyed grizzly hackle, gold Flashabou
Body   Yellow hackle fuzz
Collar   Orange-dyed grizzly hackle fuzz

4   Braided Charlie

Hook   Mustad 34007, #6
Thread   Pink
Eyes   Bead chain, black on white
Tail   Pearl Flashabou
Body   Pearl braid with red Krystal Flash at sides and top
Wing   White calf tail

5   Squid Wobbler

Hook   Mustad 34007, #2
Thread   Orange
Tail   Orange bucktail, orange Krystal Flash
Eyes   Dumbbell, black on yellow
Body   Orange braid, epoxied

```
    1
    2
    3
  5   4
```

Bill Elliott

I began fly fishing at the age of thirteen, thirty-seven years ago. For many, fly fishing is a sport. For me, it has become a way of life, not only my source of relaxation but also the way I earn my living. When most people are stuck in traffic trying to make their way to work, I am casting a fly along a mangrove-covered shore listening to the nervous chatter of the white ibis and watching an alligator glide along rhythmically, skulling the water.

For over thirty years, I have earned my living painting and drawing all forms of nature. I have done work for every major outdoor magazine and illustrations for twenty-one books. Throughout my career, fly fishing has strongly directed my work.

My second passion is creating flies that are attractive and highly productive fish takers.

The variety of fish available in South Florida could keep a fly rodder working most of his or her life trying to capture one of each. Each has its own requirements in tackle and technique, with some more difficult than others. Since I moved here with my family ten years ago, the fish I've been after most is without a doubt the greatest of all game fish—the *Centropomus undecimalis*—the snook.

Large snook hold the greatest challenge to those casting flies. They are a lazy fish and placing the fly close to where they are holding is essential—as little as a foot can determine success or failure. Accurate and long-distance casts are a must for success with the line-sider.

To increase your chances I believe you need to produce a fly that looks like the food the fish are feeding on. Once in the water your fly has to convince the snook that it's a living creature that's also an easy meal. This is not easily done, but over the last five years I have attempted to tie the better mousetrap.

Two of the flies pictured here are patterns I have worked on these past five years. One is my version of a white bait. Using a variety of colors and materials, you can tie this pattern to represent species from glass minnows to greenies (threadfin shad). I am surely not the first to imitate these baitfish, but the technique I use to form the body shape is one that has produced my second largest snook on 15-pound test, a 31½-pounder, along with a 9-pound, 2-ounce sea trout this year.

The second fly is what I call my Ghost Mullet. It is a slight variation on Jimmy Nix's mullet fly, which took my largest snook so far, a 34½-pound beauty. I tie this pattern in six different color variations and have used it successfully with every species of fish I have thrown to. Although my fly box contains a hundred different patterns, I catch 90 percent of my fish on these two flies. I have recently started tying on the Eagle Claw 067 saltwater hook. Right out of the package, these hooks require very little sharpening. If you haven't tried them, I'm sure you will be pleased.

3	Ghost Mullet
Hook	Eagle Claw 067, #1/0 to 2/0
Thread	Light yellow Kevlar
Weed	
Guard	30-pound soft monofilament
Body	One white blood marabou feather and four grizzly hackles
Sides	Six to eight strands of Krystal Flash, with short tufts of red marabou for gills
Head	White deer hair, spun and shaped
Eyes	6- to 8-millimeter plastic eyes

1. Using a pale yellow Kevlar thread, wrap from the midpoint of the hook toward the bend. Apply a small amount of head cement over the thread.

2. Take a 6-inch-long piece of mono and tie it onto the shank just above the hook point. Wrap the Kevlar toward the rear so the mono follows the bend of the hook. Tie down to the midpoint of the bend and then back up to the starting point. Coat with head cement. This should leave you with a piece of mono 4$\frac{1}{2}$ inches long; use a retention spring to hold it out of the way for now.

3. Tie in a full white blood marabou feather at the starting point; it should extend 1$\frac{1}{2}$ to 2 inches to the rear. Cut off the excess stem. Tie in two pairs of grizzly hackles, one on each side of the blood feather, concave to concave. This will form a smooth body shape.

4. Tie in six to eight strands of Krystal Flash the length of the hackles. A $\frac{1}{4}$-inch tuft of red marabou is tied in on each side to suggest gills.

5. You are now ready to form the deer hair collar and head. Take a bunch of white deer hair 1$\frac{1}{2}$ to 2 inches long; holding it just above and forward of the gills, take several wraps of thread. Pull down tightly and allow the hair to spin, forming the collar. The point of hair should face the rear.

6. Pack the butt end to the rear and start the head. The thicker the head, the better it will trim up later. Once you have all the hair up to the eye, make several half hitches. I remove the hanging thread at this time as well, to allow better access for shaping the head, which is tapered front to back with a flat bottom.

7. Reattach the Kevlar thread. Glue a plastic eye on each side. Bring the mono up through the eye and tie it off. Form a small head and coat with glue.

1	Oscar
Hook	Mustad 34007, #1/0
Tail	Red marabou, short; pearlescent Krystal Flash
Overwing	Four orange-dyed grizzly hackles
Head	Dark brown deer hair left long as a collar; tan clipped deer hair; olive deer hair for the head
Eyes	Yellow-orange with black pupils

2	Juvenile Largemouth Bass
Hook	Mustad 34007, #1/0
Tail	Brown bucktail; white and red marabou
Overwing	Krystal Flash and olive marabou flanked by six olive grizzly hackles
Topping	Olive bucktail
Body	Olive deer hair, clipped
Eyes	Yellow-orange with black pupils

4	White Bait
Hook	Eagle Claw 067, #1 to 2/0
Thread	Light yellow Kevlar
Weed	
Guard	30-pound soft monofilament
Body	White FisHair
Back	Chartreuse FisHair folded back on itself at the head. Use a medium blue marker to give a darker back coloration
Sides	Four to six strands of pearl Krystal Flash
Eyes	Depending on the fly size, 6- to 8-millimeter plastic eyes
Head	Four to six coats of Hard As Nails

AUTHOR'S NOTE: All of Bill's flies are tied weedless.

Capt.
Bruce Foster

My first contact with a fly rod was in 1960, when I was seven. My grandparents would have the family over to their home in King's Point, Long Island, just about every weekend. It was a short drive from our home in East Norwich, around the corner from Oyster Bay. After my grandfather had us help cut the lawn, and before his dry martini at cocktail time, he would practice fly casting on the freshly cut grass. I remember asking him what he was doing, and he told me he was practicing. I didn't know what he was talking about and proceeded to tell him if he could wait till just before dark we could catch all the lightning bugs he wanted in the front yard around the old crab apple tree. He got a chuckle out of my suggestion and I followed him to the front hall closet where he kept the rod, right next to his Model 21 Winchester. From that time on my grandfather would share his love for the sport with me whenever he could.

My grandparents had a vacation home in Carmel, New York, in the heart of the Croton watershed. Small lakes, ponds, and streams abound in this area, and the Gypsy Trail Club, where the home was located, had two spring-fed ponds loaded with stocked brook trout. We would fish together whenever we could and my ability to dunk a worm was fast becoming a passion.

Cold Spring Harbor is just down the road from East Norwich—where, I believe, the first German brown trout were introduced—and there is a trout hatchery there. I was amazed at the size of the brood fish that swam in those concrete tanks. Each year sea-run browns would return to Cold Spring from Oyster Bay and the biologists would net them for breeding. I was sure that if I headed to the docks in Oyster Bay, I could catch one of those monster browns. Some neighborhood pals and I recruited my grandmother as chief driver and financial backer for our tackle and bait.

She'd drop us off for the day with what seemed to be an arsenal of fishing implements, buckets, and lunch. There is no doubt that we put a dent in the population of begals, sea robins, and the then plentiful blowfish. I never did catch one of those monster browns.

When I was in the seventh grade we moved to Manorville, on the eastern end of Long Island. I was in heaven. My school was in Eastport, right on Moriches Bay, and my friends and I would spend every spare moment fishing for weakfish, flounder, and snapper blues. There were also numerous ponds in the area with plenty of pickerel, bass, and bluegills. My bicycle looked like a traveling tackle store. Anything that I thought I needed for the day I somehow managed to find a place to hang or tie on its frame.

Traveling back and forth from Manorville to Eastport, I was always looking for shortcuts to give me extra fishing time. It was a long ride, about seven miles, even with my three-speed racer. On one occasion, I happened upon a new pond. Beautiful, clear, cold, and deep, its banks were covered with overhanging bushes and under them, barely visible, were what looked like huge trout. I broke out my favorite snapper rod and tied on a small Dardevle spoon my grandfather had given me. Either these were the dumbest brook trout in the world or I was a much better fisherman than I thought. Soon my stringer was filled with some very large beautiful brookies. I managed to secure this mass of fish to the handlebars and headed off to show off my catch. Not more than a couple of clouds of dust down the road, I was stopped by a man next to a small putting green. It turned out that he was the groundskeeper of the Long Island Country Club. He asked me to follow him to the kitchen at the main lodge, where I turned over my prized catch to a man dressed in white, wearing a hat that looked like a mushroom.

Long Island Country Club was a posh weekend retreat for wealthy New York financiers, military elite, and the just plain rich. There were three stocked ponds with small boathouses, a huge central mansion, and private cabins that surrounded the two-hole golf course. All you needed to join was plenty of money. The main interest for the retired elite was the trophy trout. Because almost every member seemed to be at least ninety, caddies would row them around on the ponds while they fished. I got a job as a caddie and was paid big money, $2.50 for a half an hour and $5.00 for a full hour. Each fish I cleaned was worth twenty-five cents. It was a great summertime job and one Dr. Ackerman seemed to like me; he made me his full-time caddie. His sight was as bad as his fishing, but he had boxes of flies and always tipped me with the latest pattern that he had purchased from Abercrombie & Fitch in New York. They were beautiful, and I was intrigued with them.

With some of the money from my weekend job, I subscribed to *Field & Stream* magazine. It was full of information and I was obsessed with fishing. I hadn't yet noticed girls, which left me with plenty of time to explore the articles and ads before bed. One advertisement caught my eye: Learn Taxidermy at Home—Be Your Own Boss—Northwestern School of Taxidermy—Home Study Course. This was it. I could turn that twenty-five-cent fish-cleaning fee into big money by mounting all of Dr. Ackerman's fish. I convinced my mother what a great birthday present this would be. My first lesson finally arrived and I couldn't wait to mount a prize fish. The first lesson turned out to be how to mount a squirrel. I couldn't have cared less about squirrels but wanted to get my money's worth. My racer now had both a Swiss Army knife and a plastic bag included with the rest of my gear.

Roadkills were everywhere, and I collected them all. Under more careful examination at home, I realized

---

1	Predator Popper
Hook	Mustad 77660SS Tarpon
Body	Closed-cell foam
Eyes	Doll or prismatic eyes
Finish	Silicone; glitter; colored pens
Counter-balance	Split shot, lead wire, or glass rattle
Leader Track	Plastic bar straw
Tail	Bucktail, saddle hackles, or flash material

This popper head is a slider. It's your choice of head size, hook style, and hook size; shock leader material and pound test are totally variable.

1. From a sheet of closed-cell foam, use a brass tube heated with a heat gun to cut a plug. Brass tubing can be obtained from a hobby store and comes in different diameters; I use 1-inch tubing for this popper. Remove the cylinder of foam from the brass tube. Cut to desired length.

2. Lightly heat one end of the popper body and roll it on a flat surface until the desired taper is formed. Heat a straight piece of wire and push it through the popper body to form a channel in which to insert the plastic bar straw. Coat the straw with silicone and push it through the body. Do not trim the straw at this point. This will form the channel through which you pass your leader material to the hook.

3. Insert a split shot, lead wire, or glass rattle into the belly of the popper. This will sit the popper correctly on the water.

4. Color the body with markers in the desired pattern. Lightly coat with silicone.

5. Holding the extra straw sticking out from the body, set the eyes and highlight with glitter. Let dry.

6. Put a finish coat of silicone over the body and let it dry. Trim the straw front and back. The hook can be finished with bucktail, saddle hackles, or flash material.

To rig, select a popper body and a piece of leader material. Slip the leader through the straw and attach it to your hook. I use this popper on big cobia. Plastic-coated wire serves as my shock leader; I crimp the loop and hook ends with wire crimps.

---

that many of the fly patterns that my grandfather and Dr. Ackerman had given me had hairs, feathers, or parts of things that I could identify. Our tool shed now started to look like something from *The Silence of the Lambs*. What was not crudely immortalized was reduced, stored, and labeled for future use. A seed was planted at that time that remains to this day. I experimented then with everything I had collected and started to tie my first flies. As I think back, these are the most memorable days of my life.

We moved again when I was in the ninth grade, to Cumberland, Maryland. My vest was filled with Dr. Ackerman's tips and there were some great mountain streams in western Maryland. I fished the Savage, Youghiogheny, and Casselman Rivers with passion but was most interested in football, dating, and music. After graduation, I moved to Pungo, Virginia, on Back Bay near Virginia Beach. I got a job on a charter boat in Rudee Inlet, Virginia. Captain B. G. Smith on the *Hustler* taught me a lot about ocean game fish. Fly fishing was not popular; trolling and casting were. I did, however, catch many speckled trout and puppy drum in Lynnhaven and Rudee Inlets on flies. Late fall into January, B. G. would troll large wooden plugs on wire lines around the Chesapeake Bay Bridge Tunnel for large stripers. He was very successful and the fishing reminded me of Montauk Point in April, when big bass could be taken under the lighthouse on Hopkin's Tin Squids. I really learned to target a particular species while in Virginia Beach. Those brightly colored Reedville and Deltaville hulls could surely raise fish with their 671TIs.

From Virginia, I moved to Ocean City, Maryland, and got a mate job on a private boat. I worked on the same boat for four years; we would winter at Old Port Cove, North Palm Beach, in Florida. I caught all kinds of fish on a fly while the boss was not around.

Suitcase living was getting to me, and I moved to Annapolis, Maryland, in 1979. Fly fishermen were few, and the Chesapeake fishery was declining. I started a full-time taxidermy business in 1982 and was lucky to catch the last few years of the really big spawners. Forty- to fifty-pound stripers were common and taken for trophies. I molded them in fiberglass and still have and use the molds to this day. This was about the beginning of the crash of striped bass on the Chesapeake. When the full crash came there was a total moratorium.

About the same time, New York State had created a tremendous cold-water fishery. King salmon, steelhead, and brown trout were invading Lake Ontario tributaries to spawn, and fly fishing was becoming more recognized. A surge in products, information, and interest pushed manufacturers and suppliers, in both fresh and salt water. Brooks, Kreh, Jorgensen, Popovics, Clouser, Borger, and Caucci joined the ranks of Father Smith, Steenrod, and Defeo. With all the materials available, every tier could experiment with patterns old and new.

It's a wonderful time to be a tier and fly fisherman. I make no claim to be an innovator or inventor. My patterns and style are my own, the credit belongs to real innovators. Thanks to all of you.

1	**Predator Popper—Soft Body**
Hook	Mustad 34007, #6/0
Body	Closed-cell foam, heated and shaped with a heat gun
Line Channel	Bar straw cut and inserted through the popper body
Balance Weight	Split shot inserted and glued into the foam belly
Body Coating	Pearl glitter covered with a thin layer of silicone
Eyes	1/2-inch silver
Tail Finish	Pearl Krystal Flash; Chinese saddle hackles; bucktail

2	**Popping Bunker Spoon**
Hook	Mustad 34007, #4/0 bent to shape
Thread	6-pound clear monofilament
Tail	80-pound hard Mason mono, looped; chartreuse blood marabou
Underbody Frame	40-pound hard Mason mono, looped to shape
Spoon Body	3/4-inch pearl mylar piping covered with epoxy
Eyes	3/8-inch silver

3	**Sweet Lips**
Hook	Mustad 34007, #6/0
Lip	60-pound hard Mason mono, bent and epoxied to shape
Thread	White Kevlar
Tail	Light gray Sea Fibers; medium silver mylar piping
Belly	White Sea Fibers
Sides	Pearl Sparkle Flash
Back	Stack wrapped and layered pink Sea Fibers, blue pearl Sparkle Flash, chartreuse Sea Fibers, and light blue Sea Fibers
Eyes	1/2-inch silver

4	**Screw Tail Eel**
Hook	Partridge CS52, #2
Thread	White Kevlar
Belly	Polar bear Sea Fibers
Sides and Back	Light brown Sea Fibers under dark brown or olive glow bug yarn
Eyes	1/8-inch yellow
Finish	Blend and cover body materials with a light coating of silicone

5	**Grass Shrimp**

Hook	Mustad 37160S, #2
Thread	White monocord and clear 2-pound monofilament
Eyes	30-pound hard Mason mono and five-minute epoxy mixed with black Testors model paint
Short Antennae	Stacked white deer tail and boar's bristle
Long Antennae	Whiskers from a hare's mask; long polar bear hair
Lip Plate	Clear plastic soda straw
Body	Dubbing loop of polar bear Partridge SLF; trim to shape
Ribbing	Twisted pearl Krystal Flash, to segment body
Vein	Twisted black Krystal Flash, tied down over back
Horn-Body Shell & Tail	Polar-bear-colored Ultra Hair, shaped and covered with five-minute epoxy
Legs	Long natural polar bear hair or hare's whiskers, bent to shape

6	**Shadling**

Hook	Partridge Sea Prince CS52, #1/0
Thread	2-pound clear monofilament
Belly	Pearl Sparkle Flash
Back	Partridge SLF Hanks: pink, chartreuse, dark olive
Eyes	1/4-inch silver

7	**Round Belly Herring**

Hook	Partridge Homosassa Special, #3/0
Thread	2-pound clear monofilament
Tail	Light dun Hi-Vis; medium silver mylar piping
Belly	White Sea Fibers
Back	Blue pearl Sparkle Flash; Royal blue and purple Partridge SLF Hanks
Eyes	1/4-inch silver

1
2
3
4
6 7 5

Jack Gartside

Poets and songwriters insist that love doesn't last, that it fades with the mist in the morning sun, that it's here today and gone tomorrow, and so on and so forth until the last trumpet shall sound or country music shall die.

This may or may not be so, but one thing is sure: My love affair with fly tying has lasted now for over forty years. Ever since I saw my first fly tied, by Ted Williams of the Boston Red Sox at the New England Sportsman's Show in the old Mechanic's Hall in Boston. The year was 1955 and I was twelve years old. And Ted was my hero.

I can't remember the fly that Ted was tying, a salmon fly, I think, or maybe a Mickey Finn. It doesn't matter. Whatever it was, it was magic to me as I leaned over the table, fascinated by the movements of his hands and fingers as he carefully and slowly—so unlike the quickness with which he swung a bat—wound bright feathers around a hook to fashion a fly to catch fish.

To me this was a revelation: to catch a fish with feathers instead of with worms or bits of clams! Who would have thunk it? But if Ted said it could be done, and this was the way it should be done, then, by golly, it was really worth looking into. He cast a spell that day that would entrance me the rest of my life. I was hooked. And the hook was set even more firmly when, after about half an hour of listening to my questions, he asked me to come behind the table to try tying a fly myself. He would show me how easy it was.

Faster than I could say yes, I crawled under the table and out the other side. Ted got up and sat me down behind his vise. I was in heaven, indeed, with my hero behind me bent over my shoulder, patiently explaining some of the basics of fly tying and guiding my hands along the shank of the hook and through the few steps it took to tie a very basic fly. The fly was a simple Woolly Worm but to me it represented every-

thing that was wonderful and magical in life. For many years thereafter I would carry it with me as a sort of lucky charm, never fishing with it but just knowing it was there in my pocket, a simple link with my boyhood and a reminder that once I was in the presence of greatness.

The day after the show, I walked to the local library and found the only book they had on fly tying: *The Family Circle Guide to Trout Flies and How to Tie Them.* It had lots of beautiful illustrations but was a bit short on instruction; in fact, there were instructions for tying only one fly, the Royal Coachman wet fly. But it was a start. And I could hardly wait.

I didn't have any of the materials or a vise or any of the tools mentioned in the book but it didn't take me long to figure out that I could improvise until I saved up enough money (my allowance then was twenty-five cents a week) to buy some proper tools and materials. Hooks weren't a problem; I already had some long-shanked flounder hooks left over from summer. Thread from my mother's sewing basket would also do for the time being. And for a vise, I would make my own from two of my grandfather's micrometers, clamping one with another to the edge of a table; the hook would be held in place by tightening the micrometer's screw mechanism (which actually worked fairly well, but I found out from my grandfather in no uncertain terms that it was not an especially good use for a micrometer). For materials, well, there were always the neighbor's chickens, and down by the beach there were seagulls. And I had a dun-colored cat. This was all I needed, I figured, to get started in tying flies. I wasn't far from wrong.

Now forty years have passed. Forty years of fly tying and fishing. Forty years of playing around with feathers and furs and fish. And I've loved it all: the dry flies, wet flies, nymphs, and streamers; the trout flies, bass flies, and salmon flies; bonefish, tarpon, and striper flies. And all the other types of flies I've tried my hand at. And I've loved the fish that have fallen for these flies and the waters that these fish inhabit and the lands through which these waters flow or touch upon. And my love, like a parent with many children or a lover with many mistresses, has known no favorites. Each was special in its own peculiar way.

However this may be, I now hasten to add that one of my favorite fish is the striped bass. Not only for its beauty and strength and willingness to take a well-presented fly, but also because of its proximity (I live only a few miles from the sea) and its propensity for swimming in the waters I most enjoy fishing, the estuaries, flats, and off-isle sandy shores of New England, especially those areas in and around Boston.

I have had a difficult time deciding which of my favorite flies to include and have settled on four—four versions of a sand eel imitation that I enjoy fishing in my home waters.

On the Northeast coast, the sand eel (more accurately, sand lance —*Ammodytes americanus*) is one of the more common baitfish. Wherever found, it is fed on eagerly by stripers and other predatory fish.

Sand eels grow to a maximum length of about ten inches but they're more commonly found in lengths of five inches or less. Their color varies in different waters, ranging from creamish (in waters where light sand predominates) to olive, bronze, bluish green, and purple, often with bright silver sides and a creamish belly. And so I generally tie my sand eels in sizes and colors reflecting the coloration and size of the naturals found in the area I'm fishing.

Apart from imitating color and size, I also tie my sand eel imitations in varying degrees of realism, sometimes fairly exact, at other times impressionistic, with an emphasis on materials having lots of inherent movement.

3   Gartside Sand Eel (aka Corsair Sand Eel)

Hook	Mustad 34007, 34011, or equivalent; #6 to 1/0
Thread	White #6/0
Body	1/4-inch white Corsair tubing, tapered, length to vary
Tail & Insert	Five to six strands of Glimmer, Flashabou, or Fire Fly; tail length to vary
Eyes	Black on yellow
Body Color	To vary, depending on the color of naturals; olive or gray lateral line

1. Slip the Corsair tubing over the hook shank. Note the white thread lines on each side of this tubing. Tie down the rear portion of the tubing with these thread lines; push the tubing back over itself and tie down its front portion.
2. Draw the Glimmer, Flashabou, or Fire Fly through the tube.
3. When coloring the tubing, I recommend using art markers such as those made by Design, Pantone, ChartPak, and so on. Use broad-nibbed pens for general coloring, chisel points for the lateral line.
4. After applying color, buff it into the material and wipe off the excess.

This pattern is a fairly realistic representation of the sand eel. It can be tied with a long body and a short tail, or with a short body and a long tail (when you want a fly with more inherent action). This fly comes into its own when a very realistic imitation is needed; when you're fishing clear, low water; or when the stripers are being very selective. It's also productive when you're fishing strong rips or surf and you need a fly that will keep its sand-eel-like shape no matter how tempest tossed or turbulent the water. As well, it's very effective when dead-drifted.

Though effective under a variety of circumstances, this fly's one drawback is that because it's formed largely with rather stiff tubing, it doesn't have a lot of built-in action. When you're not fishing in the circumstances described above, I recommend fishing this fly with a lot of rod action, to give it a lifelike movement.

1	Gartside Marabou Fishhead Sand Eel
Hook	Mustad 34007, 34011, or equivalent; #6 to 4
Thread	White, #6/0
Tailwing	Sparse olive marabou, length to vary
Sideflash	Pearl or olive Flashabou, two or three strands on each side
Skirt	None
Fishhead	¼- or ⅓-inch Corsair tubing
Eyes	Black on yellow
Color	Olive, green, or brown on top; olive lateral line

The Featherwing and Marabou Sand Eel patterns come into their own when you want a fly that combines realism with behaviorism, when you need a fly that is more active than the Corsair Sand Eel yet retains some of the imitative realism of that pattern. I fish this fly less with my rod tip than with hand-stripping motions to bring out its action.

It's difficult for me to say which of these patterns is better. Each has its own merits and I often use them interchangeably. The marabou pattern produces very well (and perhaps best) when fished slow, teasingly; the featherwing performs best when fished very quickly, with sweeping rod motions to accompany an active hand retrieve. Marabou, of course, is quite a bit more active in the water than saddle feathers, but it does have one drawback as a material: its fragility.

2	Large Chartreuse Fishhead Sand Eel
Hook	Mustad 34007, 34011, or equivalent; #1 to 1/0
Thread	White, #6/0
Tailwing	Four narrow, matched chartreuse saddle or neck feathers (two pairs, tied in with concave sides facing each other), often faced with a chartreuse-dyed grizzly feather on each side
Sideflash	Pearl or olive Flashabou
Skirt	White marabou beneath the tailwing, chartreuse marabou above, length to about the middle of the tailwing
Fishhead	½-inch gold or ⅓-inch white Corsair tubing, tied in fishhead-style (see Featherwing Sand Eel)
Eyes	Black on yellow
Color	Olive on top; orange or red lateral line

I often weight this fly with lead wire up toward the front of the shank. When I do, I almost always coat the lead with fabric paint, olive or blue on top and red beneath. This gives the fly an internal color that adds, I think, to its effectiveness.

As every striper fisherman in the Northeast knows, chartreuse is often an effective color when fishing for stripers, sometimes attracting fish when no other color seems to work, especially in some of the darker waters of the New England coast. I most frequently fish this fly as a searching pattern, when I'm not sure of the size and color of the naturals in the area, or when larger sand eels are common.

4	Gartside Featherwing Fishhead Sand Eel
Hook	Mustad 34007, 34011, or equivalent; #6 to 1
Thread	White, #6/0
Tailwing	Two narrow, matched saddle feathers, concave sides facing each other, length and color to vary
Sideflash	Pearl or olive Flashabou
Skirt	Two turns of the downy portion of a saddle feather, color to match or complement the tailwing color
Fishhead	¼- or ⅓-inch Corsair tubing. Tie this in by slipping it over the shank and tying down its rear portion just before the skirt. Now push the tubing back over itself and tie down its front portion to form the fishhead. Trim the excess
Eyes	Black on yellow
Color	Olive, green, or brown on top; olive lateral line

I use the term *tailwing* to refer to any wing that is tied in at the normal tailing position, believing it to be a more accurate description of this part of the fly. *Sideflash* refers to any flashy material that is tied in at the sides of a tailwing. *Fishhead* refers to that part of the fly formed into a fishhead shape by the tying in and manipulation of the Corsair tubing.

I tie and fish this fly most frequently in shades of olive, cream, dun, and tan, either using solid colors or dying grizzly saddles in the desired shades.

1
2
3
4

Scott Heywood

In 1990, a few of my fishing friends and I started a fly-fishing travel service called Angling Destinations. Committed to exploring the finest fly-fishing opportunities in the world, we started in the Bahamas because that's where we wanted to go and that's what we knew. Now we're booking anglers to Alaska, Wyoming, and Montana, in addition to five destinations in the Bahamas.

People who haven't fished for bonefish want to know what all the hubbub is about. My reply is that it combines the best of hunting and fishing (if I could just get my bird dog involved, it would be the perfect sport). To bonefish successfully, you must have the visual concentration and patience to find the fish, and a hunter's stalking ability to get within casting range. Your cast must deliver the fly quietly and precisely. You must entice the fish to eat your fly and you must develop a feel for the hookset. Usually, the fisherman with the most skill catches the most fish.

The reward for all the concentration and applied technique is the hookup—the magical moment when that ghostly shadow is finally yet firmly attached to your casting arm. The run is explosive and magnificent. You struggle for control, your line rattling through the guides in a demonstration of pure power; 50, 100, then 150 yards of backing evaporate into the mix of sizzling, tropical heat and turquoise water.

Bonefish are creatures of the flats. They respond to the rhythms of the tides, charging and retreating over beds of bright sand and blankets of turtle grass. They are sleek and slender, shy and suspicious. They blend in perfectly with the turquoise waters and the shimmering bottom, their silver sides reflecting all, giving them the ability to seemingly change color. Sometimes bonefish betray themselves by a faint ripple at the surface that anglers call nervous water, but more often they go unseen, viewed as just another mat of turtle grass or an undulation of shadow in the white sand bottom. Bonefish are splendidly designed to confuse and befuddle. Perhaps this is why when one shy and skittish bonefish tips down to forage in shallow water and his tail breaks the surface, it seems so huge, such a dramatic and positive sign of his existence. After all the hours of searching for such subtle signs, when a tail finally appears, it can be heart stopping. The air seems charged with excitement and opportunity.

As you glide onto the flats early in the morning, the heat of midday is just beginning. Everything appears still, with only a faint breeze rustling the casurina trees; next to the mangroves, the water is glassy calm. The sun reflecting off the water and off the white sand bottom refracts into dizzying patterns. Upon closer inspection, everything is in motion; the turtle grass sways and shivers, bent over by the rising tides. Heat waves form at the water's surface and rise into the sizzling tropical air, making distant cays shimmer and re-form. Your senses notch up and you begin to use your intuition as much as your vision. You observe every motion and shimmer at the surface, every ripple caused by a baitfish; each disturbance of mud, silt, or sand catches your eye. The dark forms of rays and sharks patrol near shore. A hundred yards away, you stare at a spot until you're convinced it was only a small wave reflecting a diamondlike facet of light. Just as you convince yourself, a tail pops high above the water and flutters suggestively at you. A silver sail, blue edged and bright. You begin to quietly shuffle over toward the spot where the tail has sunk once again beneath the water's surface. When you have waded within casting distance, you tell yourself to be patient. The sun is not yet high enough to allow you to see through the water to the fish itself—if you're going to find the fish again, it must show itself on the surface.

You stare and wait and are sure it's over when off to your left, the fish shows itself again. A quick roll cast and you powerfully haul on your first backcast, putting energy into the rod and again into your second cast, playing out line with each effort. On your third cast you make it—the payoff cast—and drop the fly quietly near the expanding circles that are now the only sign of your tailing fish. A quick strip on your line brings the fish to the surface again. The tail begins to quiver and flutter as it comes nearer to the spot where your fly hit the water. You strip once and again. You use short, controlled strips until suddenly another tail appears and you understand there are at least two fish following your fly.

You feel some resistance, like your fly is trying to climb over a rock or a piece of coral, but then a subtle *tick-tick* comes down the line to your hand and you know it is the fish. You wait a second, allowing the fish to mouth your fly, and with a short but sharp strip, you strike. You now have a solid connection—you're lashed to something and you power two hooksets into your rod tip, hoping to drive your fly into the jaw.

As line begins to rattle through the rod's guides, a rooster tail appears far out in front of you and quickly arcs toward deep water as the bonefish races toward safety. Your line comes up tight against your reel. The reel handle becomes a blur, its motion betrayed only by a light whining sound—you'd removed its clicker last year when it just seemed too noisy on the flat and stalking bonefish had become a way of life. Your fly line disappears off the reel and you're into your backing before your brain can catch up with your heart. Your backing begins to disappear like an ice cube in a hot tub. The fish seems impossibly far away as your line heads for a small mangrove shoot. You raise your rod over your head and the shoot disappears below the water's surface and then immediately reappears shuddering from the impact. But still the fish races on. Then the line becomes abruptly and hopelessly slack. As your backing forms a wide belly at the water's surface, you quietly defame the fish. You reel in your line, pulling backing onto the reel until your fly line appears at the spool. At leader's end, you confirm your suspicion—the fly is gone. The tippet end is abraded and opaque. With a deep breath, you turn your back to the fish and wade back toward the mangroves, wondering if you have another fly like the one you just lost.

This is bonefishing. For many anglers, after all the trout, salmon, tarpon, and sailfish, the bonefish is still the ultimate quarry. *Albula vulpes*—the white fox—brings anglers back to the flats time and time again, year after year.

Many words have been written about why we do it. Maybe it's the excitement and danger on the flats, maybe it fulfills some impulse, but whatever complicated thing it might be it's probably just damned good fun.

Flies

I tie flies for three different bonefishing situations: school fish that are cruising and milling about; large cruising singles and doubles that are traveling fast; and tailing or skinny-water fish that are usually very spooky.

School fish, although spooky by nature, are often very aggressive, and they will sometimes race a companion to eat any fly offering you pitch to them. You need to create a fly that triggers their basic predatory response. The traditional bead-chain-eyed patterns work very well.

Big, fast, cruising singles and doubles need a visible fly that will sink into their field of vision quickly. This fly must make them slow down and take a look. In this situation I employ a fairly long, quick strip, then I stop. If the fish stops or looks, I twitch the fly once, subtly. Most bonefish prey avoid being eaten by not being seen. These prey species initially avoid contact by scooting away; then they lie still on the bottom, hoping they will go undetected. You want to give the fly enough action to initially attract the fish's attention, but not so much that the fly appears unnatural. Guides will often tell you to strip, strip, imparting continuous action to the fly. Sometimes big fish will follow, but rarely will they take. My best advice is, Less is better. One quick darting movement, then let your fly hug the bottom. If your fish doesn't stop, give it one more quick strip. If he stops, but doesn't follow, give the fly one more subtle twitch.

Tailing fish often give you enough time to change flies. I prefer blind ties (no eyes) on conventional Crazy Charlie–like patterns, or very light flies with mono eyes that land quietly. Because bonefish that are tailing have their heads tipped down, the fly must be presented very close to them in order to be seen. My unweighted flies and those with split tail wings land quietly and work well on tailing fish.

Bonefishermen need to understand that sink rate is the most important aspect of fly selection. Vary your sink rate so that your fly box contains an assortment—from the lightest blind flies (for tailing fish) to mono eyes (for tailing and skinny-water fish), bead-chain eyes (for medium-depth and moderately fast-cruising fish), and the heaviest lead barbell eyes for fast-cruising singles and doubles in three to six feet of water.

It is also important to pick the right size and color of fly. As a good general rule, use light-colored flies on light (sand) bottoms and dark-colored flies on dark (turtle grass, coral) bottoms. In nature, visibility can make any animal prey. Most prey species on bonefish flats are well camouflaged, but if your fly is too well camouflaged, the fish won't see it. Subtle earth-toned flies work best on sunny, bright days in shallow water when bonefish are spooky. Bright flies (pink, orange, chartreuse) work best on cloudy or darker days in deeper water or later in the day, especially at sunset.

I like flies that have some movement of materials even when the fly is not being stripped. Hackle tips, marabou, rabbit fur, and Sili Legs all impart some subtle movement to the fly even when it is at rest. When you take a look at prey species on a flat, often they have appendages that are, although small, constantly in motion. This subtle motion is an important fly component that triggers a bonefish to take a fly.

Another important trigger is eyes. I like eyes that are very obvious and lifelike. I also like those eyes to be facing the fish; this means tying them just above the bend of the hook. If the Crazy Charlie was invented today, the eyes might very well be tied in the rear where the fish can see them. Many prey species avoid capture by backing away, facing the bonefish with their claws. I feel this eye-to-eye contact make flies irresistible to fish.

Tips to Improve Your Bonefishing

• The majority of bonefishing is done with a weight-forward floating line. These lines lift easily off the water without spooking the fish and rarely get hung up on the bottom. Use a neutral or pale-colored fly line; gray or sand is best. Very bright lines, especially fluorescent colors, can be as easy for the fish to see as they are for you. If you use bright fly lines, make sure your leader is long enough to compensate for the line's increased visibility.

• Throw a wet towel over any obstructions on the casting deck of your boat. Cleats and handles can easily snare your fly line and ruin a cast or, worse, break off a fish.

• If you are using a monofilament butt section nail-knotted to your fly line, for your loop-to-loop connection to the leader use .025-inch or heavier medium to medium-limp mono on an 8-weight. This will transfer the energy from your cast to the leader. A butt section of less than .05 causes the cast to die as the energy is transferred from line to leader.

• Using loop-to-loop connections allows you to change leaders quickly. Attach a two-foot butt section to your fly line, as mentioned above, then tie a loop in the end. Then depending on conditions, you can use a prelooped seven-foot leader if it's windy, or up to a fifteen-foot leader if it's calm.

• A 10-pound clear mono tippet works well on bonefish. Check your leader regularly for abrasion and retie your fly after each fish. Test your knot every time you tie on a new tippet.

• Bonefish have a powerful sense of smell. They can smell shrimp and crabs they cannot see. They also can smell insect repellent, sunblock, gasoline, and aftershave. Keeping your hands clean will help keep your fly clean.

Seeing and Being Seen

• Polarized sunglasses are absolutely essential for spotting bonefish. Brown or gray lenses work best on bright days; yellow or amber work best on cloudy, low-light days. Side shields will eliminate peripheral light. Make sure you use an eyeglass retainer strap to avoid losing your expensive glasses.

• Wade quietly and slowly. Bonefish can "feel" water being pushed by your legs. Use your eyes; scan constantly; you are hunting as much as fishing. You are pitted against an animal with an incredible array of sensory organs.

• Bonefish have an acute sense of vision, enabling them to see colors well and in a wide variety of light conditions. They can see motion in muddy or clear water, and whether they are stationary or traveling at top speed. That mango Hawaiian shirt looks good in pictures—but tan and pale blue will allow you to spook fewer fish. Remember to remove shiny jewelry. Also, don't hesitate to cast from your knees or to crouch if fish come in very close.

• Use the wind and sun to your advantage. If possible, wade a flat with the wind behind you. If there is little or no wind, have the sun behind you. Often, after spotting fish, you have time to navigate upwind of them, but wade slowly until you are in place.

• A hat with a long bill will protect your face from the sun and also improve your vision, especially if the bill's underside is dark. A dark underside absorbs reflected light.

• Scan the water constantly for surface disturbances (nervous water); to consistently spot bonefish you must imagine that the water does not exist and look through it to the bottom.

Casting

• Don't strip out more line than you need to make your cast. Make a practice cast, then leave that measured amount of the line trailing in the water (if you are wading) or stacked carefully on deck (if you are casting from a boat). This will minimize the amount of line that can tangle on your feet or form knots. Do not pull line off your reel and stack it on the deck of the boat. If you do, the forward portion of your line is underneath the pile; when you cast with the line stacked this way you end up with a tangled bird's nest.

• If you are casting from the deck of a boat, take off your shoes. This will allow you to feel the fly line stacked on the deck and avoid stepping on it.

• False-cast away from the fish, especially slow-moving or tailing fish. This will keep your fly line from spooking them. Cast at a 45- to 90-degree angle to the direction that the fish are heading.

• If it is windy, make your false casts holding your rod as parallel as possible to the plane of the water. The friction of the wind over the water lessens the wind's velocity in the area three to four feet above the water's level. This casting technique makes it harder for the fish to see the fly line and allows for a very quiet presentation, because the fly does not drop from much height.

• Never cast too early or begin to cast when the bonefish is out of your range. Be patient; know your comfortable casting range. If you try to make too long a cast and your fly falls short, it will take too long to cast again and the bonefish will have moved on.

• It is better to cast too short and hope the fish sees the fly than to cast too long and spook the fish. In nature, prey never moves toward a predator. Never place a fly so that, when retrieved, it moves toward a bonefish. Predators chase their prey, and they expect their prey to be moving away from them. When confronted with an approaching fly, a bonefish will change roles, from predator to prey, and flee. Few fish can leave a flat as quickly as a bonefish.

• Generally, a tailing fish has its head tipped down and is already occupied; consequently, the fly must be dropped very close. In contrast, cruising fish can see a fly from a much greater distance and the fly can be presented farther away.

• Learn to strip-strike. . . . Trout fishermen (there are lots of us) usually raise the rod tip to strike a fish. Used on a bonefish, this technique will quickly remove the fly from the fish's field of vision if the fish has not eaten it. The strip strike, however, keeps the fly in the bonefish's strike zone and gives you a second chance. A one- to three-foot strip made firmly by the hand not holding the rod accomplishes the strip strike.

• When retrieving your fly, point the rod tip directly at it. This gives the fly the proper action.

• Lift your fly line quietly and slowly from the water to initiate another cast. Do not use the initiation of the backcast to load the rod tip. Many beginning anglers do this to allow for longer casts or to cast into the wind—but such a noisy liftoff will almost always spook bonefish.

• Do your homework before going fishing. Learn to cast accurately and quickly. Do not false-cast excessively. Play out line with each cast, then shoot your line accurately to the fish on your last cast. Repeated false casting over a fish in an effort to measure distance and accuracy often spooks fish and wastes valuable time.

The Hookset and After

• When a bonefish follows a fly, he will almost always take it. Other clues that a fish has taken your fly: His dorsal fin or tail flutters or quivers; he flashes his side in the sun; another fish races to the spot; he scurries away leaving his companion or school behind; and, most important, he tips down and his tail comes out of the water. If any of these occur, chances are this fish has your fly. Count off one or two seconds and strip-strike. Sometimes, if you can't see the fish, you can feel your line vibrate or jump. In that case, strip-strike again.

• If a fish follows closely but does not take your fly, change your retrieve: Speed up, slow down, or stop entirely. This change will often elicit a strike.

• A bonefish can travel twenty-six miles per hour, or several hundred feet in eight seconds. Set your drag before you cast to a fish, and once it's hooked get all the spare line safely out through the guides. Always fight a bonefish off the reel; to do otherwise invites disaster. Until the fish is on the reel, watch your line, not the fish.

• After getting the line on the reel, hold your rod high. This will create a steeper angle and help the line get over coral and mangrove shoots, resulting in fewer breakoffs.

• The harder you fight a bonefish, the harder it will pull back. If a fish gets tangled around a mangrove or in the weeds or coral, take all the pressure off it. Bonefish will usually stop. You can untangle your line and resume the fight.

• Handle a landed fish as little as possible. If you pinch the barbs on your hooks, hemostats will often let you not touch the fish at all.

When Day Is Done

• As you start to head home, trail your fly line without a fly behind the boat, to remove kinks and twists. As you reel in the fly line, pass it through a cloth soaked with fly-line cleaner and you will be ready for the next day.

• To avoid corrosion, rinse your reel and rod with fresh water at the end of each day.

9, 12	Scott's Shrimp
Hook	Mustad 3407 or 34007, Tiemco 811S, or equivalent; #2 to 6
Thread	Mono thread to match body color
Eyes	Burned monofilament or black lead barbells, depending on desired sink rate
Tail	Krystal Flash, to match body color
Body	Eight to ten strands of white, tan, root beer, pink, or orange Krystal Flash, topped with clear Larva Lace
Wing	Calf tail or craft fur. On a white Shrimp, use a white wing; for flies in all other colors, use a tan wing
Claws	Split calf tail. On a white Shrimp, use white claws; for flies in all other colors, use tan claws
Antennae	Four strands of Krystal Flash

1. Tie on a bundle of calf tail at the top of the hook bend to point downward at an angle of 20 to 30 degrees. Trim the calf tail by angle-cutting to form a smooth body, then wrap with thread. Separate the calf tail into two equal bundles and cross-wind each bundle to achieve a 90- to 100-degree spread. This produces the claws-at-the-ready posture and allows the fly to settle quietly on the water. Claws should be approximately $1^{1}/_{2}$ times the length of the hook shank.

2. Attach four strands of Krystal Flash so that they extend forward between the two claws. Trim slightly longer than the claws to form antennae.

3. To form the body, attach the Larva Lace beginning just behind the eye of the hook and wrap it back to a point where it meets the claws. Do the same with eight to ten strands of Krystal Flash.

4. Attach burned mono or painted lead barbell eyes to the rear eye position on the hook. Secure with figure-eight wraps.

5. Wrap the Krystal Flash toward the hook eye. Figure-eight through the eyes then tie off, leaving a $1/_{4}$-inch fanned portion over the hook eye. Trim to cover the hook eye and a little beyond. This forms the tail.

6. Wrap the Larva Lace to the hook eye in a similar manner. Tie off so as not to crowd the hook eye.

7. Attach a calf tail or craft fur wing. It should extend to three-quarters of the length of the claws.

An excellent fly for tailing fish that's also very easy to tie. The split calf tail wing allows it to land quietly; different eyes can adjust its sink rate.

1	Heywood's Brown Swimming Shrimp—Variation 1
Hook	Mustad 34007 or Tiemco 811S, #4, 6, or 8
Mouth	Tan rabbit
Antennae	Orange Krystal Flash
Claws	Cree hackle tips
Collar	Orange Crystal Chenille
Eyes	Lead barbells, painted
Hackle	Brown grizzly
Body	Brown mohair
Carapace	Orange scud back
Segments	Mono thread

1	2
3	4
5	6
7	8

2 Heywood's Brown Swimming Shrimp—Variation 2

Hook	Mustad 34007 or Tiemco 811S, #4, 6, or 8
Mouth	Orange marabou
Antennae	Orange Krystal Flash
Claws	Cree hackle tips
Collar	Brown Crystal Chenille
Eyes	Umpqua barbells, painted
Hackle	Brown grizzly
Body	Brown mohair
Carapace	Pearlescent flat tinsel
Segments	Mono thread

Along with Marl Bone Man (below), these are excellent patterns for fast-moving large bonefish. Cast well ahead of a fish and strip hard once or twice, then stop. If the fish stops, twitch barely, then stop again.

3, 4, 5, 6 Marl Bone Man

Hook	Mustad 34007 or Tiemco 811S, #4, 6, or 8
Mouth	Olive grizzly marabou
Antennae	Sili Legs (Krystal Flash can be substituted)
Body	Brown Crystal Chenille
Eyes	Umpqua barbells, painted
Legs	Brown Sili Legs, knotted fast-tie-style.

This effective fly can be tied in orange, pink, tan, or white. It's excellent for fast-moving bonefish.

7 Eye Gotcha

Hook	Mustad 34007 or Tiemco 811S, #4, 6, or 8
Mouth	Pearl mylar tubing
Eyes	Medium silver bead-chain eyes
Body	Pearl Krystal Flash with V-Rib, or pearlescent flat tinsel with V-Rib
Heart	Pink floss
Wing	Tan craft fur

Basically, this is just a Gotcha with the eyes facing the fish. It evolved with the help of Patrick Roberts, the head guide at Sandy Point, Abaco, Bahamas. He likes the eyes at the back, I like the heart. I think fish trigger on this; in the original Gotcha, I think this is what the pink nose represents. I caught a nine-pound bonefish with this fly at Sandy Point on my last visit.

8 Little Pinky

Hook	Mustad 34007or Tiemco 811S, #4, 6, or 8
Mouth	Tan sheep fleece
Antennae	Pearl Krystal Flash
Eyes	Lead barbells, nickel plated then painted black
Body	Pink floss
Segments	Gold wire
Carapace	Pearlescent flat tinsel

10 Mohair Shrimp

Hook	Mustad 34007 or Tiemco 811S, #4, 6, or 8
Mouth	Sheep fleece
Claws	White hackle tips
Antennae	Krystal Flash
Eyes	Burned monofilament
Body	Gray mohair yarn
Carapace	Scud back
Segments	Mono thread
Wings	Sheep fleece

The following flies imitate two shrimp species common on bonefish flats. They are best fished with a strip-and-stop retrieve. A flat, black, small barbell eye can be tied at the hook eye if either fly is intended to be fished in deeper water. The claws of the Mantis Shrimp can also be sculpted to resemble the folded-back attitude of the natural's claws; the bucktail represents the claws in the extended position.

11 Heywood's Ghost Shrimp

Hook	Mustad 34007 or Tiemco 811S, #4, 6, or 8
Mouth	Tan sheep fleece
Antennae	Pearl Krystal Flash
Collar	Pearl Crystal Chenille
Eyes	Burned monofilament, painted
Hackle	White saddle hackle
Body	White mohair, or dubbing with gold wire

13 Biclops Shrimp

Hook	Mustad 34007 or Tiemco 811S, #4, 6, or 8
Eyes	Burned monofilament, painted
Antennae	Hackle stems and Krystal Flash
Mouth	Tan sheep fleece
Body	Gold wire with sparkle dubbing
Wing	Sheep fleece

A very simple tie and very effective on tailing bonefish. It can be cast very close to tailing fish.

14 Heywood's Golden Mantis Shrimp

Hook	Mustad 34007 or Tiemco 811S, #4, 6, or 8
Eyes	Burned monofilament, painted
Mouth	Yellow marabou
Antennae	Light orange Krystal Flash
Claws	Brown/yellow bucktail
Collar	Brown Crystal Chenille
Hackle	Yellow grizzly
Body	Gold wire, dubbed
Beard	Sheep fleece

9	10
11	12
13	14

Capt. Brian Horsley

I grew up in northeastern North Carolina, forty-five miles from the Outer Banks. I became a full-time resident of the Outer Banks in the winter of 1974, and in the late 1970s started fly fishing for big bluefish. Twenty years later I was fly fishing for most species. In 1991, I was lucky enough to break the 20-pound tippet record for bluefish with one of 16 pounds, 9 ounces. Somehow the record still holds.

In 1992, I started the Outer Banks Fly Company, a wholesale semicustom fly-tying operation. At one time I serviced twenty-five shops in five states. In 1992, I started a wading guide service as well. Demand was surprisingly high, but after one season I knew wading was not for me. We caught fish wading, but the wind was a big problem. The next year I purchased an eighteen-foot Hewes Redfisher, painted FLAT OUT on her hull, got my captain's license, and became the first full-time saltwater fly-fishing guide in North Carolina.

Charters are available from April through November. Our target species is speckled trout, along with redfish and flounder plus Spanish mackerel, alberts, and cobia. The Outer Banks of North Carolina will become a mecca for the saltwater fly fisherman in the years to come. As for now, the area is relatively undiscovered.

A fellow from Pennsylvania had called me to book a trip two days before he was to arrive. There was no time for him to mail a deposit, and, because I don't take credit cards, I told him to come on down, but please don't stand me up. When the day arrived I arose at 4:15 A.M., drove twenty-five miles to Oregon Inlet, and launched my boat. No party. I was just about to put my boat back on the trailer when a friend suggested we go look for some alberts. Away we went, he in his boat and me in mine. It was a twenty-minute run to the artificial reef, with no signs of alberts when we arrived. After thirty minutes of looking, I turned my boat back toward the inlet. It was slick calm, a beautiful morning. On the way back I saw lots of cow-nose rays finning their way up the coast. One bunch looked different, and I wheeled the boat over to get a closer look. Boy, was I surprised! Three cobia from thirty to fifty pounds were tailing along. I grabbed a 10-weight rod with a red and yellow Big-Eye Deceiver rigged up for big red drum and moved the boat parallel to the fish. This was too easy—no way these fish were going to bite. First cast, the biggest cobia gobbled my fly on the second strip. After an hour's battle, no gaff or net, the fifty-two-pound fish was in the boat. While I was fighting it, I saw other fish everywhere. When I finally got back to the dock at 11:00 A.M., I had caught and released two fish in the thirty-pound range. I ended the day thankful that customer hadn't shown up.

1	**Big-Eye Deceiver**
Hook	Mustad 34007 or Tiemco 811S or 800S, #1 to 6/0
Thread	Danville flat waxed nylon
Tail	Three to four pairs of saddle hackles or grizzly neck hackles
Body	Diamond Braid or chenille
Wing	Bucktail
Top	Bucktail, then peacock herl
Head	Build up with thread, apply Dave's Flexament, let dry, apply prismatic eyes, then cover the head with epoxy
Flash	Fire Fly Tie on each side of the tail; Krystal Flash between the wings and top; prismatic flash down each side; and red Krystal Flash for the throat

This is my version of Lefty's famous fly. I added the prismatic eyes and epoxy head for extra flash and durability. By turning the fly in your hand, you can achieve the head shape that looks good to you.

2	**Outer Banks Sand Flea**
Hook	Mustad 34007 or Tiemco 811S or 800S, #4 to 1
Thread	Brown Danville monocord
Eyes	Lead eyes, small to medium, unpainted
Tail	Gold or copper Krystal Flash
Body	Tan medium chenille
Wing	Orange kip tail

Tie down the lead eyes $3/16$ inch back from the hook eye so the fly will ride hook-up. Tie a $3/4$-inch bunch of Krystal Flash (twenty strands) just above the hook bend. Tie the chenille on top of the Flash. Wind the chenille forward, then wrap it around the lead eyes. Continue back and forth until the fly looks fat and round. Tie off the chenille above the eyes. Take a small clump of the kip tail and tie it in front of the lead eyes. This acts as a wing to keep the fly riding hook-up, and also gives it the color of the egg sac on a soft-shell sand flea.

This fly imitates the mole crab, or sand flea, which is found in the surf. It works well for pompano, sea mullets (kingfish), flounder, croakers, and spots. It has also fooled its share of bonefish.

3	**Plug Fly**
Hook	Mustad 34007 or 34011, or Tiemco 811S; #1/0 to 4/0
Thread	Brown Danville monocord
Tail	Grizzly neck hackles 3 to 4 inches long; bucktail
Body	Deer body hair for spinning
Eyes	Lead eyes, medium to large, painted yellow with black pupils
Flash	Flashabou or Fire Fly Tie

You can tie this fly in any color; my best are pink, red-and-yellow, red-and-white, and black. Start by tying the eyes $3/8$ inch back from the hook eye. Take a $2^1/2$-inch-long piece of bucktail and attach it over the hook bend. On each side of this, tie in the grizzly neck hackles so they splay out. Add a few strands of Flashabou or Fire Fly Tie to each side. The next step is to start spinning or stacking the body hair. After each bunch, pack it down. It's not important to get this too tight; you want this fly to sink and swim. Continue spinning or stacking until you reach the lead eyes. I change colors at this point; I like my Plug Flies to have red heads. When all the spinning is finished, trim the basic shape with curved scissors. For the final trim, I use a double-edged razor blade. Be careful not to overtrim.

This fly is my version of a MirrOlure. I like to use it over deep-water grass flats. It is a good finger mullet imitation and works well on bigger speckled trout, stripers, and cobia. I have also had success in the surf with it.

4	**Big-Eye Streaker**
Hook	Mustad 34007 or Tiemco 811S or 800S, #1 to 6/0
Thread	Danville flat waxed nylon
Tail	Three to four pairs of saddle hackles or grizzly neck hackles
Body	Diamond Braid or chenille
Wing	Bucktail
Top	Bucktail, then a pair of peacock swords
Head	Build up with thread, apply Dave's Flexament, let dry, apply prismatic eyes, then cover the head with epoxy
Flash	Fire Fly Tie on each side of the tail; Krystal Flash between the wings and top; prismatic flash down each side; and red Krystal Flash for the throat

This version of the Lefty's Deceiver gives a wider profile, like that of a threadfin shad, a menhaden, or any baitfish with a wide, deep profile. It's tied the same way as the Big-Eye Deceiver except that in place of the peacock herl, I add a pair of peacock swords.

5	**Big-Eye Mullet**
Hook	Mustad 34007 or Tiemco 811S, #1 to 4/0
Thread	Danville flat waxed nylon
Tail	Long clump of bucktail
Body	Diamond Braid or mylar
Wing	Bucktail
Top	Peacock herl
Head	Build up with thread, apply Dave's Flexament, let dry, apply prismatic eyes, then cover the head with epoxy

I tie this durable fly for big bluefish; the smaller versions work for speckled trout, Spanish mackerel, and alberts. It's tied like a Deceiver, but to make it more economical I use bucktail for the tail. By turning the fly in your hand, you can achieve the head shape that looks good to you.

```
1   2
3   4
  5
    6
```

6	**Wanchese Crab**
Hook	Mustad 34007 or Tiemco 811S, #2/0
Thread	Brown Danville monocord
Eyes	Medium lead eyes, unpainted
Body	Root beer Estaz
Tail	Four pairs of grizzly neck hackles; orange kip tail; gold Krystal Flash
Body	One long webby grizzly neck hackle

Tie in the lead eyes $1/4$ inch back from the hook eye. Attach a few strands of long Krystal Flash above the hook bend; on top of this add a sparse bunch of $1^{1}/_{2}$-inch-long kip tail. Then take two $1^{1}/_{2}$-inch-long neck hackle tips and tie on each side of the kip tail so they are splayed out. Before you move the thread forward, tie the webby neck hackle butt-first at the same place you tied in the other neck hackles. This hackle will be palmered later. Move the thread above the lead eyes, tie in the root beer Estaz, then form a body around the hook shank and lead eyes. Finish in front of the lead eyes. Now put a couple of whip finishes in the thread. Take the webby neck hackle, palmer it forward above the lead eyes, and tie off. With your scissors, cut the hackles off the bottom of the fly.

I designed this pattern after using the Chernobyl Crab. I have had great success with it in spring and early June. It's particularly good over the grass flats in June when there are lots of small crabs. Excellent for redfish, flounder, and speckled trout, this fly will win no beauty contest, but it catches fish!

Bill and Kate Howe

Having fished since childhood with all types of equipment, sometimes to the point of obsession, we constantly search for information on the subject and that search is almost as pleasurable as the fishing. Reading all of the material by the authors of the day on fishing, lure construction, and tackle is never a chore. And being able to adapt a technique into our own and write about it is satisfying.

Growing up in California, we fished both salt and fresh water. Later travels took us to work, live, and fish all over the western United States, Canada, Alaska, Mexico, and the Hawaiian Islands. Many times we had the opportunity to combine work and fishing and we learned just enough about fishing not to be dangerous.

The Flies

Being intrigued with the various tying materials available, and many that are not intended for this purpose, we think a lot about the properties and idiosyncrasies of materials: durability, buoyancy, the ability to trap air or expel it, bulk, ease of tying, color, and so on. Knowing as much as you can about materials is a must if you are going to be able to predict motion, action, and fishability once a fly hits the water.

We made the change to synthetic materials not because natural materials aren't as good, but because they just don't hold up as well as synthetics and are too unpredictable in their densities. Our particular patterns are designed as swimming flies, so we prefer the almost neutral buoyancy of nylon.

Today's synthetics, especially crinkle nylons, have some very unique properties. The colors available in both opaque and translucent are endless, allowing us to match the colors of any bait. The length and density of today's materials have allowed us to use some tying methods that have been around for years and to

develop our own style of tying. The method that lends itself best to nylons is what we call the Hi-Ti.

The Hi-Ti goes back many years. It is constructed by tying several sets of wings on top of the hook shank, one right after the other. It allows us to create a wide dorsal/ventral silhouette while maintaining a slim, light-weight pattern. Combining the Hi- and Lo-Tie styles with crinkle nylon required a slightly different approach. Nylons are quite dense and do not compress when tied down, as hollow materials such as bucktail will. We have developed a method of folding this material back on itself as it is tied in. This method is not entirely new, but the manner in which we use it is unique and our own innovation, hence the ALF style of flies.

Originally, we tied baitfish imitations for striper fishing in strictly generic forms. But after being contacted by Ed Rice and Danny Byford of International Sportsmen's Expositions and asked to tie some flies for the first ISE Invitational Bluewater long-range trip, we decided to expand on our generic synthetic striper fly and the ALF was born.

The ALF, which originally stood for "Anchovy-Looking (expletive!)" and was later shortened to "Anchovy-Looking Fly" for obvious marketing reasons, then became a style of fly rather than a specific pattern. We are able to imitate endless types of baitfish with this style of tying.

The samples we sent for the trip were so well received that we ended up sending about seven dozen along. The immediate success of these flies in an open-ocean fishing situation, including multiple species catches and a couple of world records, prompted us to expand the line. It now includes everything from tiny inshore flies designed for bonefish on the flats to baitfish imitations that have been proved time and again for tarpon in the Keys and imitations that measure 14 by 18 by 6 inches, tied on #10/0 by 9/0 tandem rigs for black marlin off Australia. The style also adapts extremely well to impressionistic ties for bottom fish, squid, and shrimp.

We use an adapted Lo-Ti version of the ALF style to create viable tube fly patterns as well. The Lo-Ti adaptation helps center the tube fly in the water, making possible patterns that do not roll or spin when fished.

In our continuing effort to perfect this pattern for offshore fishing, we spent several seasons experimenting with adding flash materials to schooling baitfish—their flash. It is this reflecting and refracting of light that shows the movement in these baits and helps game fish locate them in schools or alone. The final adaptations of these flies contain what many might think is an excessive amount of flash—up to one-half of the total profile. But these flies have far outperformed those of the same silhouette with only an average amount of flash.

FPFs or Flashy Profile Flies are again just another style of tying and not a particular pattern. This style may be adapted to patterns incorporating any number of natural or synthetic materials. It is just as productive in large offshore flies as it is in small flashy baitfish imitations. By adding several layers—up to one-half the total volume of the fly's bulk—of pearlescent flash and holographic mylar to the center of your baitfish pattern, you will form a reflective/refractive center that will pick up any and all light that penetrates the water column. Use standard tying materials above and below the center to form the back and belly, and to help support the flash. We tie this fly in sizes up to #10/0 tandem—18 inches long with 6-inch-deep profiles. These are serious baitfish imitations.

To tie good fishing flies you need to repeatedly field-test them until you get it right. Creative tiers get their patterns into the hands of many competent fishermen to test them under all conditions.

One person we count on is Dean Butler of Cairns, Australia. In his sportfishing business, he has the opportunity to put our flies in front of many species of game fish, from dogtooth tuna to three-hundred-pound marlin, and we have been able to add his knowledge to our design concepts. In fact Dean and his teammates won the first Australian Billfish Open using our FPFs. Dean's continued pursuit of marlin on the fly has shown us the need for indestructible flies that are light and castable, but able to withstand the rigors of several hours of play and fight with these leviathans. Besides being tough, these flies must excite fish and hold their interest, so we continue to design *big* flashy flies that imitate the large baitfish. We now have gathered—through photo and verbal accounts of hours of having these big fish hooked and fighting—the information we need to construct the imitations that will entice strikes and hold up during prolonged battles.

The Fish

Know your place in the food chain. Fish are primitive creatures whose behavior is based solely on instinctual reactions to stimuli. They react to our flies at a very basic level, and we sometimes give them way more credit than they deserve.

In hunting, fish use all of their senses. The one that we fly fishermen rely on most is their sense of sight. For dark or clouded waters we often tie flies with elements that help them create sounds detectable by the fish's auditory systems. When we move a fly through the water, we are hoping to elicit an investigative response. If the fly pattern we are using is recognized as prey and nothing goes wrong, feeding takes place.

We should, as educated fishers, sharpen our senses to what goes on in the fish's world. Avoid the tendency to anthropomorphize the prey; learn about their basic needs and how to fill them. Remember, a fish acts the same whether we are present or not.

Most species of saltwater fish are worth going after with the long rod. There are very few fish in the oceans of the world that don't offer the fly angler a challenge. The act of fishing for the pure joy of it far outweighs how glamorous a species may or may not be.

The great barracuda stalked in shallow, clear flats is one of our favorites. A cautious yet inquisitive predator, the barracuda moves with great speed. One quick blink and it's gone, only to reappear at your flank or behind you to reverse the roles of predator and prey. Fishing for billfish, standing up and slugging it out from a small boat, can be incredibly rewarding, regardless of who is the victor. Tuna have such strength and energy for their size, while trevally command respect for pure endurance and determination.

As light-tackle fishermen, we owe our quarry our respect and understanding. A hooked fish is fighting for its life and it is our responsibility to honor that life. Fight your battles fast and hard; don't be afraid to push yourself or your tackle to the limit. Allow these gallant players to be released in top condition so they may survive to fight again.

Fishing Techniques

Fishing techniques and styles are as varied as those who fish them. The most important aspect of fishing is knowing your quarry. Once you understand the habits of the species you seek, then the best method is the one that gets your fly to the fish and keeps it in the strike zone for the longest period of time.

We have experienced success fishing our baitfish imitations with little or no applied action. Rather than constantly casting and stripping, we prefer to let an artificial sink and drift, only occasionally adding a little enticing motion by twitching the rod. This has proved to be as good a searching method as any we know. In order to best deliver your fly to the desired depth, carry a full range of lines, from floaters to high-density lead-core heads.

By using different-density lines we are able to get consistent results, from the surface to thirty fathoms. Understanding how different lines function in salt water, you can easily get your flies into depths that will surprise you. If you want greater depths, add small egg sinkers to your leader. Add the sinker to your leader above a #10 swivel, then add the desired amount of leader to your fly. Cast this rig well upcurrent and allow it to sink during the drift. This may be considered taboo by some but to those of us who view fly fishing as a constant learning experience it is just another method to achieve a goal. The most effective fisherman is the one who is just as comfortable casting an 800-gram shooting taper and hardware as a floating line and small surface flies. Don't be afraid to experiment!

The single most important technique you can develop is the ability to detect and adapt to the ever-changing conditions. Sharpen your perceptions. Water temperatures, weather, light, and tides all play an active role in fish activity. The fish are constantly adapting to these changes; their survival depends on it. So does your success.

Tackle Systems

Offshore fishing, more than any other type of saltwater fly fishing, will test tackle and angler endurance. To make your fishing easy and fun, use simple tackle to set up systems for your terminal gear.

A secure system begins at the reel. Start by tying a long-looped (at least 2 feet), fifty-turn Bimini twist knot in the end of your backing. With the loop doubled, go ahead and tie a standard backing to the spool knot, allowing about eight to ten inches of doubled backing after the knot is tightened down between spool and Bimini. This will double the strength of your backing knot and also provide a little shock absorbency should you need it. As you explore the offshore world of game fishing, you'll see this knot sooner or later! Backing to fly line is connected in much the same way. Tie another fifty-turn Bimini in your backing and use the doubled loop to tie an Albright knot. To make it secure, we suggest you finish this knot by improving it. To improve any knot, tie the equivalent of a four- to six-turn uniknot back up the standing line with the tag end, and pull down tight against the knot. For connecting fly line to butt section we also use the improved Albright knot. Butt sections of 50-pound mono are the best lines of 10-weight and higher. Choose monofilament that is somewhat stiff and abrasion resistant. The butt section is often overlooked by anglers as just a connection between the fly line and the leader. Often the reason a cast fails is that the butt section is too light and it hinges and does not allow the power of the cast to continue through the leader. Finish the butt section up with a perfection loop and you're ready.

The twenty-turn Bimini twist in your tippet, when tied properly, adds a little forgiving stretch and toughness for pulling on hard-charging fish. With a little practice the Bimini is no harder to tie than your shoelaces. Although the IGFA allows for a minimum of fifteen inches of tippet between these Biminis, we prefer tippets of twenty to thirty inches, depending on fishing conditions, fly size, and casting distance.

Bite leaders, twelve inches including the knots for the IGFA, are also very simple—or should be. They may either be attached to your bottom tippet Bimini with a Huffnagle knot or, for lighter bite

2, 3	The ALF (Anchovy-Looking Fly) and FPF (Flashy Profile Fly)
Hook	For singles: #1/0 to 6/0, Gamakatsu SS15, Octopus or Trey Combs Tandem rigs to #10/0 x 10/0
Weed Guard	#6 (.016) single-strand wire (optional)
Weighting	3-amp fuse wire (.028) lead wire
Primary	
Body	Best Way Crinkle nylon and Super Hair
Flash	Dyed pearl Flashabou; 1/32 holographic mylar, Krystal Flash, angel Hair on smaller ALF patterns. Alternate Flash for back and top of fly: bronze Flashabou and black Krystal Flash
Gills	Red FisHair
Head	Tying thread
Eyes	Witchcraft prismatic stick-ons, 3- to 10-millimeter, depending on fly size; silver iris, black pupil, or similar

1. For tandem rigs secure chosen hooks at the desired length using multistrand nylon coated wire. Crimp with sleeve close to front hook after passing through eye of front hook and back through back hook eye, then fold again.

2. Common sense should tell you that for short flies of 3 to 8 inches (singles or small tandems) overall, you can start tying on the front hook. Very long and larger flies will need to be started on wire somewhere between front and back hooks. This all depends on length of tandem and how long the nylon belly will be and length of flash tail. A 16-inch fly needs belly material only 12 inches long; the rest should be flash.

To form a deep, thin, body, apply successive material bunches atop each other in six- to eight-strand clumps for smaller flies and larger clumps for bigger FPFs. Wrap Crinkle nylon atop shank at midclump, rear ends extending belly length past hook bend.

Fold forward strands back; wrap down atop fold. Lift and trim unevenly so that material has graduated lengths and does not get that "hacked off" paint-brush appearance. For smaller or larger flies everything is relative.

3. Should you need a little extra material to fill in the belly, now is the time to tie in a clump that will fill in the sides by laying the nylon on the side of the hook ahead of the sleeve. Take a couple of wraps and cross over top of hook and down the other side; secure with a couple of wraps. Repeat this on top of hook and under, which will fill in belly portion very well.

4. Flashy profile is next, using whatever flash you prefer. We use Pearl Flashabou or Heavy Saltwater Flash in large clumps with uneven ends and folded after initial tie-in. Really big flies require three sections of flash; lots of holographic mylar should be added over last section and allowed to veil or halo flashy profile.

5. You can tie in some belly material if needed. Start completing the top of the fly, which is nothing more than sections of nylon tied and folded then tied again. Super Hair works nicely when combined with regular Crinkle nylon on large flies. Smaller flies tie well with just Super Hair. Pearl Flashabou is available in many colors. Holographic mylar will give all the flash needed. The iridescent flash that fish give off from their scales can be duplicated with pearl Flashabou and holographic mylar; no other material is required. Holographic Flashabou is also very handy for top line or lateral lines. Mylar eyes will work well. We use CA glue (superglue) with kicker spray (accelerant), and coat the head material with extra think head cement to set. There is a nice balance when material amounts are correct. Remember that when you're using high and low tying and folding material, you can achieve tremendous proportions while maintaining balance.

Tips:

All materials are folded, using a very old high and low tying procedure. Each layer is measured for length, based on how you want the fly to look for the intended application, and laid on hook or wire secured with a couple of wraps, folded over and secured again.

If the material is tied and cut off and held together with epoxy, you are not tying an ALF or FPF. Shortcuts are not acceptable. The synthetic material does not compress, so the folding keeps the material where it belongs instead of pulling out. The deep profile is achieved by layering above and below; keep front view thin, side view as deep or narrow as needed.

leaders and light leaders, with a loop-to-loop connection that allows you to change flies that have pretied bite leaders quickly. To connect the fly, we use a loop and prefer the Homer Rhode knot. Although this is only a 50 percent knot, it is still one of the best connectors for bite leader to fly for monofilament of 50 to 100 pounds. Even at 50 percent the breaking strength of this knot is 25 pounds in 50-pound-test mono—which is stronger than the maximum 20-pound leaders you will be fishing.

Attaching wire bite leaders takes a little more practice to master. For easier casting, we keep our wire leaders short. If fly-fishing wire is used to protect your leader from the fish's teeth, six inches is more than adequate most of the time. In the case of wahoo and large sharks, however, you should practice casting twelve-inch wire leaders so that you can handle them when you need them. Use haywire twists to attach single-strand wire to fly and fix a small 50-pound, black barrel swivel to the other end. You can then quickly attach your fly to your leader with the loop-to-loop system. Twisted wire, when

| 4 |
| 5 |
| 6 |
| 7 |
| 8 |

used, should be attached to the leader by means of an Albright knot. This knot pulls down nice and tight and gets a good bite in the soft plastic coating on this wire. Tie your fly to this wire by means of a figure-eight knot and you're ready to go.

It is never wise to exceed your tackle's capabilities. Leaders of more than about 20 pounds limit your ability to break off a fish; you usually break something instead.

Both fly fishing and fly tying are fun and easy if you allow them to be. Well-tied flies go right along with well-constructed leaders and well-tied knots. Don't be afraid to explore the saltwater environment. Just remember that nothing improves your fishing skills like practice, and nothing will make for a great trip like being prepared.

1   Tarpon ALF Green Back

Hook	Eagle Claw 254, #4/0
Thread	Flat white Danville flat waxed nylon
Weed Guard	Coffee-colored stainless wire, #6, doubled
Body	Best Way Super Hair: polar bear, gray, smoke, olive, dark green, black
Flash	Pearl Flashabou; 1/32-inch holographic gold mylar
Cheeks	Dark red FisHair
Eyes	2-millimeter prismatic stick-ons, black on chartreuse
Head Color	Black waterproof marker
Glue	CA with accelerant for eyes and head
Cement	Jolly Glaze

2   Flashy Profile Fly (FPF)

Hook	Tandem-rigged Gamakatsu Octopus, #7/0 and 6/0
Thread	Flat white Danville flat waxed nylon
Rigging	140-pound plastic-coated wire, doubled and crimped with #7 sleeves
Body	Best Way Super Hair: white, polar bear, light blue, seafoam green, bright green, dark green, black
Flash	Best Way saltwater pearl mylar; 1/32-inch holographic silver mylar; 1/32-inch holographic gold mylar; pearl Krystal Flash; fluorescent green Krystal Flash; bronze Flashabou
Cheeks	Dark red FisHair
Eyes	10-millimeter prismatic stick-ons
Head Color	Black waterproof marker
Glue	CA with accelerant to set eyes and head
Cement	Jolly Glaze

3   Original ALF

Hook	Eagle Claw 254, #4/0
Thread White	Fluorescent white Danville flat waxed nylon
Body	Best Way Super Hair: white, polar bear, gray, smoke, light blue, lavender, bright green, royal blue, dark blue, black
Flash	Pearl Flashabou; 1/32-inch silver holographic mylar; mixed-color Krystal Flash; bronze Flashabou
Cheeks	Dark red FisHair
Eyes	6-millimeter prismatic stick-ons, black on silver
Head Color	Black waterproof marker
Glue	CA glue to set eyes and head; accelerant to speed up setting time
Cement	Jolly Glaze

4   ALF TOO Silverside

Hook	Eagle Claw 254, #2/0
Thread	Flat white Danville flat waxed nylon
Body	Best Way Super Hair: polar bear, smoke, tan, olive
Flash	Pearl Flashabou; 1/32-inch holographic silver mylar
Cheeks	Dark red FisHair
Eyes	4-millimeter prismatic stick-ons, black on silver
Glue	CA with and accelerant to set eyes and head
Cement	Jolly Glaze

5   Baby Bunker

Hook	Gamakatsu Octopus, #5/0
Thread	Yellow Nymo, size A
Body	Best Way Super Hair: polar bear, smoke, tan, olive, brown, light blue
Flash	Pearl Flashabou; 1/32-inch holographic silver mylar; bronze Flashabou; black Crystal Hair
Cheeks	Dark red FisHair
Eyes	6-millimeter prismatic stick-ons, black on silver
Head Color	Black waterproof marker
Glue	CA with accelerant to set head and eyes
Cement	Jolly Glaze

6   American Eel

Hook	Eagle Claw 254, #4/0
Thread	Flat white Danville flat waxed nylon
Weed Guard	Coffee-colored stainless wire, #6, doubled
Body	Best Way Super Hair: white, yellow, gray, tan, light brown, olive, dark brown, black
Flash	Pearl and bronze Flashabou
Cheeks	Dark red FisHair
Eyes	4.5-millimeter prismatic stick-ons, black on silver
Head Color	Black waterproof marker
Glue	CA with accelerant to set eyes and head
Cement	Jolly Glaze

```
        9
        10
          11
  12    13
  14    16
      15
```

7   Tarpon ALF Blue Back

Hook	Eagle Claw 254, #4/0
Thread	Flat white Danville flat waxed nylon
Weed Guard	Coffee-colored stainless wire, #6, doubled
Body	Best Way Super Hair: polar bear, lavender, light blue, seafoam green, royal blue, black
Flash	Pearl Flashabou; mixed-color Krystal Flash
Cheeks	Dark red FisHair
Eyes	2-millimeter prismatic stick-ons, black on chartreuse
Head Color	Black waterproof marker
Glue	CA with accelerant for eyes and head
Cement	Jolly Glaze

8   ALF TOO Blue Back

Hook	Eagle Claw 254, #2/0
Thread	Flat white Danville flat waxed nylon
Body	Best Way Super Hair: white, olive, light blue, royal blue
Flash	Pearl Flashabou, $1/32$-inch holographic silver mylar; silver or blue Krystal Flash
Cheeks	Dark red FisHair
Eyes	2-millimeter prismatic stick-on, black on chartreuse
Head Color	Bright blue and black waterproof markers
Glue	CA with accelerant to set eyes and head
Cement	Jolly Glaze

9   Attack Mac

Hook	Gamakatsu Octopus, #7/0
Thread	Flat white Danville flat waxed nylon
Body	Best Way Super Hair: white, lavender, bright green, dark green, black
Flash	Best Way saltwater mylar; pearl Flashabou; purple-mix Flashabou; green Fire Fly; black Crystal Hair
Cheeks	Red FisHair
Eyes	7-millimeter prismatic stick-ons, black on silver
Body Color	Black waterproof marker
Head Color	Colored waterproof markers
Glue	CA with accelerant to set eyes and head
Cement	Jolly Glaze

10   ALF Tube Fly

Tube	Rigid plastic, 2.5-millimeter OD tubing, $2^1/2$ inches long
Thread	Flat white Danville flat waxed nylon
Body	Best Way Super Hair: white, light blue, seafoam green, royal blue, bright green
Flash	$1/32$-inch holographic silver mylar; combed silver mylar tubing; Best Way saltwater mylar
Cheeks	Red Super Hair
Eyes	8-millimeter prismatic stick-ons, black on silver
Glue	CA with accelerant to set eyes and head
Cement	Jolly Glaze with holographic powder

11   Boss Squid

Hook	Gamakatsu Octopus, #8/0
Thread	Flat red Danville flat waxed nylon
Body	Best Way Super Hair: purple, polar bear, light brown
Flash	Best Way saltwater mylar; copper Flashabou, $1/32$-inch holographic silver mylar; Tiewell gold/red rainbow
Eye Panel	Witchcraft fly wing
Eyes	10-millimeter prismatic stick-ons, black on silver
Cement	Jolly Glaze with holographic powder

12   Syntheceiver

Hook	Gamakatsu Octopus, #5/0
Thread	Flat white Danville flat waxed nylon
Tail	White Super Hair; pearl Flashabou; Witchcraft fly wing
Body	Silver Japan braid coated with CA glue
Wing	Best Way Super Hair: chartreuse, royal blue
Wing Flash	$1/32$-inch holographic silver mylar; $1/32$-inch holographic blue mylar
Eye Panel	Witchcraft fly wing
Eyes	4.5-millimeter prismatic stick-ons, black on silver
Head Color	Colored waterproof markers
Cement	Jolly Glaze

13   Squid

Hook	Gamakatsu Octopus, #5/0
Thread	Flat white Danville flat waxed nylon
Body	Best Way Super Hair: purple, light brown
Flash	Pearl Flashabou; $1/32$-inch holographic silver mylar; Tiewell gold/red rainbow
Eye Panel	Witchcraft fly wing
Eyes	6-millimeter prismatic stick-ons, black on purple
Cement	Jolly Glaze with holographic powder

14   Seafood

Hook	Eagle Claw 254, #3/0
Thread	Fire orange Danville flat waxed nylon
Claws	Best Way Super Hair: red and orange mixed
Eyes	Plastic bead-chain eyes, black
Body	Super Hair: orange, tan, red
Cement	Jolly Glaze with holographic powder

15   ALF Mini

Hook	Tiemco 9394, #8
Thread	Monocord, #3/0
Body	Best Way Super Hair: polar bear, olive
Flash	$1/32$-inch holographic silver mylar
Eye Panel	Witchcraft fly wing
Eyes	15-millimeter prismatic stick-ons, black on chartreuse, cut to fit wing
Cement	Jolly Glaze with holographic powder

16   Bottom Dweller—Halibut

Hook	Eagle Claw 254, #3/0
Weight	Spirit River brass dumbbell, medium
Body	Best Way Super Hair: dark brown, seafoam green
Flash	Copper and bronze Flashabou
Eyes	2-millimeter prismatic stick-ons, black on chartreuse
Glue	CA with accelerant to set eyes and head
Cement	Jolly Glaze with holographic powder

Joe Howell

Since I first wet a line over forty years ago, I have been fishing the lakes, rivers, and saltwater estuaries of Oregon, primarily on the Umpqua River system. For the past fourteen years I have made my home on the North Umpqua River, where I own and operate the Blue Heron Fly Shop.

Salmon and steelhead migrate from the sea to spawn in the main Umpqua. In the spring there are huge runs of shad, and striped bass in modest numbers, in the estuary and tidal flow of the lower river.

The tide affects the Umpqua for almost sixteen miles upriver. It was here that I fished for striped bass in the mid-1960s and 1970s. There was a large population of stripers then, and very little sportfishing. As the numbers of fish increased, so did the sport- and commercial fishing. Thirty years have passed and there are still stripers, though not as many. There are still enough for the sport fisherman, but we probably will not see large numbers of fish again in the lower Umpqua.

One unforgettable evening in 1964, I was fishing a short distance down from the town of Scottsburg. For a quarter of a mile down to the bend of the river and bank to bank, there were fish showing all over the surface. As far as I could see, stripers were churning and slashing baitfish. Big stripers, twenty to thirty pounds on average, and a few so big they were scary! There were stripers to the left, to the right, and in front of me.

This was to be my introduction to striper fishing! I grabbed a rod and jumped into a little twelve-foot rowboat and, with a few strokes, was out in the middle of the river. As I rowed out I wished I had brought my fly rod, but the spinning rod and plug I'd borrowed would have to do. The tide changed and I drifted downriver casting the plug to the bank. Wham! Fish on! Oh no! Pulled out! Reel, reel, reel, fast! Another cast. Wham! Fish on! Solid hookup! Thirty-five pounds of pure muscle. . . . I thought I was going to lose him when I slipped the net under him. Rod in one hand, net in the other, boat wobbling side to side—man, this was great! As I rowed back upriver in the dark, the striper lay at my feet, a beauty glistening in the light of the moon. What a day!

When my four years in the U.S. Air Force ended I was back, fly rod in hand. Back then the striper flies were pretty simple. Krystal Flash, Flashabou, and all the other shiny trimmings had not yet been invented. Most of the flies I tied were with bucktail or polar bear as long as I could find. The Joe Brooks's Blonde style of flies with long tails and wings was easy to tie, and these were the ones I most often used. Simple color combinations of red and white, black and yellow, green and white, or blue and white all worked. At times all-black or all-yellow caught fish.

The area we fished most was the bay formed by the Umpqua and Smith Rivers. There are large islands and train trestle and highway bridges to fish around, and stripers can usually be found at sloughs at the mouths of Schoefield and Butler Creeks. The areas around and between some of the islands became mud flats at low tide. That's when I've always had my best fishing. Schools of stripers would cruise the drop-offs as the tide ebbed. As the flats lost water, the stripers waited for anything edible diving off the edge of the flats. We looked for structure that might offer baitfish some protection. Trestle pilings, drop-offs, and downed tree snags were good places to fish. The seams around some of the islands as the tide was going out also sometimes produced.

We tied flies on #3/0 to 5/0 saltwater hooks with short shanks and wide gaps. Most of the flies I tied were in the 4- to 5-inch range. I found them to produce better for me than flies of 2 to 3 inches. The bay is a natural rearing area for a variety of baitfish and crustaceans, everything from Dungeness crabs to bullheads, suckers, perch, and squawfish, or chubs, as we locals call them. Young perch of three to five inches and chubs of four to six inches could be found around the pilings of trestles and backwater areas. The small perch were often rainbow colored while the chubs had dark, greenish brown backs with sides tinged silver and yellow. Those two particular baitfish often have some yellowish color to them. As a result, I found myself favoring flies that were yellow or had some yellow in them. It's probably just one of those fisherman's quirks.

In the early 1970s there wasn't a lot of tackle to choose from, at least not tackle that I could afford to buy. A Pflueger 1498 or Martin Model 72 Multiplier reel, and #10 or 11 full-sinking weight-forward lines or shooting tapers were most common. A nine-foot fiberglass Fenwick rod completed my state-of-the-art outfit. I crammed large plastic boxes full of my homemade offerings of hair and feathers. The boxes then, as is true today, contained far more flies than I needed or used, but part of the fun is in tying and trying a new creation.

The Baby Perch fly is one of those passed on to me by a friend, who got it from someone else, who heard about it from who knows whom. I wish I knew! We all had our own color combinations and at one time or another they all worked. The Baby Perch is a bushy, broad-shaped fly that looks more like an old shaving brush. Ocean perch are more flat and oval shaped. Also known as pink-finned ocean perch, they enter the brackish water bays of West Coast rivers in the spring. Upon entering their birthing areas they give birth to several dozen babies averaging 1½ inches. As the perch grow in size throughout the summer, they become another source of food for the stripers before and during their migration to the ocean.

Tying in bucktail layers of different colors, you can achieve a broad, somewhat oval-shaped fly. A well-appointed bushy-tied fly will hold its shape even when wet. Bucktail colors include layers of white, red, yellow, and blue in the tail, and the same sequence in the wing.

A large, painted, yellow-and-black eye completes the fly. I use a waterproof model paint. I feel that the painted eye is just as important to the Baby Perch fly as the bushy, oval shape and should always be included in the pattern.

Another pattern I favor is the River Chub, a simple, bright attractor fly. It is tied with a long yellow tail and matching wing, and a silver or gold body with a bunch of peacock herl over the top. Large cheeks of lemon wood duck complete the fly. If lemon wood-duck feathers are not available, then substitute a dyed mallard. A painted eye of yellow and black is sometimes added to enhance a baitfish look.

The River Smelt is a good all-around searching pattern. It resembles a variety of forage fish present in the estuary at different times of the year. It is tied with a tail of long bucktail, first white, then a little pink over it. The wing is white bucktail under, followed by a thin layer of pink, and topped off with a larger amount of blue bucktail. A large natural pearl mallard feather tied on both sides as a shoulder completes the fly. As in the chub fly, the painted eye is also optional on the smelt pattern.

My friend and fishing partner Roger Paul liked to use large pink-and-white or red-and-white flies. These were usually tied with bucktail and sometimes palmered with several saddle hackles, which made them quite bulky. He was using such a fly early one morning at low tide as we fished directly across from Butler Creek Slough near the remains of an old waterlogged tree. A few limbs, slimy with algae growth, hung over the surface of the water. The remaining structure of the tree disappeared into the murky depths of the river. A perfect striper hangout! We silently edged the boat to within casting distance. I quietly let the anchor out as Roger began to cast. His first cast was right on target, only his fly did not sink! What a bummer! We both chuckled about his floating powder puff of a fly. Not expecting anything to happen, he made a couple of foot-long tugs to try to sink that fly—which still did not sink, but bobbed back to the surface with each strip he made. One more strip and a huge striper broke the water, slashing the fly. This so surprised Roger that he swung his rod a mighty 180 degrees, stumbling backward over the seat and nearly falling out of the opposite side of the boat. I lunged and seized him by his coat sleeve. Then we realized that the striper was no longer there. The fly was still floating!

On another occasion, I had a big striper follow a River Chub fly right to the side of the boat. In the haze of the dawn, the dark shape stared at me as it hung suspended by the boat. I was still staring at its beady little eyes when it sank slowly beneath us. Roger had also seen the giant and in our excitement we estimated it to be forty to fifty pounds.

1

2

3

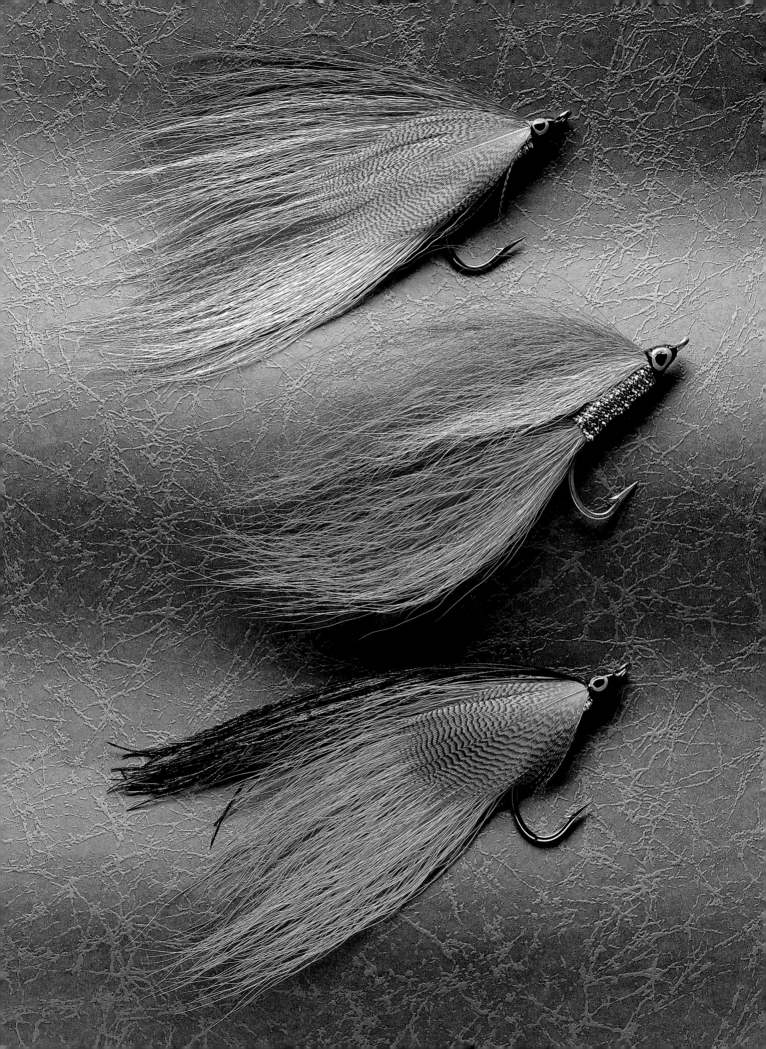

I've often wondered whether, in the dimness of the morning light, we had seen a giant striper . . . or had it been a seal?

Over the years I've fished for salmon and steelhead in Oregon, Washington, Idaho, and British Columbia, and I've made a couple of trips to the Florida Keys to fish for tarpon with Billy Pate. They were all enjoyable times, and I have many stories to tell. I still hope that the striped bass population on the Umpqua will return to what I once knew. The numbers seem to be slowly increasing in recent years. Who knows—maybe there is still a fifty-pound striper out there with my name on it!

3	River Chub Streamer
Hook	Eagle Claw 254N or TMC 800S, #2/0 to 4/0
Thread	Black Danville, #3/0
Tail	Yellow bucktail
Body	Gold Diamond Braid
Wing	Long yellow bucktail topped with several strands of peacock herl
Cheeks	Natural lemon wood-duck flank feathers
Head	Black thread
Eyes	Painted, yellow with black pupils

1. Wind a thread base onto the hook shank to a point above the barb. Coat with head cement.

2. Tie in a thick bunch of dyed-yellow bucktail, fairly long, to form the tail. Depending on the size of the hook, the overall length of the fly should be 3 to 5 inches. Cement.

3. Tie in a 10- to 12-inch piece of Diamond Braid 1/4 inch behind the eye of the hook. Wind to the tail and back again toward the eye. Cement.

4. Tie a long, thick bunch of dyed-yellow bucktail extending at least to the middle of the tail, or slightly longer. Cement.

5. Tie in several strands of peacock herl as a topping over the bucktail. Cement.

6. Select two large natural lemon wood-duck flank feathers. Tie in the whole feathers, one on each side, for the cheeks.

7. Shape and finish the head with thread. Tie off, cement, and let dry.

8. Paint the eyes yellow and let dry. Paint black dots for the pupils.

1	River Smelt
Hook	#3/0
Thread	Black
Tail	White with pink bucktail over
Body	Silver oval tinsel
Wing	Bucktail: white, pink, white, then blue
Cheek	Mallard flank feathers
Head	Black thread
Eyes	Painted, yellow with black pupils

2	Baby Perch
Hook	#2/0
Thread	Black
Tail	One bunch of each of (bottom to top) white, red, yellow, and blue bucktail
Body	Wide silver oval tinsel
Wing	One bunch each of (bottom to top) white, red, yellow, and blue bucktail
Head	Black thread
Eyes	Painted, yellow with black pupils

AUTHOR'S NOTE: Joe's flies were developed at a time when most of the synthetics used today were not around. He used materials that were readily available, durable, and dyed in the colors needed to match the local baitfish. His flies have the look of the old-time classics used for striped bass, right up there with the Gibbs Striper Fly and Joe Brooks's Blondes.

Tom Kintz

Like most kids I grew up with, I was introduced to fishing by my father. I enjoyed fishing in fresh and salt water and had several fishing buddies when I was in grade school in southern California. We spent many hours catching bluegills and crappies in the local ponds, and trout in mountain streams. Most of the monthly Boy Scout outings involved travel to distant fishing locations, and it was during this time that I became interested in fly tying and fly fishing.

I didn't have much money so the idea of catching fish on a homemade lure rather than a store-bought device intrigued me. I discovered fly tying in the outdoor magazines. Using a pathetic vise I had constructed with a clothespin and some rubber bands, I tried to tie my own flies, but without instruction and particularly demonstration, I couldn't assemble anything that I thought worthy of fishing.

About the time I was in the eighth grade, I finally attended fly-tying classes. A fishing buddy's older brother and uncle were members of a fly-fishing club in Orange County. This club sponsored fly-tying classes with some notable fly tiers. My friend's older brother, Jim Steinbergs, was a respected tier and fisherman, and he and his uncle, Jim Molitor, became my mentors. In addition to teaching me to tie flies, they introduced me to saltwater fly fishing, as we pursued the surf perch and corbina off Laguna beaches. Since then, surf fishing has been my favorite kind of fishing—regardless of how many fish I catch.

I went off to college in King's Point, New York, where I learned an entirely different kind of saltwater fly fishing—northeastern inshore fly fishing. I often found striped bass and bluegills near the school's docks, and I fished them in my limited free time. After college, I settled in Connecticut and fished mostly fresh water. I learned important lessons using deer hair poppers for

bass, pickerel, and sunfish, did some surf casting with spinning gear, and longed for the chance to use a fly rod on some of those bass. But the rocky Connecticut shoreline seemed uninviting, and I did not realize the opportunity that was before me the whole time.

I worked along the Connecticut waterfront at General Dynamics—Electric Boat Division in Groton. On my way to and from the submarines, I often caught sight of striped bass feeding on the local staples. During the lunch period, it might be bits of chicken or bread, but normally it was silversides, sand eels, juvenile bunker, or small squid. Although I have avoided creating any bread or chicken flies, observing the natural bait in action helped me develop some productive patterns.

At work and on the beach, I met several fine fly fishers who influenced my tying. Mark Twiss, a fellow employee, is a fine fly tier, fishing buddy, and trusted friend with whom I exchange tying ideas, fishing techniques, and local fishing reports. Jane Timkin is a well-traveled and experienced fly fisher. I enjoy fishing with Jane because she so thoroughly relishes hooking these wonderful fish. Tom Gaudreau, a fellow employee and fly rodder, provides valuable commentary on my flies and reminds me of the shortfalls of being a purist. Steve Burnett, another Electric Boat employee and revered saltwater fly-fishing guide, and I exchange fishing reports and feedback on how my fly patterns perform. Mike Sisco, a talented artist and painter who is well known for his surf casting, is an excellent fly tier and fishing buddy. The camaraderie I find in fishing is one of life's finest experiences.

Moving to Westerly, Rhode Island, was the luckiest stroke of my fishing life. Here there is world-class fishing just minutes away from home. The beaches, surf, and local jetties have become my fishing bailiwick, and I'm in my glory. I had never caught such large fish on a fly rod, and so many! As I began to fish the local waters, I learned that fly fishing is the most effective way to catch these fish, and no longer were the rocky areas off limits.

I discovered the little tuna, or false albacore as it is locally called (sometimes bonito by mistake). I pursued this fish in an effort to catch something that would stretch out my backing line. Arguably the hardest-fighting fish for its size, this fish taught me to make sure my stripping basket is out of the way while I'm on a jetty. While hooked up to a large albie and unable to see where I stepped, I fell on the rocks twice as I ran after the fish, barely keeping the last of my backing on the reel.

I am most impressed by the diversity of baitfish that pass through this area. Growing up on the West Coast, I observed a wide variety of baits there as well. The marine environment is so well stocked with species that it presents quite a challenge to me as a fly tier. The differences among the species fascinate me and I have developed fly patterns to match them. Although I do most of my fishing in New England, I often tie patterns that are intended for Pacific fish as well as those in the Atlantic.

I took up professional tying and for some time supplied the local shops, but as I began writing on the methods I use to tie some of the flies I have developed, demands on my time increased. I've had to reduce my fly manufacturing and concentrate on designing flies and writing. Now I enjoy having my young helpers at the workbench while I tie. It also leaves more time to enjoy fishing from the boat. Yes, surf fishing is my favorite, but boat fishing is more consistently productive and usually gets me larger fish. On the boat my children get closer to the fishing, too, because they're not big enough to wear waders.

The Flies

My fly patterns are usually the result of a recent fishing experience. I normally develop a pattern to appear just as the natural, adding a few design features to enhance the fly's performance. Occasionally, I'll concentrate on a particular feature of a fly. Major Bunker is one example. This pattern's feature is size—beginning with super-long saddle hackles, progressing to a double collar configuration to increase bulk along its length, then finishing with an epoxy head to reduce the thinning effect of streaming in the current.

One aspect that I find particularly frustrating in flies with long materials is their tendency to foul if not tied properly. I build in a few details to reduce this tendency. The double collar technique of tying is very effective in reducing fly tangling. The rear collar keeps the long saddles in place and prevents hook wrapping. This method is used in the Major Bunker, Watch Hill Squid, Natural Squid, Linesider Licorice, and Doll-Eyed Reef Demon.

Another antifouling method is to reduce the length of the material so that it does not extend beyond the hook bend and become fouled in the hook. This method is used on the Anchovy Flies and Little Butterfish. The keep-it-short method is also used in combination with another popular method, called Hi-Ti construction, in the Breachway Minnow. The Hi-Ti method works because the material bunches tied closer to the hook bend impede the motion of the bunches tied progressively forward, reducing the chance that the long fibers will get caught.

Certain materials can help reduce fouling of the fly. Corsair, though it lacks the action of more limber materials, is usually stout enough to prevent the materials from wrapping around the hook. Tying the materials back as close to the top of the hook in the bend as possible reduces fouling by requiring an extreme bend in the materials for them to become caught. This also applies to the Epoxy Bait patterns and Seaside Minnow—the epoxy actually "ties" the materials as far back as the epoxy is applied.

I tie my patterns to fish them. For this reason, I make the flies durable and castable. I also incorporate weight, as necessary, to obtain the desired sink rate and compensate for bulk. For the Reef Demon, for example, I meld a few tying techniques to assemble a fly that sinks fast, is not a burden to cast, is durable, and supports a larger eye than the average Deceiver-style pattern. Since I prefer fishing the flies to tying them, the Reef Demon represents a successful attempt to reduce the number of flies I need to tie by putting more qualities into each one. But as long as bluefish have teeth and rocks have snags, I'll need to tie flies.

The Bait

The coastal baitfish in my local waters are numerous and often predators will feed on a certain type of bait. Sometimes the fish will feed on several baits at the same time. Like all things in nature, the varieties and quantities of baitfish are subject to seasonal changes. For example, striped bass in May and June feed on squid, juvenile sea robins, crabs, silversides, and herring. In July and August the fish eat mostly silversides, sand eels, squid, and herring. With September come large quantities of butterfish and anchovies. These and very small squid are the favorite foods of the false albacore caught off the reefs. Inside, near the beaches and jetties, they devour sand eels and silversides. The eastern bay anchovy is a favorite of the little tuna. Because there are schools of these tiny baitfish for the fish to choose from, a fly fisher faces quite a challenge. Bass and blues target squid, butterfish, and silversides until the end of October, when they'll also feed on large menhaden, finger mullets, herring, and the usual sand eels and silversides. This is the general trend, at least; there are far more baitfish than can be explained here. Keep this in mind when you're preparing patterns for the coming season.

The baitfish found near the beach are different from those a mile offshore. The shallow beach areas are more frequently filled with smaller sand eels and silversides than larger baits. You'll rarely catch sight of a squid while wading in the surf. Though they sometimes come in close, squid prefer deep water. Butterfish are also less common inshore than they are off the reefs, but small herring or menhaden that look similar to the butterfish are often present.

Being prepared and flexible are the keys to success. Matching the hatch can involve creating dozens of patterns, which keeps any fly tier busy. Knowing the general seasonal trends you can tie the appropriate fly patterns ahead of time and have them on hand when the action gets hot. Occasionally, an unexpected bait will appear and you'll have to select the most suitable pattern from your fly box—inspiration for your next visit to the tying bench. Challenge, frustration, and inspiration all contribute to the development of a suitable collection of patterns.

Materials

It's important to know the properties of fly-tying materials you use so you can tie them correctly. The taper in natural materials such as bucktail and saddle hackles makes them particularly useful when assembling a portion of the fly that you don't want to see foul. The gradually increasing limberness from butt to tip in such materials leaves the tips to move freely while main-taining the core shape of the material adjacent to the hook. Synthetic materials, typically strandlike, are normally of uniform diameter throughout their length and bend from wherever they are tied in, unlike tapered strands such as bucktail. Take more care when using synthetic material to ensure that the fly does not tangle. I often use synthetic material to add colorful or flashy trim to the fly, tying it in places where its path to the hook bend is cushioned with natural bucktail.

I stick to a few materials as my tying mood dictates. I have been using more craft fur lately. Simple and effective, a more perfectly matched material for the creation of small bonito flies is hard to find. Corsair is another great material I used with fabulous results during a trip to Martha's Vineyard with Mark and Tom. I found it effective in imitating a number of small baitfish and excellent for fishing at night. It's a stout material and makes a tangle-free fly.

I use natural materials such as bucktail and saddles frequently. I prefer earth tones like cream/white, gray, black, green, and tan and use brighter colors to trim the pattern and provide accents. I also use flashy material such as Krystal Flash and Flashabou for subtle enhancements.

Fishing Techniques

Every location has certain quirks and types of fish, which require special methods to draw a strike. Often, a cast and strip over a known good location is all that is necessary to produce results. This works over reef areas when no surface activity is visible and inshore when you're just fishing the structure. On other occasions, you may need to make modifications. In situations with large numbers of baitfish it is better to cast and swim the fly. Swimming the fly is keeping it among the baitfish, stripping in ever so slowly to keep from snagging the bottom. You can use the current to help. Cast across current, strip in the slack, and twitch the rod tip to give a swimming motion to the fly. As the predators move in to attack, the baitfish dart away, leaving behind only the vulnerable single fly. If you fish atop a jetty, you'll be able to observe. This method requires patience, because the hungry, active game fish and scampering bait may cause you to move the fly away too quickly.

Bluefish can be more finicky than their reputation would indicate. Typically, they prefer a fast action on a fly. The blues seem to enjoy attacking other fish, and do so when they are traveling in large schools. Recently, bluefish numbers have been low, and the smaller schools do not seem to feed so recklessly. These fish can often be taken with a slowly fished fly or one that is placed near a feeding fish. When only smaller numbers of fish are available, placement of the fly becomes more important, and patterns must be

---

2   **Big Reef Squid**

Hook	Tiemco 911S, long shank, #2/0 to 4/0
Thread	Clear monofilament
Tentacles	Six long genetic white saddle hackles
Rear Collar	White bucktail and pearl Flashabou
Underbody	.032-inch lead wire, 8 to 10 wraps
Body	Pearl Bill's Bodi Braid
Head Collar	White bucktail
Topping	Pink, tan, or other color craft hair to evenly cover head collar
Trim	Fine black and/or red permanent marker
Eyes	White doll eyes, 10 or 12 millimeters

1. Place the long-shanked hook in the vise and wrap it with the monofilament thread. Position the thread above the hook barb to tie in the tentacles.

2. Assemble six hackles so that the tips are aligned. Split the group into two and place the curved sides against each other so that the tips of the hackles spread out. Tie the hackles in so that they extend the maximum length. The feather butts should cover three-quarters of the hook shank to act as an underbody. If desired, apply head cement to the thread wrappings.

3. Select a hefty bunch of short, crinkly bucktail hair. The rear collar length should be one-third to one-fourth the length of the saddle hackles. Tie in this bunch with a loose wrap of thread right over the tail wrappings. Tighten the next wrap to let the hair roll around the hook in a controlled fashion, evenly distributed around the hook shank. Finish tying with several tight wraps. Again apply head cement if desired.

4. Wrap the body with 8 to 10 turns of .032 lead wire. This is for density, compensating the fly and allowing it to sink properly in heavy tides. Tie in a length of pearl Bill's Bodi Braid to cover the tail wrappings, rear collar, and lead wire. Wrap the mylar to 3/8-inch behind the hook eye.

5. Select a large bunch of white bucktail. Short, crinkly bucktail is preferred to maintain body density. The hair should reach to the midlength of the rear collar when in place. Tie in the head collar first with a loose wrap and then with successively tighter wraps to distribute the hair evenly around the hook. Repeat this method with a large bunch of tan or pink craft hair.

6. Use a red or black marker to dot the pattern on the body and tentacles. Whip-finish the head and apply head cement. Finish the fly by using Goop to glue the eyes to each side of the rear collar.

---

more representative of the predominant bait than flies that work well in big-school situations. An epoxy silversides, for example, may be more effective than a bright orange popper, but just the opposite is true when the fish are in a large school and are competing for the larger, more tempting helping.

Little tuna and bonito are more selective feeders. They love to eat little squid, silversides, anchovies, sand eels, and butterfish. When you're fishing from a boat, the type and size of your fly make less difference than when you are inshore. That is, until the anchovies come in. Once the large brown clouds of bait appear, the false albacore feed almost exclusively on them. A squid fly that worked the day before will be rejected in favor of an anchovy pattern. Delivering your fly using the swimming method is especially effective, because these fish often attack large schools of bait. One other very important reason to use this method is that this kind of fish moves so fast. These fish can miss and come back in a split second if the fly is kept in the target zone. When pursuing the little tuna, I have excitedly stripped the fly away from the fish only to see the fish return and maraud the spot. If you're fishing from shore, you'll get too few opportunities for these fish, and a miss can be frustrating.

Striped bass can be particularly fussy about the way the fly is delivered. The striper is perceptive and often a certain retrieve will suit its fancy. Typically, I start with the cast-and-strip method, then proceed to the swimming method should it be necessary. Sometimes, the bass do not like the pulsation of the fly when it is stripped in. Situations like this call for a steady retrieve, accomplished by placing the fly rod beneath one arm and stripping smoothly, one hand after another. There are so many variations to the delivery based on the actions of the fish, bait, and fly being used that experimentation has to be ongoing. Certain tips will help you determine the preferred method of retrieve. For instance, when fishing at night, a swimming retrieve or slow stripping action is more effective than a fast retrieve. Not only does this keep the fly in the zone longer, but it also enables the fish to see it better. Increasing the speed of retrieve also means more casting, which can result in more in-flight fly fouling during the course of the night. A fouled fly rarely gets taken and is hard to correct in the darkness. When conditions require searching for

fish that are not showing, a cast-and-strip method is effective for covering more water.

Remember, saltwater fish are typically migratory and constantly on the move. When casting to open water, the best delivery is one that covers water and puts the fly where the fish will find it. It's a statistical game and you'll improve the odds if you keep the fly in the target zone as long as possible.

1   Major Bunker

Hook	Tiemco 811S, #4/0
Tail	Long cream saddle hackles
Rear Collar	Gray bucktail trimmed with pearl Flashabou and topped with brown Streamer Hair (Icelandic wool)
Underbody	.032-inch lead wire
Body	Wrapped pearl braided mylar
Front Collar	Gray bucktail trimmed with pearl Flashabou and topped with brown Streamer Hair (Icelandic wool)
Final Topping	Black Streamer Hair
Head	Five-minute epoxy; darken the top with a black pen
Eyes	White doll eyes

3   Natural Squid

Hook	Mustad 34011, #3/0
Tail	Light cree saddle hackles
Rear Collar	Tan elk hair or bucktail
Body	Wrapped pearl braided mylar
Front Collar	Tan elk hair or bucktail
Eyes	Yellow solid plastic

4   Squid-O-Fur

Hook	Mustad 34011, #3/0
Tail	White or gray saddle hackle
Underbody	.032-inch lead wire
Body	Acrylic fur
Eyes	Clear solid plastic
Trim	Dot the body and tail with a fine black permanent marking pen and red markers

5   Squid Flash

Hook	Tiemco 811S, #2/0
Tail	White saddle hackle
Rear Collar	White calf or bucktail
Body	Pearl Estaz
Eyes	Solid plastic

6   Anchovy Fly—Type 3

Hook	Tiemco 811S, #6
Tail	Pearl Krystal Flash
Body	Wrapped pearl braided mylar
Underwing	Tan craft fur
Topping	Brown craft fur
Head	Five-minute epoxy
Eyes	Adhesive mylar

7   Anchovy Fly—Type 2

Hook	Daiichi 2456, #4
Tail	None
Body	Wrapped pearl braided mylar
Underwing	Pearl Krystal Flash
Collar	White craft fur
Topping	Layered pink and brown craft fur
Head	Five-minute epoxy
Eyes	Adhesive mylar

8   Seaside Minnow

Hook	Mustad 34011, #2
Underbody	Wrapped pearl braided mylar
Body/Tail	Layered polar bear and chartreuse nylon fiber, topped with olive Krystal Flash and covered with five-minute epoxy
Gills	Red Krystal Flash
Eyes	Adhesive mylar

9   Seaside Minnow—Pacific Anchovy

Hook	Mustad 34011, #2
Underbody	Wrapped pearl braided mylar
Body/Tail	Layered nylon fiber: polar bear, light blue, dark blue; top with black Krystal Flash. Trim the underside with pearl Flashabou, covered with five-minute epoxy
Gills	Red Krystal Flash
Eyes	Adhesive mylar

10   Epoxy Bait—Bay Anchovy

Hook	Tiemco 811S, #6
Tail	Pearl Flashabou; pink and brown nylon fiber
Body	Pearl Flashabou covered with five-minute epoxy; color the top brown with a marker
Gills	Red Krystal Flash
Eyes	Adhesive mylar

```
 6
8    7
     9
10   11
12   13
14   15
```

11   Epoxy Bait—Silversides

Hook	Daiichi 2456, #4
Tail	Narrow white saddle hackles and epoxied-down wing
Body	Pearl Flashabou and wing covered with five-minute epoxy
Wing	Pearl Krystal Flash; olive nylon fiber
Eyes	Adhesive mylar

12   Hot Shrimp

Hook	Mustad 34011, #4
Eyes	Melted nylon darkened with pen
Underbody	Wrapped pearl braided mylar
Ribbing	Palmered white saddle hackle, clipped to appear as legs beneath
Wing/ Antennae	Gray craft fur
Body	Hot glue

13   Little Mullet

Hook	Daiichi 2456, #2
Tail	None
Body	Wrapped pearl braided mylar
Underwing	Pearl Krystal Flash
Collar	White craft fur
Topping	Olive craft fur
Head	Five-minute epoxy
Eyes	Adhesive mylar

14   Anchovy Fly—Type 1

Hook	Daiichi 2456, #4
Tail	None
Body	Wrapped pearl braided mylar
Collar	White craft fur
Topping	Cinnamon craft fur
Head	Five-minute epoxy
Eyes	Adhesive mylar

15   Little Butterfish

Hook	Tiemco 800S, #1/0
Tail	None
Body	Wrapped pearl braided mylar
Collar	White craft fur
Topping	Gray craft fur
Head	Five-minute epoxy
Eyes	Adhesive mylar

Bob Lemay

I came to South Florida to attend school in 1971. I had no idea what saltwater fishing was all about. My early years on the water had been on the TVA lakes of Alabama, fishing for panfish and bass. Imagine my first saltwater session. I found myself on a pier in the middle of a charge of jack crevalle with everyone hooked up at the same time. That day I caught my first jack, about ten pounds of pure muscle and determination, and after the excitement died down I noticed that my light spinning reel wasn't working properly. The repairman said that the shaft was bent and my expensive German reel just wouldn't hold up to this kind of fish. Clearly I had a lot to learn and lost no time in that new classroom.

I was lucky enough in those days to be able to spend forty hours a week on the water, although occasionally college would interfere. Almost immediately I fell in with a rowdy crowd that fished day and night off the old South Beach pier. Those guys fished mackerel in the morning, bonito and jacks in the afternoon, sharks or snappers or snook at night. I swear some of them lived on that pier!

A look at the local form of shark fishing might give you an idea of their determination. Each afternoon just before dark they'd take turns setting out the baits. This consisted of paddling several five- to ten-pound chunks of bonito or other bloody fish out on a surfboard one or two hundred yards in front of the pier. The baits would be dropped off and the lucky angler would return to the pier to rejoin his friends. Since sharks ten feet long were common, I never wanted to be the one on the surfboard.

One of the fellows on the pier, although only about seventeen years old, was an accomplished rod builder. Ronnie Lee Armstrong would go on to become a professional fisherman and one of the best mates on boats that sailed out of Miami. I was lucky enough to learn rod building and tackle repair from him. Fly fishing was still a few years away for me. Our world in those days was light and ultralight spin and plug casting, and I still have one or two of the rods that we built. Because we couldn't buy what we needed ready made, each one was designed to a specific purpose. South Florida is where many advances in sportfishing were taken and are being made. As a fishing junkie the next step was natural: That first winter I got a job at a local tackle shop and began learning the business side of fishing while also learning to repair reels, rig baits, clean bait tanks, and continue my education. Reef Tackle on Seventy-Ninth Street is still a local landmark and a good place to learn.

After a year or so there I took the next step and got a job on one of the charter boats out of Haulover docks; I eventually wound up working on boats sailing out of the Castaways docks. The lessons I learned there were important to me years later when I began tying flies for tackle shops and guides. Captain Gary Hall on the charter boat *Rave* was the best teacher. His lessons were simple: The first was that each fish encountered might be the only one you'd see that day, and the second was that each bait or lure had to work perfectly for that one chance. With this kind of attitude we were hard to beat, even with beginning anglers.

Several years after I left charter boats, I ran into one of the guys I had worked with in Islamorada. Captain Bouncer Smith by the mid-1970s was on his way to becoming one of the area's best guides and charter boat captains. He noticed that I didn't have any fly rods and encouraged me to try it. Within a year I was learning to fish all over again.

By then I had joined the Tropical Anglers Club, based in South Miami. One of the oldest competitive clubs in the area, it claimed more than a few world-famous anglers as members, former members, or those just passing through on their way to exotic destinations. For a fellow just learning how to handle a fly rod in salt water it was heaven!

My first fish on a fly was taken off Smith Shoal Light, about eighteen miles from Key West. In those days the fish there were so hungry that the only way to keep your fly from being chewed to pieces was to keep it in the boat.

The great thing about the club was that it contained anglers of all skill levels, from beginner to master, and most of the members would help a novice as long as secret spots were not disclosed. Because the club always had competitions going, you were encouraged to catch a variety of fish on every kind of tackle. As a result I began trying for every species possible.

Along with learning how to use the fly rod, I began to tie my own flies. Ronnie Armstrong had taught me to make my own lures and tie my own jigs years before, so I had a good start. My next great teacher was Bob White. The founder of the club years before, he was also the premier lure maker in all of South Florida and the club's fly tier. Bob was a retired schoolteacher who spent many hours each week in his shop making lures and jigs, tying flies, and taking time to answer the many questions that beginners like myself were asking. He taught me about the various kinds of materials and where to obtain them. In those days hardly any shops carried fly-tying materials and, if they did, the variety was limited. When I left the club in the early 1980s, I had already begun to tie for one or two shops. I had also begun to teach fly tying at a local junior college.

When I think of those who influenced my tying, several masters come to mind. Harry Friedman, a contemporary of Joe Brooks, helped me tie my first bonefish fly. Bob Kay furthered my education when I began tying for shops where he was working. Each new order presented a challenge of some kind or other.

I've always enjoyed tying for guides and anglers who have very specific needs. Each new pattern provides the seeds for additional ideas, and with guides you hear very quickly what works and what doesn't. As I began to reach out and work for shops in other areas of Florida, one thing became clear. Each area has its own preference for patterns. The real criterion should

---

6	Summer Blues
Hook	Long shanked, #1
Thread	White
Throat	Pink Krystal Flash
Wing	White bucktail; pearl Krystal Flash; blue FisHair
Eyes	Painted, yellow with black pupils, epoxied

1. With white mono thread, tie in a bunch of pink Krystal Flash for the throat.

2. Tie in a bunch of white bucktail for the wing. On top tie in pearl Krystal Flash. Tie in a bunch of blue FisHair for the top of the wing.

3. Paint on the eye: a black pupil on a yellow background. Epoxy the head.

This pattern was designed for mackerel and bluefish that are hitting on the surface or close by. It is tied with 4-pound mono and intended to be used without a wire leader. I try not to let the fish get a good look at it—I strip it a few times, then pick it up. After it disappears a few times the fish are ready to blast it when it comes into view.

---

be "Does it work?" with every other consideration secondary. The best-looking fly is useless if the fish refuse it or it fouls on every cast. A fly must also be durable and have a hook that is suitable for its intended target. In the backcountry the same fly may work for a three-pound fish and one that weighs thirty. When tying for specific purposes you have to consider fly-rod size and tippet strength. Consider how a carpenter matches the size of his or her hammer to the size of the nail. After drawing a strike from a target fish, you still have to hammer that hook home.

Tying for salt water is quite different from tying for fresh water. Most of the anglers and tiers I know came from quite different traditions than trout anglers did. While many freshwater anglers started with and prefer fly tackle, the saltwater types come to fly fishing after fishing with other types of gear. They are far more likely to regard the fly rod as one of a variety of tools. I know more than a few who reach for the long rod only when fishing is hot; they use other means to locate fish.

Some of the most successful patterns have been influenced by what has been successful with other types of tackle. If a gold spoon really works for redfish on the

1
2
3
4
5

flats, you want to design a fly of the same size with heavy amounts of gold flash and a similar action. More than a few of my own patterns have been so inspired.

One difference between tying for salt water and for fresh is the materials needed to tie the larger patterns. Most hackles are bred these days for freshwater use. They are narrow, clean, and quite useless for tying tarpon flies. The feathers that I look for are wide, webby, and usually come from a cape or saddle that anyone tying a dry fly would reject without a second glance. Recently a few breeders have begun to raise birds just for the saltwater market. These are capons and do provide some really nice neck hackles that are just right for tailing tarpon flies.

The only other alternative is to look through grade-3 necks for the ones that are suitable. When I'm looking for neck hackles in solid colors, I generally go to inexpensive strung neck hackles in as large a size as I can find. With the great variety of synthetics available these days, it's no wonder that some of the most innovative new patterns are for the salt. With no need to match the hatch except when tying crab patterns, results are the only measure of success.

For my own patterns I've developed a few elements that add to a fly's performance and appearance. Because I started as a rod builder (and still build everything from fly rods to big-game rods), I usually use Flex Coat as the finish for my larger patterns. Although the flies must rotate in a fixture for two hours after the finish is applied, the results are well worth it. I also use quite a bit of Crazy Glue at critical points in my work.

For painted eyes I use an alkyd enamel for its gloss and color. The stuff is labeled quick drying, which means twenty-four hours per coat unless I take a shortcut. I usually use a mobile solar oven (my car) to accelerate the process. On a good sunny day the first coat will dry in about four hours, as will the second.

I use lead eyes in many of my patterns. Using the same enamel, I've developed a method for baking large numbers at one time. Each coat takes thirty minutes in the oven at 225 degrees; the windows need to be open for ventilation. This, of course, is not done while anyone else is home.

Weed guards are essential for any backcountry pattern. Mine are made from #5 coffee-colored stainless leader wire. A wire weed guard provides greater durability and a slight keel effect. One guide reported that an angler caught thirteen fish one morning on one of my flies. Each time the wire was bent back into position and ready for use. Of course, tying with a piece of wire sticking out is like handling a porcupine. You'll probably need a few Band-Aids before you get the hang of it.

Almost all of my bonefish and permit patterns have weed guards. These are made of mono and are my own design. Tied in properly, they should all pass the lawn test—tying the fly to a leader and dragging it slowly across a patch of grass without hanging it up.

Here's one last item that has greatly improved my tying over the years. Each time I complete an order for a new pattern, either mine or someone else's, I save a sample. Then each time I prepare to tie one fly or one hundred of the same pattern, I've got a standard to work from. These masters are carefully saved and listed for each customer. If I find a way to improve a pattern I replace the master with the improved fly. Gradually my flies have improved, because I have kept a standard to work from. Now if I only had more time to use them! I do wish to have enough time and opportunity to pass along some of the things I've been lucky enough to learn. I've been helped along the way by so many real craftsmen that I can never repay what I owe.

6
7   8
9
11   10
12   13

1	Glass Slipper
Hook	Tiemco 800S, #2/0
Thread	White
Tail	White FisHair; pearl Krystal Flash
Wing	Grizzly neck hackles
Collar	Orange marabou; grizzly hackle fluff (from the base—soft)
Eyes	Painted, yellow with black pupils, epoxied

This new pattern is a dramatic departure from the other twenty-five patterns that I tie. Unlike the others the tail is tied flat and the whole fly is tied with 4-pound mono. If you look closely you'll find crimped nylon, Krystal Flash, Lite Brite, and marabou, along with the usual saddle and neck hackles. The pattern was designed for spooky fish in clear, shallow water. Only a few guides have samples to date, and it hasn't seen a season's use yet. I have high hopes for it.

2	Blue Sunrise
Hook	Tiemco 800S, #3/0
Thread	Blue
Tail	Blue calf tail; pearl Krystal Flash
Wing	Yellow neck hackles
Collar	Orange hackle fluff
Eyes	Painted, white with black pupils, epoxied

This bright pattern was developed for a top angler who wanted a fly different from any other-colored fly the fish were likely to see; it's used on those days when fish refuse all the usual offerings. It also comes in a pink form.

3	Orange & Grizzly
Hook	Tiemco 800S, #2/0
Thread	Fluorescent orange single-strand flat floss
Tail	Burnt orange calf tail; pearl Krystal Flash
Wing	Orange grizzly neck hackles
Collar	Orange grizzly hackle fluff (from the base—soft)
Eyes	Painted, yellow with black pupils, epoxied

This is another basic pattern that will take fish almost everywhere.

4	Blue Claw
Hook	Tiemco 800S, #3/0
Thread	Green
Tail	Blue calf tail; pearl Krystal Flash
Wing	Blue grizzly neck hackles
Collar	Green grizzly hackle fluff
Eyes	Painted, yellow with black pupils, epoxied

Crabs are a large part of a tarpon's diet. This pattern was designed for migrating fish off the upper Keys in the spring.

5	Furnace & Squirrel
Hook	Tiemco 800S, #2/0
Thread	Fluorescent orange single-strand flat floss
Tail	Furnace neck hackles; fox squirrel tail; pearl Krystal Flash
Wing	Furnace neck hackles
Collar	Well-marked fox squirrel
Eyes	Painted, yellow with black pupils, epoxied

This Cockroach-style pattern has taken fish everywhere. Many anglers use almost nothing else, only changing the size of the fly or the color. It was designed, like most of my tarpon flies, to be snelled, and should not foul when cast.

7	Uptown Crab
Hook	Mustad 3407, #6
Thread	Brown
Claws	Grizzly hackle tips
Body	Grizzly hackle fluff; apply Flex Coat on its bottom
Legs	Brown rubber bands
Eyes	Lead dumbbells

I also tie this one on #4 hooks for bones, and a larger version on #2 to 1/0 hooks for permit. This has some of the characteristics of the Glider—its design causes it to dive for the bottom and land upright like a real crab. Its ingredients include four hackles, 30-pound mono for the ribs, Flex Coat, silicone, and 15- to 20-pound mono for the weed guards. I don't think this one will ever be produced in great quantities.

8	Silhouette
Hook	Tiemco 800S, #1/0
Thread	Red
Tail	White saddle hackles; pearl Krystal Flash
Body	White hackle fluff, with palmered red hackle in front
Eyes	Lead dumbbells, white with black pupils

This fly is a universal pattern and, like the Deceiver, is as much a method of tying as a specific recipe. I tie it in every size from #2 to 5/0. The idea is to match the shape of the bait that is available. In fluorescent green it has taken record-size redfish in the Indian River. I use it in white at night around the bridges. In a bright blue version one angler off Jupiter, Florida, has had strikes by large black-tipped sharks. Tied in bright yellow it is a very effective searching pattern in Florida Bay and the backcountry. One guide uses a large black Silhouette on a #4/0 Tiemco hook for big tarpon with great success each year.

9	R.U.B. Fly
Hook	Mustad 3407, #6
Thread	Gray
Antennae	Pearl Krystal Flash; short grizzly hackles
Body	Grizzly hackle fluff, then grizzly hackle
Eyes	Lead dumbbells tied at the hook point, yellow with black pupils, epoxied

This was developed for one of the best guides in Islamorada, Florida. Its full name is the Randy's Ugly Bug.

10	Redfish Rabbit
Hook	Mustad 3407, #2
Thread	Red
Body	Pearl ice chenille
Wing	Pearl Krystal Flash; a white rabbit fur strip
Collar	Red grizzly hackle fluff
Eyes	Lead dumbbells, yellow with black pupils

Another pattern for sight fishing, this one is a variation of Steve Bailey's Bonefish Bunny. With an outrigger weed guard it is very effective in the heavy grass of Florida Bay.

11	Sand Bear
Hook	Mustad 3407, #6
Thread	Tan
Body	Fluorescent orange chenille, then tan chenille
Wing	Tan bear hair; cree neck hackles
Eyes	Painted, white with black pupils, epoxied

This pattern uses bear hair and cree neck hackles. The weed guard is unique and makes it completely weedless. This outrigger weed guard must be spread at a 45-degree angle and also inclined forward at a 45-degree angle to be effective. This angler who holds five out of six world records for bonefish on a fly has been using it with great success. Chico Fernandez's Snapping Shrimp was the inspiration for this pattern.

12	Glider
Hook	Mustad 3407, #6
Thread	Tan
Tail/Body	A cree neck hackle tied on the bottom; apply Flex Coat on its bottom
Wing	White calf tail; orange marabou; pearl Krystal Flash; tan marabou
Eyes	Bead-chain eyes

The first time you cast an epoxy fly at a tailing fish (and it runs in terror for deep water), you'll find that it is just a bit noisy upon landing. This pattern is not. It is also not epoxy; it uses Flex Coat and, when wet, sinks just like its name implies. I have caught many good fish with it in the area of Key Biscayne, where nine-pound fish are average. Color variations are brown and pink, and brown and tan, all over a grizzly feather instead of a cree.

13	Marabou Special
Hook	Tiemco 811S, #4
Thread	Chartreuse
Tail	White marabou; pearl Krystal Flash
Collar	Chartreuse marabou
Eyes	Lead dumbbells, yellow with black pupils

I use this pattern in the winter on the inside where the water is almost totally fresh. Most of the forage for snook, tarpon, reds, and so on is quite small this time of year and the water is very clear. The fly is tied in white or yellow with different colors of hackle, including grizzly. Many days, this is the pattern I use for tarpon to thirty pounds, snook to ten pounds, and more. One bonus is that it can be easily cast with a light rod.

Ted Lewis

It was 5 A.M. and the fog was thick, a dark, cloudy, miserable day, just the way I like it. As I climbed through a maze of rocks and small cliffs covered with barnacles, I couldn't stop thinking about the striper that had straightened my hook the day before. As I reached my destination, a cormorant flew up from the water right where I fish. Everything seemed right. I watched the wave action for a while, making sure it was safe to approach the edge.

The fly I chose was a large pollack pattern designed in a Catherwood style. I rigged this one up with a wire tippet. I had heard that bluefish were being caught in this area and was hoping that a large blue might take my offering. I like to fish near cliffs and rocky places where the water drops off to thirty and forty feet.

I use a fast-sinking lead-core shooting taper attached to a hundred feet of 30-pound braided mono. This is attached to 250 or 300 yards of 30-pound backing.

A good habit to get into before you start fishing is to pull thirty to forty feet of line off your reel, stretch it, and let it drop by your feet. Now while holding the rod under your arm, transfer the line into a stripping basket, starting with the line closest to the reel. This will make your first cast a lot easier.

I had been casting for about an hour, and couldn't understand why I hadn't caught any fish. I could see my fly drifting with the tide. As the wave came in I stripped in line, and when it turned to go out I let the fly drift around. All of a sudden, out of the dark green depths, came a huge striper.

I want to tell you, my imagination went wild. I could have sworn that fish was at least six feet long. I could see the huge head and mouth open to take the fly not more than ten feet in front of me. As I set the hook, the fish turned and took off. As the line flew out of the stripping basket, I thought, Please don't tangle on me

now! Within seconds the fish was out to the backing and the reel was screaming.

I remembered how the day before I had horsed that big one and ended up with a straightened hook. This time I applied side pressure and let the fish run, palming the reel. I kept the rod low and the pressure on until the fish started turning and coming back in my direction. I pumped the fish in and reeled like crazy.

When you're cliff fishing, before you start casting, it's important to find a spot where it's possible to land a fish. With waves breaking against the steep rock formations, you'll need all the help you can get.

As the big striper approached the rocky coastline where I stood, I had to keep it out of the barnacle-covered rocks where it might break me off. You can't just lift a big fish out of the water—for sure the line will break! The best way to land a fish in this situation is to ride it in on a wave over the rocks. Just like surfing.

But the wave action this morning was not all that great. The waves were too small and it took at least six tries. Each receding wave would carry the fish back out, and I would have to line it up again for the next one. Finally a large swell came in and, as I lifted the fish, the wave carried it up to a flat section of rock. When the wave went out, the large striper was left lying there. What a fish! It turned out to be forty-two inches long, and weighed about twenty-eight pounds. What a way to start the day.

You might want to buy some special equipment for this kind of fishing. You don't want to go rock hopping without something substantial on your feet. I wear rubbers with aluminum cleats over sneakers. They're available from Orvis or L. L. Bean. I put them on when I reach the slippery areas and take them off for climbing. I also wear inflatable suspenders. If you ever fall in the water, they could save your life. You'll need a rod with some backbone; I find that 9- and 10-weights work well. A reel with a good drag system is important. Also, if you intend to land stripers in this kind of cover, you should use a heavy leader. I use a 30-pound Maxima for a butt section; three to five feet will do. I've had big fish drag the line across the rocks and never even nick this line. Finally, I attach a 16- or 20-pound tippet, about a foot long. Change the tippet if you feel any nicks and expect to change it often.

This is exciting fishing, not for the faint of heart. Be very careful, watch the waves, and when you least expect it a forty-pound striper may come calling.

---

2   Hair-Head Deceiver—Herring

Hook	Tiemco 800S, #3/0 to 4/0
Thread	White monocord, #3/0
Body	Long saddles: white or gray
Topping	Peacock herl
Collar	Marabou; deer body hair
Gills	Pink craft fur
Head	Natural deer body hair
Eyes	1/4- to 1/2-inch EM eyes

1. Wind white monocord to just above the barb; this will be your tie-in spot. Tie in a piece of white bucktail off the end of the hook. Tie in three or four long saddle hackles (white and gray) on each side of bucktail. Add silver flash on each side.

2. Keeping the same tie-in spot, add twelve to fifteen strands of peacock herl for the topping. Add silver-gray marabou for collar. For the gills, add pink craft fur on each side of tie-in spot; a little of this goes a long way.

3. Now comes the hair head. Take a bunch of natural deer body hair about an inch in diameter. Clean all the fuzz from base of hair with pet brush. Next, while surrounding the hook, push the hair up the hook shank until it pushes back on the marabou and hackle. Wrap thread around hair once, lightly. On the second wrap pull down on thread; hair will flare. Pull the hair back with your other hand, work the thread through the hair, and make a couple of wraps. Spin the hair to the eye of the hook, packing it as you go. Form this head into a fishlike shape; secure the eyes with Goop.

---

1   Pollack

Hook	Tiemco 800S, #4/0
Thread	Monocord, #3/0
Collar	Marabou: olive, brown, off white
Wing	Olive schlappen; gold Krystal Flash
Throat	Red saddle fibers
Head	Green and white deer hair
Eyes	9-millimeter EM eyes

---

3   Tinker Mackerel

Hook	Tiemco 800S, #4/0
Thread	Monocord, #3/0
Wing	Green and blue saddles or schlappen; grizzly hackles down the side
Body	Marabou: white, silver-blue, pink, green, blue
Collar	Blue deer hair
Throat	Red saddle hackle fibers
Head	Blue and white deer hair
Eyes	9-millimeter EM eyes

---

4   Sar-Mul-Mac

Dan Blanton

Hook	Tiemco 800S, #4/0
Thread	Monocord, #3/0
Tail	White bucktail; silver Flashabou
Wing	White saddle or schlappen
Sides	Grizzly hackles
Wing Topping	Gray and pink bucktail
Collar	White bucktail
Throat	Red chenille or saddle fibers
Head	White chenille
Eyes	9-millimeter EM eyes

1
  2
3
  4

Glen Mikkleson

I began fishing with my father when I was five or six. He was an avid surf caster who ran the south shore beaches of Long Island in his green Willy's Jeep, a popular beach buggy at the time. He was quite successful. There were a lot of bass around in the early 1960s and his key to success was keeping in touch with the surf. There is no substitute for time spent on the beach.

Later we began freshwater fishing for trout and bass and made the evolution from bait to lures to flies. I was introduced to fly tying by a neighbor, Harold Johnson, when I was thirteen. We were intrigued with deer hair and because he had a whole hide to share, most of my early flies were of spun deer hair. We used the book *Fly Tying* by William Bayard Sturgis.

I kept tying and fishing through high school and sold flies to a local tackle shop for a while. I took a fly-tying course from Woly Wolyniec, who had a marvelous gift for teaching and getting people involved. He later helped me get a job at Fireside Angler, the only local source for fly-tying materials. Primarily a mail-order business founded by Eric Leiser, Fireside had been bought out by Hank Nellen. As manager there for six years, I learned a great deal, and I owe thanks to John Goodleaf, Gus Nevros, Bob Sater, and Arch Walker, along with Hank and the many knowledgeable customers.

One of the greatest influences on my fly tying was Dave Whitlock. I had read his articles and I embraced his theory that nearly anything a fish eats can be imitated and fished on a fly rod. All his flies had that distinctive Whitlock look. Strong silhouette, beautifully blended colors, and excellent fishing performance all combining to make a Whitlock pattern a durable fly that the average tier could learn to tie and catch fish with. Looking at a lot of new patterns today makes me believe Whitlock has been the most influential innovator in the last twenty-five years. Dave also happens to be a heck of a nice guy who is always there to share and teach others in his humble, low-key style. Thanks, Dave.

I started saltwater fly fishing in the mid-1970s because there were a lot of opportunities to do so around Long Island, and I began to meet a few people who were involved in the sport. I knew Walter Kurpiel as a customer at Fireside and was aware that he fly-fished the salt. When I would run into him at the beach, he would quietly call me aside and point out something or show me a good fly. It seemed that he was willing to help if you were willing to put in the time and effort to learn. His modest attitude and soft-spoken manner shrouded his immense talents from those who didn't know him well, and that's the way he liked it. When I fish today, I realize most of my technique and tactics I learned from Walter all those years ago.

I've learned a lot from many people through the years, and I've also enjoyed passing what I know along to others. And that's the way it should be for us to get the most enjoyment from our sport. The outdoor experiences and the people we befriend make our sport so much more than just catching fish.

Long Island

I fish mostly the eastern half of Long Island. A look at a map will reveal that this area contains hundreds of miles of coastline. There are so many types of fly-fishing water that you need a variety of tactics and tackle setups to experience them all. For the shorebound angler, Long Island is an ideal place to fly-fish because there is always a beach in the lee within a half hour's drive.

The north shore offers the most opportunities for fly rodding. It is usually calmer than the south shore, because it doesn't get the ocean swells directly from the Atlantic, and generally easier to wade. There are boulder-strewn beaches as well as those with pure sand or gravel or combinations of all three. Mussel beds, rocky points, offshore bars, coves, and creek and harbor mouths all provide structure to hold bait and predators alike. Beyond your backcast might be a tall, eroding sand bluff, or a tidal marsh, or a line of houses, bungalows to mansions. Prevailing summer southwest winds usually make the Long Island Sound waters calm. Sometimes they're like a mirror. A nor'easter can turn things ugly but often productive, pushing bait and game fish right onto the beach.

The south shore of Long Island is mostly pure sand barrier beaches pounded by the Atlantic surf. A north wind can lay the surf down and fly fishing can be quite easy, but the south shore can demand more of the fly angler in skills and perseverance. There are also a number of good-size inlets that are excellent places to fly-rod. The bays behind the barrier beaches have many flats and deep channels to explore all summer long.

Between the forks is generally calm water of varying depths. Some locations have tremendous tidal currents. Fly-fishing these rips from a boat requires specialized tactics but can be productive for a number of species. Small harbors and salt ponds dot the shoreline here and all can provide good action, especially in the early season before waters warm to summer highs and brown tides tend to slow things down.

Montauk, the east end of the south fork, has been a mecca to anglers for many years. The reason is simple—Montauk has it all: pounding surf, sheltered bays, boulder reefs, points, long straight sandy beaches, deep water and shallow flats, tons of bait and all the game fish. There are many skilled captains to take you inshore or offshore. And almost all of this fishing can be done with a fly rod. An angler could spend the whole season fishing east of East Hampton and probably have more success than by traveling all around the Northeast.

The Fish

Most of the time fly rodders are targeting the striped bass. Populations have been high in recent years and they can be found almost anywhere there is salt water at one time or another through the season. Most caught will be schoolies in the fourteen- to twenty-eight-inch range; the spring run, however, can have fish to around the forty-inch mark and groups of even larger fish are encountered every fall. The best times are June through mid-July and mid-September through November.

Bluefish, although declining in numbers in recent years, still provide fly rodders with lots of thrills. In the spring we get a lot of fish in the three- to seven-pound range. Surface flies and slashing blues provide a less serious type of fishing but are always lots of fun for both the novice and expert. These same small blues can frustrate even the experts when they gorge themselves on dense schools of $1^1/2$-inch-long sand eels. Both large and small blues can be caught in the fall. The large ones are usually chasing the larger baitfish such as bunker, herring, and tinker mackerel as they make their migration southward.

Weakfish have begun to make a comeback in Long Island waters in the last three years. The south shore bays and Peconic Bay between the forks have had good runs of weaks. Some areas have fish in the two- to five-pound range, and others have fish in the eight-pound range. As time goes on, if the fish continue to flourish, the sizes will probably go higher. At the end of the last weakfish population cycle in 1985, I had caught some that were well over twelve pounds. Most daytime weakfishing is done in deeper water, but they do feed in the shallows after dark.

Perhaps the most challenging of the inshore saltwater species in our area are the small tuna: bonito, false albacore, and Spanish mackerel. It seems that there are more and more of these speedsters visiting our waters each season. Their feeding habits coupled with excellent eyesight make them all very difficult to fool. Their power and speed help them win their share of the battles. The unpredictable frenzies will keep you on your toes and you'll use your finest casting skills. The south shore inlets, the Montauk area, and the whole north shore are the most likely places to encounter these fish.

Spanish mackerel can be found here from mid-July till mid- to late September. Of the three, the macks seem to have the lightest runs and can be the hardest to find on any consistent basis. They can also be the hardest to hook and land with flies, because they slash through baitfish pods with lightning speed and their teeth rival those of the bluefish and barracuda. It is quite a sight to see their bright silver-and-blue bodies, studded with metallic yellow spots, reflect the sunlight as they clear the water while feeding. Sometimes they'll come out straight up, like a missile launched from a submerged submarine! They usually run two to six pounds, but specimens on either side of this range can be caught. Unfortunately for them, they happen to be my favorite fish to take home for dinner.

Bonito also arrive in Long Island Sound around the middle of July and stay the latest, sometimes into November. They might be found by themselves or in mixed schools of Spanish macks, bluefish, or false albacore. They can be very fussy at times, requiring the angler to match the bait more closely or go down in tippet size to get strikes. Their pointy, conical teeth will not slice your leader but can nick it enough to break, so extended battles are not recommended. Some schools early in the season might contain smaller fish—say, from three to six pounds—but at the end some hefty ones up to ten or eleven pounds are not uncommon. Bonito are also a good eating fish.

False albacore are my favorite species of the three. They tend to be larger, usually in the eight- to twelve-pound range, and can peel off a hundred yards of line in the first run in a matter of seconds! In my area they seem to be the most consistent in their habits and therefore more predictable. You might find that they relish nasty weather and really seem to go nuts when the waves are high and the wind is blowing a gale in your face. I use a canoe a lot when conditions permit, because they sometimes will feed all day long just out of range of beach fishermen. Most fly fishers have their best luck using small baitfish imitations, but sometimes the fish will prefer a very bright attractor fly when they are blitzing heavily. Large streamers, poppers, and even small crustacean patterns have been known to work at times, so it pays to be observant of the food they're feeding on and experiment. The best time for the false albacore, or little tunny, is September and October. Some years they are around for the whole eight weeks, but most often it is a shorter run of three to four weeks. Millions of tiny bay anchovies are usually what bring them into our inshore waters, and the cooling water temperatures of autumn are what drives them away. They are less leader-shy than others and their teeth, which are very small and embedded in the gums, pose little problem for your tippets. I usually recommend a stout 10- or 11-weight fly rod, so you can fight these fish hard and get them in without a prolonged fight. It's better for releasing them and you can get back to the action faster. Albies make a poor meal, even for a dog I'm told, so try your best to release them with enough energy to survive.

Bluewater fly fishing can be done in the waters south of Long Island, and there are plenty of knowledgeable charter captains willing to take you out. You can set your sights on yellowfin and bluefin tuna if you own the proper tackle. Some years there are a lot of white marlin in the area, as well as blue and mako sharks. During the last few seasons, a few fly rodders scored well on dolphinfish, because there were many coming in fairly close. The offshore boats will also encounter Spanish mackerel, bonito, and false albacore, as well as skipjack tuna, as side action to the larger predators. The offshore season is generally mid-June through September but can vary because of water temperature—the most important variable in this type of fishing.

The Flies

I've heard it said that saltwater flies are much easier to tie than freshwater flies. I think more depends on the particular pattern and its intricacies than on which water type or fish it is intended for. The larger size alone might cause them to be easier. After concentrating on saltwater flies for the last fifteen years, I'm sure I'd find myself clumsy at #22 ants, although at one time I could turn out these tiny terrestrials in less than two minutes each. There are different problems facing the saltwater tier.

The question of durability is one. A saltwater fly has a harder life than its freshwater counterpart. It has to withstand more rugged use. Bulkier materials have to be attached to the hook in a stronger fashion than do tiny wisps of hackle and fur. Saltwater casts are also longer and more powerful than those for fresh water. A poorly tied fly can flutter apart as it makes that sudden high-speed U-turn. Saltwater fish are generally larger and rougher on the fly, too, and the saltwater environment can be more demanding. Sand, boulders, heavy currents, and the corrosive salt water itself put more demands on the tier to produce a durable product.

Castability is a very important consideration for the saltwater tier. Excess weight, extreme bulkiness, and wind-resistant materials can make some patterns unfishable except in the most ideal of circumstances. Almost any large fly can be tossed thirty to forty feet from the stern of a boat or tip of a jetty on a calm day. But that same fly might be impossible to use from the shore with a high beach or boulders in your backcast. Forget it if you have to reach seventy feet beyond a set of breaking waves. Even a mild breeze from the wrong angle will render that mammoth fly useless. Sometimes small flies are made more difficult to cast if you use materials that add unnecessary weight and bulk. Glass eyes, large lead eyes, thick coats of silicone, wide stiff mylar strips, rabbit fur strips, and large doses of marabou are all very popular in saltwater flies. I tend to avoid them because of the weight and bulk they contribute. True, they are used and catch fish, but I've never seen them outfish flies of a more castable design. The arrangement of the materials on the hook contributes to or detracts from a fly's castability. Flies designed with most of the material flowing back from the eye will tend to wrap around the hook bend while being cast. Naturally, this fouling can be frustrating. Shorter-shanked hooks may help. Applying silicone or another flexible adhesive to the wing to stiffen it can also aid in eliminating some fouling. A better fly design is to have the bulk of the material streaming back from the rear of the hook shank. The time-honored Lefty's Deceiver is a popular example of this design. Even these flies may foul on occasion, so the flexible glue at the base of the tail is a good idea.

Most saltwater flies attempt to simulate fish foods swimming in the water. Your flies must swim also. A baitfish imitation tied with a dark back and white belly should be balanced so it will travel through the water that way. The center of gravity, which is usually the hook bend or a weighted shank, has to be lower than the bulk of the more buoyant materials. This center of gravity will act much like the heavy keel of a sailboat in keeping the fly upright as it's retrieved. Additionally, when the point of leader attachment (hook eye) is above the center of gravity, the fly is more assured of riding correctly when fished. (Look at a simple bucktail jig.) Inverted-hook fly designs such as a Clouser Minnow or various bonefish flies are better tied on downturned-eye hooks. These put the line of pull above the center of gravity, even on sparse patterns whose wing will supply little buoyancy. On other flies such as shrimp—whose bulk may damage hackle legs on the bottom and whose hook bend is thus intended to ride down—an upturned eye will help keep its back on top. The crab fly presents special problems for the fly tier. Its flat disklike shape needs a weight as ballast so the fly will settle to the bottom or swim with its back on top. The line of pull should be in line with this weight so the crab can be retrieved swimming sideways in its flat position without inverting or spinning like a propeller in the currents. Large bunker and herring patterns, with as much bulk tied under the shank as on top, may tend to lie flat in the water. At times these may be just the ticket for catching fish, but if your intention is to have the fly swim upright, you may have to weight it somewhere for ballast, or bend the eye upward, or both. Similarly, foam poppers and deer hair slab-sided types cannot be made too tall or they may also float on their sides.

We labor over our flies to make them closely imitate the bait. Sometimes this exactness might be what brings success, but most often close is good enough. Matching the size, color, and silhouette of a bait can all be important to varying degrees under different conditions. I've experienced times when none of these details meant a thing. How the fly was manipulated through the water was the secret. Other times fishing through an exact location was the only reason for success. Constantly changing conditions dictate that the reasons for success will always change. What works today might or might not work tomorrow. Thus the mystery and also the fun. When fly fishing you're forced to use your head. When it is the fly that makes the difference, the art of exact imitation comes into its own. Observation of the bait and its size, colors, and particular shape are translated into feathers, hair, and tinsel by the astute fly tier. It adds a special thrill when such a creation proves to catch when others fail.

Flies that fall into the attractor category can sometimes be quite effective. Bright unnatural colors tied in combinations that in no way resemble the natural forage can catch fish after fish, while the closer imitations get strikes less fre-

	1	
2		3
	4	

quently. When this happens it's hard to explain why with any certainty, but we all form theories. Perhaps fish strike not only out of hunger but also out of rage or curiosity or playfulness. A fish might use its mouth the way we use our hands. I have had great success night fishing for fussy stripers by using flies predominantly red in color. The fly doesn't really resemble an average baitfish, so maybe this is because the fly stands out from the naturals, or the color gets them mad. Fluorescent yellow has also been a good color. Perhaps what we see out of the water is a lot different from what a fish sees in the water. The clarity of the water and the light conditions are always changing, as are the depth and bottom coloration. What we think is outlandish and gaudy might look good in the depths. Or maybe gaudy is just what fish want that day. It pays to experiment.

Another quality that's important to me is how the angler likes the fly. I'm in the business of selling flies, so they have to look good enough to buy. They have to catch the anglers. Many flies are sold on recommendation, while others look good enough to sell themselves. A fly that looks good gives the angler confidence before he or she uses it. And a confident angler is often a successful one.

1, 2, 3, 4 Acrylic Deer Hair Crab

Hook	Mustad 34007, #4 to 2/0. Bend the front one-quarter of the shank down 20 degrees so that in the finished fly the hook will ride up
Thread	White, size A
Body	Cover the shank with thread, then spin natural deer hair along its whole length. Trim to shape, leaving the bottom flat and the top plane at about 30 degrees to the bottom instead of parallel. Study the crabs you wish to imitate, because they all have different shapes and colors. After you have trimmed, soak the deer hair body with thinned acrylic glue and let it set up for a little while
Claws	Webby hackle of the appropriate color trimmed to shape and coated with acrylic glue to hold its shape. These are then glued to the fly's underside
Legs	Neck hackles, left natural for movement, also glued in underneath
Eyes	Heavy monofilament melted at the ends and glued into the hair at the front
Antennae	Two pieces of 10-pound monofilament glued in the hair between the eyes
Ballast Weight	Lead tape cut to shape and epoxied to the flat bottom
Size Variations	Very small for a floater, larger for a swimming crab, and larger still for one to be fished on the bottom
Color	Paint with nail polish to suit the species. Speckling can be added with fine-tipped permanent markers

---

10 Lavender Sand Eel

Hook	Mustad 34007, #1/0 to 8
Thread	White, size A
Tail	Sparse white bucktail
Tail Flash	Mixed silver and light purple (#12) Krystal Flash
Body	Silver mylar braided yarn, over which is wrapped four strands of pearl-dyed lavender (#6968) Flashabou
Wing	Lavender bucktail under olive dun bucktail
Wing Rib	Pearl-dyed lavender Flashabou
Head	Painted with pearl, lavender, and olive dun nail polish
Eyes	Witchcraft stick-ons, silver mylar with black pupils, #2
Gills	Tiny bits of red (#6911) Flashabou
Coating	Three coats of two-ton epoxy. The eyes and gills are set into the second coat when it tacks up

1. With white thread, tie in a tail of sparse white bucktail.

2. For the tail flash, tie in mixed silver and purple Krystal Flash.

3. Wrap the body with silver mylar braided yarn.

4. For the wing, tie in lavender bucktail to the desired length; on top tie in olive dun bucktail of the same length.

5. For the wing rib, wrap on pearl-dyed lavender Flashabou.

6. Paint the head with pearl, lavender, and olive dun nail polish. Give the fly one coat of two-ton epoxy.

7. Place the stick-on eyes and bits of red Flashabou for gill slits.

8. Give the fly two more coats of two-ton epoxy. Take special care to epoxy the body past the end of the hook bend; this will keep the wing from tail wrapping.

5
6
7
8
9
10

5	Acrylic Spearing
Hook	Mustad 34007, #1/0 to 3/0
Thread	White, size A
Tail	Pale dun bucktail
Tail Flash	Krystal Flash: silver, black, olive, pearl
Body	Silver mylar braided yarn covered with pearl Flashabou
Wing	Pale olive bucktail
Wing Rib	Wing lashed to the body with one strand of pearl Flashabou
Head	Pale olive and pearl nail polish
Body Coat	Thin coat of *clear* acrylic caulking. Let cure for twenty-four to forty-eight hours
Eyes	Witchcraft stick-ons, silver mylar with black pupils, #2½
Gills	Small bits of red Flashabou on the underside of the head
Lateral Line	One strip of Saltwater Flashabou, over which is one strand of black Krystal Flash
Final Coat	Light coat of two-ton epoxy over the body after the caulking has cured

6, 7	Acrylic Squid
Hook	Mustad 34011, #1/0 to 5/0
Thread	White, size A
Tail	Two long saddle hackles around which are eight short saddle hackles tied as a skirt
Tail Flash	A mixture of Krystal Flash
Body	Tapered poly yarn, colored with markers or nail polish, then covered with a thick coat of *clear* acrylic caulking and shaped with your fingers. Allow this to cure for twenty-four to forty-eight hours
Eyes	Witchcraft stick-ons, silver mylar with black pupils, #4½. Set the eyes into the caulking at the rear of the body
Fins	Sections of webby saddle or neck hackles trimmed to shape and glued to the sides
Coating	A light coat of two-ton epoxy over the cured caulking
Speckling	Fine-tipped permanent marker on the body, fins, and tails. Use black and other colors to match the Squid
Color Variations	Red, gray, white, orange, and pink

8	Acrylic Tinker Mackerel
Hook	Mustad 34007, #1/0 to 5/0
Thread	White, size A
Tail	White bucktail; pearl and silver Flashabou
Body	Silver mylar braided yarn wrapped to the middle of the shank
Middle Wing	White and fluorescent green bucktail; silver, fluorescent green, electric blue, and kelly green Flashabou
Body	Continue silver mylar braid up to the head area
Front Wing	Navy blue bucktail
Belly	White bucktail tied sparsely and shorter than the wings under the head gills; a small bunch of red Flashabou
Undercoat	Tie off the head and coat the body area with *clear* acrylic caulking. Work well into the hair to form a nice taper, not too fat
Top Wing	Dyed grizzly neck or saddle hackles, dark blue-green over fluorescent green. Tie in at the head and glue along the body, caulking with thinned caulking cement. Let the caulking cure for twenty-four to forty-eight hours
Head	Pearl, fluorescent green, dark blue-green, and black nail polish
Eyes	Witchcraft stick-ons, silver mylar with black pupils, #3 or 3½
Final Coat	Light coat of two-ton epoxy over the body after the caulking has cured

9	Red/Black Epoxy Baitfish
Hook	Mustad 34007, #1/0 to 8
Thread	Red, size A
Tail	Red bucktail
Tail Flash	Mixed red and black Krystal Flash
Body	Red mylar braided yarn
Wing	Black under red bucktail
Wing Rib	One strand of red Flashabou
Head	Red nail polish
Eyes	Witchcraft stick-ons, silver mylar with black pupils, #2
Coating	Three coats of clear two-ton epoxy
Color Variations	White, for a spearing; lavender or blue, for a sand eel; fluorescent yellow and white; fluorescent green and white; fluorescent green and yellow; black; olive and white; light olive and pearl; red and black; pink and white; blue and white;, brown and white; blue and green

I began working with clear acrylic caulking made by Red Devil paints a few years ago and have been pleased with the results. For large flies, a thick coat can be laid down over an underbody to give a translucent bulk without the weight of clear epoxy. Acrylic can be worked and shaped much like silicones (a little Fotoflo on your fingers helps) but is much more transparent, as the name suggests. It sets up semirigid—somewhere between epoxy and silicone. I also make a flexible glue for many applications by thinning it with a high-strength lacquer thinner. I still have the first fly I made with this material. It caught a forty-inch bass in the surf three Novembers ago and is now stuck on my bulletin board.

This fly has become a workhorse type of pattern for me; it has rivaled the Deceiver, which is still my favorite type of saltwater fly, for the number of bass caught in a season. It is really an updated version of the old Blonde series. Modern mylar tinsels and eyes, the wing lashed to the body for a slimmer profile, and three coats of two-ton epoxy are all that separate this fly from those that Joe Brooks developed back in the 1950s and used with great success on many species worldwide. The Blondes caught plenty of fish for me, too, so making a few improvements with modern materials was a natural step. I tie this fly in about fifteen different color schemes and vary the profile somewhat to simulate the naturals. So here's an old fly with a new lease on life.

Brian O'Keefe

I was born and grew up in the Seattle area. My first fishing took place in local waters, where I fished for perch, crappies, and bass. I used to bring some of the bass I caught during my lunch hour to the Bellevue High School home ec class.

During my teens I spent summers in Montana with my dry-fly-purist, Orvis-cane-rod-wielding, silk-line, Mucilin-stained grandfather, who lived in Missoula.

At the age of nineteen I headed for New Zealand, where I stayed for eleven months and walked a thousand miles from the Bay of the Islands on North Island to Stewart Island, south of South Island. During my travels I lived on trout, berries, and oatmeal.

I left New Zealand for Australia where I spent five months working and, when I got tired of that, wandered up to Kashmir, India, and became the first ski instructor in the Himalayan ski resort of Gulmarg, Kashmir.

When I returned to the states, I attended college in Corvallis and Bend, Oregon.

I spent six great winters as a ski bum/ski patrol at Mount Hood and Mount Bachelor in Oregon and Sun Valley, Idaho. During the summers I guided trout and steelhead trips on the Deschutes, North Umpqua, and Klamath Rivers. I also spent some time guiding around Iliamna and King Salmon, Alaska.

I started a fly-tackle rep company when I was thirty and, for the last twelve years, have represented Umpqua, Buck's Bags, Orvis, Simms, Lamson, Patagonia, Barbour, and many others. At present I am the northwest and Alaska rep for Scott Rods and Scientific Anglers.

While on my travels I've had many opportunities to take photos of what I have seen. *Field & Stream, Fly Fisherman, Flyfishing, Fly Rod & Reel, Trout, Fly Fishing in Salt Waters, Gray's Sporting Journal,* and *Outside* have published my work.

I have done catalogs and ads for Patagonia, Orvis, Umpqua, Simms, Kaufmanns's, Hunter's, and Westbank Anglers, to name a few, and dozens of posters, postcards, and travel brochures.

As a fisherman I have traveled and fished in Alaska (300 days), Belize (150 days), New Zealand (180 days), the Bahamas (150 days), and made numerous visits to fish Costa Rica, Christmas Island, the British Virgin Islands, Baja, the Yucatán, Venezuela, Bonaire, Tonga, Canada, Florida, Montana, and Idaho. I have lived in Washington and Oregon all my life.

I've combined my fishing travels and my background in photography and fishing tackle into a high-tech, fast-paced, four-projector, dissolve-slide program that equals *fun.*

I don't consider myself much of a fly tier. I know what works, where, when, and why. My flies are rough stuff that I can't buy in the area I live. I like small, sparse Charlie-style flies for Christmas Island. For big Bahamas bones that cruise the lumpy, soft, half-grass/half-marl bottoms, the home of the double-digit bones, I have done better with large flies tied with long tails and eyes at the back, done up in tan, light brown, and ginger colors. For sand flats in the Bahamas, Belize, and Venezuela, I fish standard stuff: Gotchas, Charlie variations, Clousers, Puffs, Horrors, and some of the new patterns by Tim Borski.

The three flies here have accounted for many big bonefish and also work on my favorite fish—a tailing mutton snapper. They have also caught permit in the Yucatán and Belize.

The reason I don't put a high priority on my own fly tying is that I really like using other people's creations. In a way it's like going fishing with them.

---

3   **Bonefish Bugger**

Hook	Mustad 34007, #6
Tail	Tan marabou flanked by tan grizzly hackles, splayed
Eyes	Bead-chain eyes tied on top of the shank, just below the hook point
Body	Tan fur

1. With tan thread, tie in the silver bead-chain eyes just above the hook barb.

2. Tie in a small tuft of tan marabou.

3. At the same spot, tie in two tan-dyed grizzly hackles, splayed.

4. For the body, dub the thread with tan fur and wrap the entire body with this dubbing.

5. Tie off the head and cement.

---

1   **Bonefish Cruiser**

Hook	#6
Tail	Two strands of tan Krystal Flash; tan craft fur; grizzly hackles, tied and splayed
Eyes	Bead-chain eyes
Body	Tan thread
Wing	Orange Krystal Flash and tan marabou

---

2   **Bonefish Turd**

Hook	#8
Tail	Pearlescent Krystal Flash; tan fur with green bars
Body	Pink dubbing
Eyes	Brass with yellow eyes and black pupils
Wing	Tan marabou
Head	Tan thread

1

2

3

Gail
Pucciarelli

I started tying flies about four years ago only because as an artist I thought flies were an art form in themselves. I bought a beginner's tying book and began tying as many flies as free time allowed, using patterns in books and samples for reference. When I started showing my flies to others (including some great tiers), I was encouraged, but they all told me, "you've got to fish your flies, see them wet." Well, I thought I'll throw them in the tub. I'd never fished and had no intention to. The thought of fishing back then brought to mind images of worms and beerbellies. I had no clue. Finally, after a lot of persuasion from other tiers (one of whom promised me fishing would not be as painful as a trip to the dentist) and from my obsessed fisherman, Scott, I decided to try it.

It was the fall of 1994. I remember spending a lot of time undoing wind knots and tangles, and freeing flies from trees. And not catching fish. This went on for a couple of weeks, but I'm patient so I kept at it. One morning started out pretty typically. I lost half my flies when I dropped my fly box upside down in the river, and I slipped off a moss-covered rock and went for a swim. My left side was soaked from my waders on up, but I kept fishing. It was soon dusk and I remember sitting on a rock, trying to tie a blood knot with cold, numb fingers, thinking, What am I doing here, I could be home warm and dry, I'm never going to catch a fish. I finished that blood knot (an accomplishment in itself back then) and got back in the river. It was dark, so I figured I'd just take a couple of casts. Well, maybe the fish felt bad for me that night, I don't know, but that's when it finally happened: *my first fish*. Actually my first three fish, three in a row, a brookie and two land-locked salmon. I'll never forget how it felt, catching those first fish. If you had been on the river that night, you would have heard my screams of delight. I some-

times still have those days when nothing goes quite right, but not as often. And to the women out there who are considering taking up this sport, do it! I regret not doing it sooner.

That winter I started tying commercially. I tied both fresh- and saltwater flies for a few shops. The orders for saltwater flies really picked up as spring neared. When the stripers arrived in Maine, I had my first experience fishing the salt and was immediately hooked. I love the ocean, and we moved up here from Massachusetts to be on the coast. That first time out I got eight fish in a half hour—not because I'm a great fisherman, but those hungry little stripers will eat anything when they first get here. I was encouraged. When the season kicks in, I'm so busy tying it doesn't allow me a lot of time to fish. I'm often racing against the clock to finish an order in time to catch a tide, usually late night. Being in Kennebunk is an advantage. I can drive ten minutes and be at one of several great spots, catch the tide, and fish productively for a couple of hours without giving up too much tying time. I did all my fishing from shore last year and though I had a few nights when I caught forty to fifty fish in a short time, the largest one was only twenty-eight inches. I'm hoping to catch-and-release a keeper this year.

Toward the end of that summer I started working at Eldredge Bros. Fly Shop. It has been a good experience. I've learned a lot more about gear and fishing, met some great people, and heard a lot of fish stories. I've also learned how to build rods and just completed my first.

About the time I started working at Eldredge's, I came up with my mackerel fly. It is another version of the Bunker, Grocery, or even an overgrown Deceiver. I spent a lot of time working with dyes on grizzly and bucktail and tied a couple of dozen before I was satisfied. I gave out samples to people to try, and have had

5	Gail's Sand Eel
Hook	Mustad 34007, #1/0
Thread	Black
Body	Silver tinsel
Wing	White bucktail; pearl Fire Fly, olive bucktail; peacock herl
Throat	White bucktail and a small tuft of red marabou
Eyes	Black on yellow

1. With black thread, tie in the silver tinsel and wrap the entire body.

2. With the thread just behind the hook eye, tie in a wing of white bucktail to the desired length. On top, tie in pearl Fire Fly. Then tie in a top wing of olive bucktail. Over this tie in three or four strands of peacock herl.

3. For the throat, tie in white bucktail three-quarters of the length of the wing and a small tuft of red marabou.

4. Paint on the eyes.

5. Epoxy the head.

some good feedback. One friend who fishes from a boat caught eight fish over thirty inches in one afternoon. Scott caught one just under keeper size, and I had two large fish follow the fly but retreat when they saw me. Even though I developed the fly toward the end of the season, it has done well at the shop and has continued to do well through the winter. Trout Unlimited has asked me to demonstrate tying it at one of its meetings.

There are times when stripers will hit almost anything and others times nothing at all. The most important features of a fly, I think, are shape, size or silhouette, and the retrieve used. Overall color is probably next. I like eyes on my flies. It is true that an eye gives a fish a focal point, so an eye gives me an advantage. I like to try to keep the eye close to the point of the hook. I usually use a red throat on my saltwater flies. Although I use some synthetics, I prefer natural materials because I've had better luck with them. Smaller amounts of flash seem to make a fly look more realistic in the water. When it comes to color, a lot depends on where you fish. Chartreuse was a great color last season in Maine, but olive and white were more productive on Cape Cod. Two flies I have not yet fished but plan to test this year are the Grocery, tied with turkey marabou, and the Hair Head Baitfish, with spun deer hair. The others here are my favorites and my most productive. I do enjoy tying something new that works well.

Though most of the commercial tying I do is for the salt, I like the variety of tying. I tie and frame large streamer flies and donate them to Trout Unlimited and the American Museum of Fly Fishing in Manchester, Vermont. I also do some classes and, when I can, try to squeeze in some artwork.

The future of the striper is somewhat of an unknown. I have talked with people who fished them in the 1960s and 1970s who say populations aren't close to what they used to be, although the fish have started to come back. Let's hope commercial fisheries don't change this. And, please, catch and release.

I have met so many wonderful people, too many to name, great tiers and those involved in this sport who have influenced and encouraged me along the way. Thanks to all of you, and a special thanks and love to my parents for their patience and understanding (they rarely see me during the season), and to Scott; without his love for the sport I might have never fished or tied a fly.

1	Gail's Hair Head Baitfish
Hook	Mustad 34007, #1 to 1/0
Thread	Chartreuse
Tail	White bucktail; twenty white ostrich plumes; pearl Fire Fly; two chartreuse hackles, flanked by two olive gray hackles
Body/Head	Clipped deer hair: white on the bottom, chartreuse and olive on top
Eyes	Painted, black on yellow

2	Grocery Fly
Hook	Mustad 34007, #5/0
Thread	Chartreuse
Tail	Yellow bucktail, then two white saddle hackles
Wing	Two yellow turkey marabou feathers; yellow bucktail; pearl Fire Fly; olive bucktail; peacock herl
Throat	White bucktail and a small tuft of red marabou
Eyes	Painted black on yellow

3	**Gail's Tinker Mackerel**
Hook	Mustad 34007, #5/0
Thread	White
Tail	White bucktail; two white saddle hackles; two aqua green saddle hackles
Wing	Aqua green bucktail with black bars; tinsel flash; peacock herl
Sides	Short purple bucktail
Throat	Pearl Fire Fly; white bucktail; a short tuft of red marabou
Eyes	Painted, black on yellow

4	**Gail's Slider**
Hook	Mustad 34007, #5/0
Thread	Black
Tail	White bucktail; pearl Fire Fly, two white hackles; four dyed-green grizzly hackles
Body/Head	On the bottom, clipped white deer hair; on top, clipped green deer hair
Eyes	Painted, black on yellow

1	
2	
3	
4	
5	

Carl Richards

I grew up in Columbus, Ohio, during the 1940s and 1950s; there was little trout fishing around, but some fairly good smallmouth bass fishing. A lady in the neighborhood took me fishing on the Scioto River when I was five years old and I caught a fifteen-inch smallmouth on a minnow and a cane pole. After that I was hooked.

When I was a youngster I read *Just Fishing* by Ray Bergman. He talked a lot about fly fishing and it sounded like a lot more fun than bait fishing, so I began hanging around Hall's Hardware, which was the equivalent of today's fly shop. I would listen to the local experts and learned much more from them than I could on my own. Along with the hammers and nails, Hall's sold fly-tying material, and I bought some every week. The store's owner, Harold Hessler, was the best fly fisherman and fly tier in the state and one day he said, "Hey kid, how would you like to tie some flies for the store? I'll give you a dollar a dozen." That sounded pretty good to me so he asked me to tie a dozen McGinty wet flies, which I delivered the following week. I'm sure he threw away the first eight dozen but after a while the flies must have been good enough, because I saw them in the case. I tied flies for Harold for the next eighteen years.

I graduated from Ohio State University in 1958 with a degree in dental surgery. The main reason I became a dentist was so I could be my own boss and live where I wanted. I promptly left Ohio and moved to Michigan, where the trout fishing was better. I lived then and now in the city of Rockford, fifteen minutes from the Rogue River, thirty minutes from the Muskegon, and two hours from the Au Sable. I fish a lot.

Several years after moving to Michigan, I met Doug Swisher and we became fishing companions. We were having trouble getting fish to take our flies on certain hatches, especially #24 blue-winged olives. We decided to study the hatches in a scientific way to see if we could develop some new patterns that would be more successful than the standard. This study resulted in the publication of *Selective Trout,* followed by *Fly Fishing Strategy, Stone Flies,* and *Emergers.*

We became interested in saltwater fly fishing in 1970 when we began fishing with Captain Bob Marven in Key West. About fifteen years ago Doug decided to spend his summers in Montana and winters in Florida. We began fishing the Ten Thousand Islands near Naples. At that time there were many richly colored saltwater patterns that did not seen to resemble anything the fish were eating. We had no reason to pick one over another, other than whim. I decided to study the prey forms that the various saltwater game fish eat, much as we studied the trout's diet before writing *Selective Trout.* This study resulted in the publication of *Prey* and *Backcountry Fly Fishing.* I found that certain saltwater game fish prefer certain prey. This is usually because that particular prey is the most numerous in the area, often in swarming numbers.

One good example is the rock mantis shrimp on Turneffe Reef in Belize. I walked the reef one day at low tide trying to capture whatever was there. Mantis shrimp were everywhere. I returned home and designed a pattern to imitate this shrimp that does not look like a shrimp or swim like a shrimp; it looks a lot like a preying mantis. I made another trip to Turneffe Reef the following year with a group of friends. The new Mantis Shrimp pattern outfished everything else ten to one. Toward the end of the trip we were running out of the flies and had to cut our other flies apart for materials to make more Mantis Shrimp. The bonefish on the inside of this reef have always been thought picky and spooky, but I believe these fish were difficult because the anglers were spooking them with unnatural flies.

11	Spanish Sardine

Hook	Mustad AC 34068, #3/0 to 6/0
Thread	Dynacord and transparent Coats & Clark, #3/0
Rear Wing	Polar bear Fish Fuzz
Body	Hollow, pearlescent Everglow tubing
Front	
Underwing	Polar bear Fish Fuzz, over which is white silk brick
Overwing	Polar bear Fish Fuzz; under ivory glow-in-the-dark Flashabou; under green Fish Fuzz; under gold Flashabou
Side	Two strands of pearlescent Krystal Flash
Gills	One strand of red glow-in-the-dark Flashabou
Eyes	Large press-on eyes
Cement	Five-minute epoxy and Crazy Glue
Weight	Lead wire (optional). This is sometimes used on the New England coast when fishing for stripers or blues

1. Tie in a batch of polar bear Fish Fuzz at the bend of the hook so it slopes slightly down from the horizontal. This is to help create the deep belly.

2. Tie in a cylinder of Everglow tubing at the bend and wrap to the head.

3. Tie in a thin batch of Fish Fuzz under the hook at the eye so it extends back to the bend.

4. Tie in a bunch of silk brick on each side of the Fish Fuzz under the hook. This procedure completes the deep belly, which is opaque, glistening white.

5. Tie in a batch of polar bear Fish Fuzz on top of the hook at the eye to extend back to the end of the hair that was tied in at the bend of the hook.

6. Switch the thread to the transparent Coats & Clark and tie in five strands of pearl Flashabou (this glows green in the dark).

7. Tie in a small batch of green Fish Fuzz over the Flashabou.

8. Tie in a smaller batch of gold Fish Fuzz over the green.

9. Tie in two strands of pearlescent Krystal Flash on each side of the body at the midline to extend the entire length of the body.

10. Tie in one short strand of red glow-in-the-dark Flashabou on each side of the body in the gill position.

11. Tie off the head and cement with five-minute epoxy.

12. Paint two paste-on eyes with a thin layer of yellow acrylic paint and draw a black line around the outside of each eye.

13. Place the eyes on the top of the head.

14. Paint five-minute epoxy on the eyes and head, being careful to use only enough to keep the eyes firmly cemented. As I am tying the pattern, I cement each step with Crazy Glue for durability. If you paint Crazy Glue on the head or eyes, you must wait a day before you place the epoxy, because the two compounds will react with each other and become too gummy.

I believe a good pattern should resemble, as closely as possible, the most numerous prey form in the area, because that is usually what the fish are feeding on. The fly should be constructed of materials that allow for as much movement in the water as possible, and be designed to swim like the natural it is imitating.

Other than fresh water, I fish in Florida, the Bahamas, Belize, and Ascención Bay in Mexico for tarpon, snook, redfish, bonefish, and permit. Recently in Belize, fishing out of the Golden Bonefish Club, I scored a Grand Slam—tarpon, bonefish, and permit all in one day. What was unusual about this slam was all the fish were caught on the same fly, my Spanish Sardine pattern, which closely imitates a common and widespread baitfish. Lots of anglers get Grand Slams, but I have never heard of getting one on the same fly.

I sold my practice in 1991 and now practice dentistry just three days a week. This gives me more time to study, research, and write about saltwater prey forms and freshwater aquatic insects. I want all you trout fishermen who are becoming interested in saltwater fishing to know that as much as I love the salt, trout are still my first love. I am presently writing a book on caddisflies.

For you who are serious about saltwater fly fishing and are interested in acquiring a flats skiff, I would like to leave you with the first commandment of the CSW (Competent Southern Waterpersons). We advise that in saltwater areas you should fish where birds are, because that's where the baitfish are, so that's where the game fish are. In shallow water, however, this can be fairly hard on the hull of your flats skiff. When you are thus running two miles out in the Gulf of Mexico and see a flock of birds in the water, you may think they are swimming. At low tide they are probably walking. The commandment: Don't Drive Your Boat Where You See Birds Walking!

1	Goby

Hook	Mustad 34007, #6
Thread	Brown
Tail	Latex
Body	Brown pheasant body hackles
Wing	Sparse Krystal Flash and brown pheasant body hackles
Throat	White craft fur
Overwing	Brown craft fur
Eyes	Gold stick-ons

2   Green Crab

Hook	Mustad AC 34068, #2/0 to 8
Thread	White monocord, #3/0
Legs, Belly, and Claws	Liquid latex
Carapace	Olive fly yarn
Eyes	Burned monofilament

3   Common Blue Crab

Hook	Mustad AC 34068, #2/0 to 8
Thread	White monocord, #3/0
Legs, Belly, and Claws	Liquid latex
Carapace	Sand-colored egg fly yarn
Eyes	Burned monofilament

4   Mud Crab

Hook	Mustad AC 34068, #2/0 to 8
Thread	White monocord, #3/0
Legs, Belly, and Claws	Liquid latex
Carapace	Dark brown fly yarn
Eyes	Burned monofilament

5   Porcelain Crab

Hook	Mustad AC 34068, #2/0 to 8
Thread	White monocord, #3/0
Legs, Belly, and Claws	Liquid latex
Carapace	Light brown fly yarn
Eyes	Burned monofilament

6   Baby Lobster

Hook	Mustad 34011, #1
Thread	White Dynacord, #3/0
Eyes	Burned monofilament
Antennae	White latex with red spots
Carapace and Abdomen	Light pink sheep fleece or Fish Fuzz
Walking Legs	Long, light blue hackle
Swimming Legs	Short, tan, webby hackle

7   White Swimming Shrimp

Hook	Mustad AC 34068 or Dai-Riki 700B, #3/0 to 8
Thread	White Dynacord, #3/0
Weight	Flat lead wire (optional)
Eyes	Burned monofilament
Antennae	Boar's bristles
Carapace and Abdomen	Light gray sheep fleece or Fish Fuzz
Rostrum	Tan hackle turkey biot
Walking Legs	Long, light brown cock hackle
Swimming Legs	Short, tan webby hackle
Antennal Scal, Antennul, and Stylocerite	Speckled tan-and-brown hackle tips (these look like a lower lip below the eyes, but are really the base of the various antennae)

8   Immature White Swimming Shrimp

Hook	Mustad AC 340068, #10
Body	White mohair
Hackle	None
Wings	White sheep fleece under tan sheep fleece
Eyes	Burned monofilament
Antennae	Boar's bristles and Krystal Flash

9   Mantis Shrimp

Hook	Dai-Riki 700B, #246
Thread	White Dynacord, #3/0
Eyes	Burned monofilament
Antennae	Boar's bristle, moose mane, or equivalent
Legs	Hackle tips
Walking Legs	Long, stiff, cream cock hackle
Carapace and Abdomen	Fish Fuzz or sheep fleece in olive, tan, or black
Swimerettes	Short, webby badger hackle
Tail	Fish Fuzz
Weight	Flat lead strips or lead eyes

10   Minnow

Hook	Mustad AC 340068, #6 to 8
Thread	Coats & Clark transparent
Wig	Polar bear Fish Fuzz
Eyes	Paste-ons

```
  1
2   3
4   5
```

```
    6
    7
       8
 9
       10
11
```

Scott Sanchez

I started fly fishing and fly tying at the age of twelve and have worked in the fly-fishing industry for fifteen years. I have been assistant manager at Jack Dennis Sports, tied flies commercially, helped with video and book production for Snake River Books, consulted for Dan Bailey's, worked at the Austin Angler, and served as the Texas rep for Scott Rods. I made the video *Understanding Fly Tying Materials,* do fly-tying demonstrations, and teach fly tying and fly fishing. I am now the wholesale manager at Dan Bailey's. I've fly-fished salt water in Texas, Belize, California, the Virgin Islands, Hawaii, and France.

Double Bunny

The Double Bunny is my favorite big-fish fly. It works in fresh or salt water and brings out the fish you don't usually see. The idea for the Double Bunny came to me nine years ago on a fishing trip to Belize. John Hanlon and I were trying to catch barracudas that were not being cooperative. The two flies that ended up working the best were a Kiwi Muddler and a FisHair 'cuda fly, and we wondered, What if we put together the pulsating action of rabbit fur and the undulating action of a 'cuda fly? If we added the profile of a large baitfish, we would have a fly that looked alive in the water. I didn't have the materials to tie the Double Bunny on that trip, though, so it had to wait.

The following couple of summers as I fished for trout the idea of the super barracuda fly came back to me, and the first Double Bunny soon came out of my vise. I've used it successfully ever since. It's a great fly for finding and catching large fish. So far it's caught cutts, rainbows, hybrids, browns, brookies, and macks. On the nontrout list there are snappers, groupers, tuna, mackerel, jacks, 'cudas, snook, redfish, speckled sea trout, tarpon, salmon, stripers, pike, large- and smallmouth bass, and even a catch-and-release fly-rod-record channel catfish. The 1992, 1993, and 1994 Jackson Hole fly contests were also won on a couple of Double Bunny variations.

The great thing about this fly is that it can be fished very slowly. The rabbit pulsates and moves like an injured baitfish in the water. On the Texas coast it can be used for fishing channels, potholes, and deeper flats. It does a good job of imitating mullets, piggy perch, and croakers. The eyes on it help prevent short strikes. I've found sinking lines to be a good asset for fishing this fly in waters over four feet in depth. For bass I tie in a mono or wire weed guard. For salt water, I use stainless hooks. Originally I tied the flies with Zonker strips, but now I generally glue whole hides together and strip them out. If you do this, a plastic box knife with adjustable blade depth works great. For most tiers, though, Zonker strips will be more economical and allow you to tie different-colored Double Bunnies. The glue I prefer for the rabbit hide is Val-a brand latex contact cement. Barge-type contact cement will also work well, but the fumes can get to you.

Here are my favorite colors for Bunnies, the back color first and then the belly:

- Chinchilla/white—This works as a baby white-fish, shad, and mullet imitation.
- Olive/white—Use for trout, bass, and salt water.

- Olive/gray—This is my one-fly winner.
- Blue/white
- Chartreuse/white

Duct Tape Squid

The Duct Tape Squid evolved from an epoxy/hot-melt glue squid that I have tied. While on a trip to Hawaii, I needed some squid flies to catch tuna. I didn't have any epoxy in my travel kit, but I did have some white duct tape. I used it for the carapace on the squid and found it was a lot quicker to tie, lighter in weight, and easier to cast than the epoxy carapace; it also had less tendency to twist. It's a good fly for reefs, blue water, jetties, oil rigs, and other areas where you find squid.

Lipstick Minnow

The Lipstick Minnow came out because I needed a small minnow that was quick to tie and still had a translucent, epoxy-type look. While in the hardware store, I saw some clear vinyl tubing that looked like it might do the trick. I've tested it since on tunny, bonefish, sea trout, redfish, jacks, and a variety of other, smaller inshore species. Bass, crappies, and sunfish eat it, too. With a weed guard, it can be fished on flats or in vegetation. The original fly had a hot-melt glue head, but I now use epoxy for the head. With a rotisserie these are quick to tie. If you don't want to use epoxy, solid plastic eyes can be put on with Aquaseal or Goop. This fly lands on the water softer than a full epoxy-bodied fly. It is very effective for fishing speckled trout under the lights at night and can also be effective when redfish are being finicky. It is a good imitation of glass minnows and small silversides and has worked very effectively for tunny.

Scott's Tubing Shrimp

I started tying my shrimp as a quicker version of the Nix Epoxy Back Shrimp. In its unweighted form it lands in the water much softer than the epoxy shrimp. The sink rate can be changed by weighting it with lead wire to make it sink quicker or by dressing it with more Crystal Chenille to make it sink slower. I've tied this fly from #8 to 3/0. It works great on finicky bonefish and is an excellent fly for redfish and sea trout. I vary the weed guard mono by the size of the hook it's tied on. It is a good fly to fish in the summer when the shrimp and redfish are in shallow water in numbers. Using shooting tapers, I've also caught specks off deeper oyster reefs. Friends have used this fly in the Northwest for rockfish.

Prism Diver

The Prism Diver is a modification of the Dahlberg Diver. The great thing about divers is that they are both surface and subsurface flies, which makes them great to fish in varying conditions. I wanted to make this Diver float longer when it gets waterlogged (with any luck by fish), and to improve its underwater appearance. The idea for the foam/prism tape wing came when I was bass fishing and was tested almost immediately with good results. The foam keeps the fly at the surface when you want it there, and the partially water-saturated deer hair lets it dive well. The lure tape gives it a crankbait look underwater.

I generally tie this fly on Dai-Riki 930 stainless hooks. This allows me to fish them in fresh or salt water, and they don't rust when I forget and put my flies away wet. This heavier wire hook helps ballast the fly, too. I usually tie this fly in white, black, gray, and chartreuse, and in #2, 1/0, and 3/0. In the smaller sizes, I will tie a tail of Wing Fiber.

This is a good fly to use when you're blind casting on a flat and light conditions are bad. The head of this fly pushes a lot of water and the flash shows from quite a distance. This can pull fish to the fly. The Prism Diver can be used for early-morning specks that are chasing baitfish on top; it has also worked very well as a subsurface fly for snook on the South Texas coast.

Sluggo Fly

I developed the Sluggo Fly to fish for bass in heavy cover. Some very popular and effective lures for large bass are the soft plastic baits. A friend of mine, Bill Jones, is a partner in a great bass lease in East Texas. He needed a fly to compete with his fishing partners, who were doing very well with large plastic worms and Slug-Gos. These baits have a soft feel to them, fish very well on the drop, and work well on finicky bass in all water depths. They are also very weedless.

I decided to tie it as a tube fly so I could rig it like a Texas Rig Worm. I found that the rabbit strip needed a little more body for casting, so I put a little clear silicone caulking on the belly of a rabbit hide and added some glitter.

The early test runs were great. Along with Bill Jones and Robert Cathey, we used Sluggo Flies to catch some very nice fish in heavy cover and over deeper grass flats.

This fly can also be used in salt water. It is a good snag-resistant fly to throw in the grass and mangroves.

---

6   Double Bunny (Trout Style)

Hook	Dai-Riki 930, #2 to 3/0
Thread	#3/0
Weight	.35-inch lead wire wrapped only on the front half of the hook, leaving a slight amount of room just behind the eye of the hook (optional)
Body/Wing	Two rabbit strips, darker on top and lighter on the bottom
Flash/ Lateral Line	Rainbow thread and Brighton to match body
Eyes	5/16-inch stick-on eyes
Adhesive for Rabbit	Contact cement
Head Cement/ Eye Overcoat	Fletch-Tite brand clear vinyl archery cement or epoxy
Weed Guard	Hard monofilament (optional)

1. Wrap lead on the front half of the hook.

2. Impale the hook point though the rabbit that will be the belly.

3. Put the hook in your vise, start the thread, and secure the lead. Secure the bottom rabbit strip by the tip just behind the eye of the hook.

4. Holding the back end of the top rabbit strip away from you, use your bodkin to put contact cement on the hide only. You don't need a lot. If you put too much on the bodkin, you will have a tendency to get it on the hair—which you don't want to do.

5. Now use your bodkin to put contact cement on the hide side of the bottom strip and the thread-covered lead.

6. Hold the tail end of the rabbit strips in your left hand and pull straight back. With your right hand, pinch the strips together and pinch them down on the lead.

7. Take a few strands of Krystal Flash double the length you want and tie them in at their midpoint just behind the eye of the hook. Tie half on each side of the hook. Finish the head and whip-finish.

8. Lightly coat with contact cement the area of the rabbit where you will put the stick-on eyes. Let this set, then attach an eye to each side of the fly.

9. Overcoat the eyes and head with Fletch-Tite or epoxy.

10. Let the fly dry, then go catch some big fish.

It can be cast and then left sitting until fish come back when they are being very spooky. It can be crawled along rock jetties without hanging up too much. In longer lengths it is a nice ribbonfish imitation and when a kingfish ruins it, who cares? It didn't take any time to tie. The Sluggo can be tied in almost any color. My favorites are black, purple, chartreuse, and gray. I will often use fluorescent-colored thread on the head to give a firetail look. The rubber legs can be tied in matching or brightly contrasting colors.

Big Lip Shrimp

The Big Lip Shrimp is a shrimp-shaped popper. Speckled sea trout, redfish, and most of the Gulf Coast game fish love to eat shrimp. A lot of times redfish can get into very skinny water. Sometimes it is hard to fish a fly in the summer when the grass has grown up on the flats and the fish are shallow; your fly is always getting hung up even with a weed guard. When your fly is hung up, you can't fish it, and you may spook fish getting it unsnagged. Brooks Bouldin of Houston has a nice caribou floating shrimp for these conditions, and the idea for the Big Lip Shrimp came from this kind of fishing. I took my own Tubing Shrimp and put a foam carapace on it. This didn't float quite as high as I wanted so I added a foam indicator—which floats it higher, but also makes it into a popper. Most of the time shrimp will make a lot of commotion escaping from predators. They will jump and skip and spray water along the surface. This noise rings the dinner bell for specks and reds. The Big Lip Shrimp mimics these actions. It can be fished on the flats, in channels, and under the lights. Glow-in-the-dark Flashabou is a nice touch for night fishing. This fly has fished well for speckled trout, redfish, and ladyfish; I haven't yet tried it for tarpon or snook, but it could be good around mangroves and docks. The Big Lip is a simple, quick fly to tie. Tan, white, and pink are good colors, but you may want try others.

Conehead the Barbarian

This conehead Bend Back combines the features of some very effective patterns to create a new fly that catches fish and is reasonably snag-proof. Clouser Minnows and other lead-eyed flies dive to the bottom quickly and have a jigging motion that seems to attract fish. However, these eyes also pick up grass and get hung up on substrata. Bend Backs, another effective pattern, work great in shallow water and with sinking lines in deeper water, but even when weighted with lead they don't have as pronounced a jigging motion. Bend-back hooks definitely pick up less grass on the hook point than standard hooks do. I've used standard bead-head beads on small Bend Backs with good results, although on larger sizes they just don't look quite right. The conehead bead is the answer: It seems to give a better profile and many times can be coaxed out of the rocks when hung up. So

I've painted eyes on the beads, painted the beads (like a jig), and covered them with tubing. Putting prism tape over the cone seems to give the best results. It forms a great minnow head, and you get some bonus gills in the process. This fly is quick and simple so you can spend plenty of time fishing. It has worked well on stripers and white bass; it's good for probing channels and deeper flats for redfish and speckled trout. Flounder love this fly.

1	Sluggo Fly
Hook	Dai-Riki 930, #3/0
Thread	Pick your favorite color; #3/0 or size A
Tube	3/16-inch vinyl tubing, available at aquarium and hardware stores. It can be dyed with a rubber worm dye, such as Dip It, available at bass-fishing stores
Body/Tail	Silicone-caulking-coated rabbit hide. I take a whole or half rabbit hide and lightly coat the skin side with clear silicone caulking. I usually sprinkle some glitter onto the thin coating of silicone. I spread this with a plastic putty knife. This could also be done to Zonker strips with a toothpick
Legs	Rubber, pick your favorite color; #3/0 or size A (optional)

1. This fly is much easier to tie if you have a vise for tube flies. I make a simple one out of a bicycle spoke. Cut the spoke off about 1 1/2 inches from the nipple end. File the sides of the unthreaded part so they are flat; this will make it easier to hold in your tying vise. Cut a piece of the vinyl tubing 3/4 inch long, and slide this onto the spoke. Screw the spoke nipple on large-end first until just a few threads are showing. Put the spoke into the vise, close the vise, and screw the nipple down until the tubing is wedged snugly between vise and nipple.

2. Start your thread on the tubing.

3. Cut a silicone-caulking-coated rabbit strip about 3/16 inch wide.

4. Tie the tip to the tubing. If desired, tie in a clump of rubber legs. Whip-finish and cement.

You can also tie this fly on a #1/0 Sproat worm hook, such as an Eagle Claw L95. For salt water use a bend-back hook, either premade or done yourself. Thread your tippet through the tube head and tie on the hook. Impale the hook point through the hide and push the eye of the hook into the tubing. I will sometimes put a small split shot in front of the fly to make it sink quicker. If you use a standard-eye hook, a bead or split shot just in front of the hook will prevent the hook eye from going up through the tubing and blocking the hook gap. This fly can be fished large or small and for any fish species that likes a fly fished slowly through cover.

2	Prism Diver Shad
Hook	Dai-Riki 930, #2/0 or 3/0
Thread	White Flymaster Plus or monocord, size A
Weed Guard	Stiff monofilament; vary to suit hook size and snag conditions
Tail	Chinchilla rabbit strip; prism flash
Body	Natural gray deer (with optional top spots of black deer)
Gills	Red deer collar; silver prism tape over a thin piece of red foam
Eyes	Doll eyes; either solid or hollow is fine
Adhesives	Superglue, Goop, and double-stick tape

1. Tie in the weed guard at the bend of the hook. It should go halfway down the bend. A drop of cement will prevent the weed guard from twisting to the side, which would make it ineffective.

2. Tie in the rabbit strip with a few strands of flash over it. I usually make it about three shank lengths.

3. Clean and stack a good-size clump of deer hair. Push this clump down onto the hook shank at the bend of the hook. You will have hair in a 360-degree spread around the hook. Flare it without spinning it.

4. Clean and stack some red deer hair for the gills. Cut off the tips before you spin it; this will make it easier to spin.

5. Put a piece of lure tape (approximately 3/4 inch by 3/4 inch) on the foam. Cut this foam into a wide triangle, then round the top edge.

6. Stick a 1/4-inch-wide strip of double-stick tape onto the point of the foam and wrap it around the foam. Peel off the tape backing. Flex the foam at the point where the sticky tape ends. Push the foam side of the foam up against the deer hair and secure it with your thread. The double-stick tape will make it easier to attach the foam. Wrap securely and cover the tape with your thread.

7. Clean a good-size piece of deer hair and flare it on top of the hook shank. Flaring will be much easier than spinning over the base of the foam.

8. Flare a clump of deer hair on the bottom of the hook shank.

9. Spin more deer hair in front of the other clumps until you are within 1/32 inch of the eye of the hook. Stack dark-colored top spots on gray hair, if desired. Whip-finish.

10. Take a double-edged razor and, with pliers, break it into two single-edged razors. Double-edged razors are sharper than anything else, but extreme caution must be used with them.

```
    1
 2     3
    4
 5     6
   7  8
```

11. Cut the belly of the bug flat. If there's a question, cut less rather than more; you can always cut off more. Be careful at the back of the fly not to cut the weed guard thread.

12. Hold the fly facing toward you. Place the razor on top of the hook and with it cut from the eye of the hook back toward the collar. This will form the top of the head. The angle of the head will be approximately 25 degrees.

13. Cut the sides of the head at the same angle as the top.

14. Round the square shape of the head by making fine cuts with the razor.

15. Hold the fly upside down and slightly round the edges of its belly. This will make it float slightly lower in the water.

16. Make a flat, shallow cut along each side of the head in front of the collar. This is where you'll glue the eyes.

17. Tie off the weed guard. Insert the fly into the vise and start your thread behind the eye of the hook. Push the mono through the eye of the hook and wrap your thread around it. Fold the mono back, wrap down, and whip-finish.

18. Pour a small amount of Goop into the eye socket and stick on the eyes. Cement the head of the fly.

The Prism Diver can be tied with other tail materials, such as marabou or hackle. For a less flashy fly, delete the lure tape.

3	Big Lip Shrimp
Hook	Dai-Riki 930, #2
Thread	Pink, #3/0
Weed Guard	12-pound Mason mono
Mouth and Forelegs	Fluorescent pink Bailey's Float Vis (a fine acrylic fiber)
Eyes	Hairbrush stems that are black on the end
Rib	Tying thread, doubled
Body/Legs	Large pink Crystal Chenille
Antennae	Glow-in-the-dark pink Flashabou; pink Krystal Flash
Carapace	Thin pink closed-cell foam
Popping Lip	Thin pink closed-cell foam

1. Cement the hook shank, start your thread, and tie in weed guard mono at the bend of the hook. The weed guard wraps should extend down one-third of the bend. You want this to be a light weed guard, just enough to keep grass out of it.

2. Tie in a piece of Float Vis as a tail at the bend of the hook. It should be two-thirds a shank length.

3. Cut the hairbrush stems off the brush at the base; side cutters or toenail clippers work well. Mash the stems flat with pliers so that they are easier to tie in.

4. Tie in the eye on the near side of the hook; it should extend just past the bend. Then tie in the eye on the far side of the hook. Flex the eyes so that they separate; figure-eight wrap to keep them separated and secure them better. Put a drop of cement on the base of the eyes.

5. Make a dubbing loop with your tying thread and pull it over to the far side. This will become the rib.

6. Tie in the Crystal Chenille and wrap forward to within an eye's length of the hook eye.

7. Tie in the Flashabou and Krystal Flash antennae at the front of the hook. Six strands of each is good. This should extend past the hook bend 1 1/2 shank lengths.

8. Cut a carapace from the foam about 1/2 inch wide. Cut a popping lip from the foam.

9. Tie in the carapace at the front of the hook. With your ribbing thread, make a wrap to secure the carapace in at the back. Hold the rib, set the popping lip on top of the carapace, and lash it down in the same spot with the ribbing thread. Make another wrap at this spot, then wrap the ribbing thread forward to secure the rest of the carapace. This will also segment the carapace. Tie off the ribbing thread with the tying thread.

10. Trim the Crystal Chenille so that the legs are longer at the rear than at the front.

11. Tie off the weed guard by putting the end of the mono through the hook eye and lashing down a few times. Adjust the weed guard to equal 1 1/2 gaps. Fold the mono back above the hook eye, secure, and whip-finish.

12. Pull the fly out of the vise. Hold it so that it faces you and trim the popping lip so that it is slightly curved and symmetrical. Cement the head; also cement around the popping lip to reinforce it.

As with most poppers, different retrieves will work on different days. The retrieve patterns that work best for me are an abrupt twelve-inch strip followed by a fairly long pause and then a frantic quick strip that skips the fly across the water. If you are getting some blowups or short strikes, fish a smaller nonfloating shrimp pattern below this, to give you the popping-cork-and-shrimp effect.

4	Duct Tape Squid
Hook	Dai-Riki 930, #3/0
Thread	White, #3/0
Tentacles	Eight hot pink saddle hackles; eight strands of large white rubber legs
Eyes	Two large strung pearl beads
Body	Pearl Crystal Chenille
Carapace	White duct tape

1. Start the thread and wrap back to the bend of the hook.

2. Tie in the saddle hackles. Attach four on each side. The curve should be facing out.

3. Tie in the rubber legs, four to a side.

4. Wrap your thread about ³/₄ inch back around the saddles and rubber as if you were tying an extended-body dry fly.

5. Cut off two connected pearl beads. Figure-eight the thread around them to secure them to the hackles and rubber legs.

6. Tie in the Crystal Chenille. Wrap around the eyes and hackle body going forward, then wrap around the hook shank, almost to the eye. Whip-finish.

7. Cut a piece of duct tape about three-quarters of the shank length, and stick to the bottom of the hook. Cut another piece of the same size and stick to the top. Push the tape pieces together firmly. Cut the tape to the shape of a squid.

Other good colors for this fly include gray, silver, and purple; and badger, root beer, and brown. I've tied it as small as #2 and as large as #6/0 with tandem hooks. A slip-on popper head can be used with it, too.

5	Conehead the Barbarian—Gray and White
Hook	Mustad 34011, #6 to 1/0
Thread	Red, #3/0; unwaxed is preferable
Wing	White Bozo Hair on #1/0 and 2, or white Bailey's Wing Fiber on #6 and 4; then silver Brighton with pearl rainbow thread; then gray hair
Throat	Red rainbow thread
Head	Silver conehead, medium on #6 hooks and large on hooks #4 and larger
Head Cover/ Gills	Pearl prism tape wrapped around the conehead. The top of the head is colored with a gray marker
Eyes	Tape eyes; the nonprismatic seem to stay on better
Overcoat	Loon Soft Epoxy (optional)

1. Bend the front quarter of the hook shank up about 15 degrees and crimp the barb.

2. Slip the point of the conehead onto the point of the hook, then up to the eye. Put your hook in the vise with the hook inverted.

3. Put a drop of superglue behind the cone and start your thread.

4. Tie in the white hair just behind the cone. This will extend past the bend of the hook about half a shank length. Tie in the Brighton and rainbow thread, then tie in the gray hair.

5. Tie the throat in opposite the wing: Take about ten strands of red rainbow thread, fold it around your tying thread, and slide it up to the hook. Secure it down, then cut it to half a shank length.

6. Make a number of wraps in front of the wing to wedge the cone in place. Put a drop of superglue in front of and behind the cone.

7. Cut a piece of prism tape ³/₈ by ³/₄ inch. Cut a half moon into the long end of the tape, then taper the sides slightly from the circular cut out, going back. This shape will make it easier to wrap around the cone.

8. Place the center of the curve on top of the cone and so that the leading edge is just behind the eye of the hook. Wrap the near side down around the bead; wrap the far side down around the cone and over the other end of the tape. This will form a tape cone.

9. The back ends of the tape will form gill covers. Holding the wing out of the way, trim the tape to the size of head you desire. Make it flush with the cone on the bottom to look like fish gills viewed from below.

10. Color the top of the head with a gray marker and put on the eyes. If desired, color the inside edge of the gill plate with a red marker.

11. Overcoat the tape with Loon Soft Epoxy, and rotate until the epoxy sets. If you don't do this, use a bodkin to put the superglue at the leading edge of the tape, on the tape seam, and at the front of the tape eyes to secure them. Thick Flexament will also work to coat the head, but you need to make sure it won't dissolve the tape eyes.

This fly can be tied in other colors to imitate most baitfish; it can also be tied in sparser or bulkier shapes to change its profile. Rabbit strip and feather wings also work.

7   Lipstick Minnow

Hook	Mustad 34011 #2 to 6
Thread	Gray, #3/0
Tail	Gray marabou or rabbit hair
Tube Holder	Pearl or silver mylar braid
Underbody	Rainbow Krystal Flash and silver Brighton
Overbody	1/8-inch ID by 3/16-inch OD clear vinyl tubing, available at hardware stores and at aquarium stores as mini airline tubing
Eyes	3/16-inch stick-on eyes
Head	Clear waterproof five-minute epoxy

1. Start the thread and wrap back to the hook bend.

2. Tie in a marabou tail about three-quarters of the shank length and cement.

3. Wrap thread up two-thirds of the shank and tie in the mylar braid.

4. Wrap the mylar braid in a figure-eight to make a lump and tie off.

5. Tie in the Krystal Flash and Brighton so that they go around the hook shank. They should go over the eye of the hook about two shank lengths. Tie off the thread.

6. Cut a piece of tubing about two-thirds of the shank length. Push this over the eye of the hook and onto the mylar lump. This will push back the Krystal Flash and form the body.

7. Attach the stick-on eyes to the hook behind the eye.

8. Coat the head with a little epoxy and turn until it's set.

I've tied this fly in #6 to 1/0. I use larger tubing (1/8 by 1/4) for the #1/0s. For a less flashy fly use Ultra Hair for the underbody. Wing Fiber or acrylic fur also makes a great-looking tail.

8   Scott's Tubing Shrimp

Hook	Dai-Riki 930, #4
Thread	Brown, #3/0
Back Legs	Brown marabou
Eyes	Burned monofilament, strung plastic beads, or—my favorite— hairbrush eyes
Antennae	Brown Ultra Hair; root beer Krystal Flash
Body	Root beer Crystal Chenille
Hackle	Brown long flash chenille
Rib	Doubled-over #3/0 thread
Carapace	Clear vinyl tubing cut to shape. This is sold in hardware and aquarium stores
Weed Guard	#8 or 9 Mason hard mono

1. Make three wraps of .025-inch lead slightly behind the eye of the hook.

2. Tie in a tuft of brown marabou about two-thirds of the shank length.

3. Cut hairbrush eyes off a brush and smash the stem with pliers.

4. Tie in an eye on each side of the hook shank. The eyes should extend just past the bend of the hook. Wrap the thread around the base of the eyes in a figure-eight to separate them. Glue the wraps.

5. With the thread at the back of the hook, make a dubbing loop. This will become the rib.

6. Tie in the Crystal Chenille and long flash chenille. Wrap the Crystal Chenille as the body and the long flash as a palmered hackle.

7. Tie in the Krystal Flash and Ultra Hair behind the eye of the hook.

8. Cut a carapace out of the tubing. It should be tapered at both ends. Push the tubing down onto the body and antennae. Hold it in place, then secure and rib with the dubbing loop. Tie off the dubbing loop.

9. Tie in a piece of #8 or 9 Mason mono. Tie this in a figure-eight like a spinner wing. Pull down both sides and post it under the hook shank. Wrap the thread in front of and behind the weed guard. Cut it so it is slightly longer than the hook gap. Smash the ends of the mono with a pair of pliers. This will make it easier to hook fish.

10. Whip-finish. Cut the long flash fibers so that they are longer at the back of the fly. Cement the head and put some cement on the carapace. Cut off the excess antennae fibers so that there are about four or five strands extending about 1 1/2 shank lengths beyond the bend of the hook.

Other good colors include olive, tan, hot pink, pink, orange, and gray. Weed guards aren't needed if you're fishing open water. Will Myers showed me that this vinyl tubing can also be dyed different colors with Dip It rubber worm dye.

Mark Sedotti

I was forced to learn to tie in 1991 when I couldn't get the saltwater flies I needed and wanted. Three friends graciously and enthusiastically taught me. Tom Piccolo is a renowned tier in his own right. Allan "Flats" Finkleman, whom I call New York City's finest flats fisherman, has caught a staggering number of ten-pound-plus bonefish on a fly. And long into some memorable nights I've chased stripers sipping on cinder worms with Jay Bobowitz. No one has more knowledge about this fascinating kind of fishing than he.

I tie flies to solve my fishing problems or copy some bait that I often see. Occasionally I'll tie a pattern on request. I'm also interested in using something that will catch big fish, which is often a big bait.

I've primarily fished for striped bass and bluefish on the western Long Island Sound but have broadened in the last few years to fishing these along with false albacore, bonito, redfish, and some bonefish over the entire Northeast, North Carolina, and, of course, the Caribbean (for bonefish). I'm now also doing more freshwater reservoir and lake fishing for trout and warm-water species. It's exciting to play with new patterns and catch some surprisingly big fish here, too. Both this and the saltwater fishing are so close to my home. I am attracted to saltwater fly fishing because it is close by and offers so much still to be explored; the fish are big and hard fighting, too, and it is so beautiful and uncrowded out there! You'd be surprised how peaceful and free it is where I fish on Long Island Sound, even though the Manhattan skyline stands within sight.

The casting has always been special, too. I love performing the long, graceful, and powerful casts. It's so Zen-like and satisfying, and every single well-performed cast still thrills me.

Since my local area has so little public shore access, I've fly-fished from boats for years, and it's this method that I prefer. Some say they feel more at one with the environment when wading. Not me! I feel more freedom in a boat, and it's floating upon the sea that best sets me at one with it. No nervous glances along the shore looking for landowners running down the beach after me either!

Some of my flies are very big, but they simply copy the naturals (menhaden, mackerel, and so on), which are often large and commonly relished by predators. Even though I've been casting giant flies long distances for five seasons now, and have written about how routine it is and can be for many, I'm still told that it can't be done, or is so difficult, or blah, blah, blah! Casting big flies is not radical. Most fishermen can do it. The problem is not the casters' abilities but their minds. They don't believe they can. Change your mind and the fly will fly! Think positive and you'll not only have the long casts, but the flies, the fish, the records, the enjoyment, and the thrills will all be yours as well!

I'm a stickler for proper length and profile in my patterns. I think both are very important if you're going to get fish to think that your offering is what you want them to think it is. I've seen fish in salt water become selective so often, I think it's routine behavior. They're tough to take until you cast something to them that looks like the bait they're feeding on. In length, profile, and color, I tie my flies to look like the naturals. They especially have to look like the real thing in the water. It doesn't matter what they look like on land. Often, though, productive flies look good in both places.

I began to tie using natural materials. I'm currently exploring synthetics and am really getting into studying color and flash in my new patterns. I've become interested in subtlety, refraction, and reflection of different materials and colors. My new flies are heavily influenced by the work of Bob and Kate Howe of La Mesa,

2, 3   Sedotti's Slammer

Hook	Tiemco 800S, #3/0
Thread	White
Weight	.030-inch lead wire, plus lead keel
Tail	White schlappen
Midfly	White bucktail
Side	White bucktail
Flash	Pink Krystal Flash; silver Flashabou
Back	Peacock herl
Head	Top, olive bucktail; sides and bottom, white bucktail
Eyes	10-millimeter doll eyes

1. With white thread, tie in a lead keel.

2. For the tail, tie in two pairs of white schlappen hackles to the desired length.

3. At the midpoint of the hook, tie in white bucktail on top (for a wing) and bottom (for the belly). In the same spot, tie in Krystal Flash and silver Flashabou.

4. With thread at the head of the fly, tie in peacock herl for the fly's back.

5. For the fly's top, tie in olive bucktail. For its sides and bottom, tie in white bucktail.

6. Glue on 10-millimeter doll eyes.

7. Cement the head.

This fly can also be tied tandem.

Lefty Kreh told me that someone tied a pattern years ago that looked like this. I tied it with no knowledge of that, however, and even if I can't take credit for its origination, it is an incredibly effective fly.

Tying materials Hi- and Lo-Ti—on both the bottom and top of the entire hook shank—produces a wide-profile fly, perfect to imitate a menhaden, which was the Slammer's original purpose. As I said, I'm a stickler for good profile, and this fly is tied in different and specific ways for each size category: 4–7 inches, 8–9 inches, and 10-plus inches (to achieve a bunker's natural shape). Each category is tied precisely, with the components and steps strategically fitting together, each making way for the next. The 10-inch-plus fly can be tied in two ways, one for narrower breadth and one for wider. Besides having lead wrapped around the hook shank, each size has a built-in lead keel that helps it track straight, cast better, and sink better, too. Wide-profile flies have a tendency to ride on their sides, and to correct this problem, Tom Piccolo suggested the keel. Although you really don't need the keel with the smaller versions, the extra weight helps them sink better. Also, a small fly with lots of lead on the shank gives a good jigging action. Make the fly heavier and it will drop better and faster than most flies with lead eyes, with the bonus that it casts noticeably better too!

I often tie the big fly longer than 12 inches and it is very castable. I routinely and easily cast it 80 to 90 feet because it's light, well balanced, and wind resistant. The main hook shank is wrapped with .030-inch lead wire. Under this, tie the keel—fifteen $\frac{1}{2}$-inch strips of the same lead wire, stacked in three rows of five. A properly balanced big fly has enough weight to be cast with good momentum. I happened upon this concept while working on getting a fly to track well.

Another reason the Slammer casts well is that it's made of natural materials and collapses when it's wet and out of the water, offering less air resistance. Once the fly hits the water, it opens up wide. Synthetic materials don't collapse and large flies made of synthetics won't cast well for very long distances.

Bob Popovics suggested I make the fly look like a fish from beneath, so I added bucktail to the sides and tied feathers over them. It really made a great three-dimensional fly. I do this for the 8-inch and sometimes for the larger version. I don't need to do it for the smaller because of its natural shape.

The fly works well whenever menhaden are around, often hooking selective fish. I've caught giant bluefish and big striped bass; I hooked an estimated fifty-pound redfish (which I subsequently lost) on the fly. The small sizes, 5 to 7 inches, are great alewife and shad imitations, too. I've used the fly to take lake and brown trout, largemouth and smallmouth bass, as well as big pickerel in fresh water.

California; Tom Piccolo of Mamaroneck, New York; and Dan "The Chief" Marini of Cape Cod, Massachusetts. Synthetic translucent materials in a variety of mixed, natural colors and reflections, plus strategic flash, along with length and profile—this is exciting!

One more thing. *Think* when you're fishing and when you're trying new flies. Keep an open mind, perform relaxed, be keenly observant, and use your intuition.

1
2
3
4
5   6

1   Sedotti's Mackerel

Hook	Eagle Claw 254SS, #6/0
Thread	White
Underbody	.030-inch lead wire, plus lead keel
Midfly	Bucktail on the sides, covered with schlappen or saddle hackle
Flash	Pearl Flashabou
Back	Peacock herl
Head	Top, green bucktail; sides and bottom, white bucktail
Eyes	12-millimeter doll eyes
Markings	Black Pantone marker

This fly is tied in the Deceiver style, but has some important twists. Like the previous patterns, the Mack has a lead-wrapped shank and a lead keel to help it track and sink well. The two long coke feathers are tied in at the back on top of the lead wrap, then four white saddles are tied in on the bottom of the lead, below the first two. This separation is very important because it gives the fly a little more of a natural profile, the colors are separate and distinct, and the final result is a fly that appears more like the natural. The saddles will also bend, first down, then up a little, providing a realistic belly shape. As on the Slammer, bucktail clumps are tied in on the sides of the keel to allow white saddles to be put atop, so the fly has a good three-dimensional quality. The Mack looks more like the natural in the water than any mackerel fly I've come across. It casts great, too. It doesn't have that many feathers, so you can toss it a mile! In the spring, up in Maine, the bigger bass just suck it in. There you may have schools of small bait, mackerel, and small stripers, all working within sight of the boat. Toss in the Mack on a sinking line, let it drop, start retrieving, and the line tightens. Bingo, big fish from below!

4   Bunker Head

Hook	Tiemco 811S, #4/0
Thread	White
Tail	Red marabou
Midfly	White bucktail
Side	Pearl Flashabou and Krystal Flash; pink bucktail
Top	Olive bucktail
Eyes	Black on white
Head	Silicone

Cut-up menhaden is by far the most popular bait in my area. Often when bluefish are feeding on and chopping up a school of menhaden, pieces of the baitfish, including many heads, drift down toward the bottom, below the activity. There you often have lazy stripers lying in wait for an easy meal.

Much of the Bunker Head is covered with silicone. This not only helps the fly keep its shape while drifting but also makes it chewy. If it feels real, maybe the bass holds onto it longer, giving you more time to detect the hit on the dead-drifted presentation and set the hook. The fly is also heavily weighted along the shank.

5   Sedotti's Flounder

Hook	Tiemco 811S, #3/0
Thread	White
Tail	Extension, 100-pound monofilament
Underbody	.030-inch lead wire, plus lead keel
Body	Bottom, white saddle hackle; top, tan bucktail
Eyes	10-millimeter doll eyes

Back when I was killing bass, I found flounder in their stomachs. There were even times when they would spit them out during the fight.

I simply extended 100-pound mono behind the hook shank and Hi- and Lo-Tied bucktail clumps and short saddles to the top and bottom along the sides. I weighted the shank heavily and added a keel, of course. Presto . . . a flounder.

6   Pinfish

Hook	Tiemco 800S, #1/0
Thread	White
Midfly	White craft fur
Side	Pink and yellow Krystal Flash
Wing	White craft fur with an olive top
Markings	Black horizontal bars
Eyes	Black on white

One evening in North Carolina when I had time to kill, I asked Bill Harris what bait he would like copied. Pinfish, he replied, and I tied it on the spot.

The Pinfish is tied with Enrico's Fish Fibers. I like this material because you can tie quickly with it, it keeps its bulk in the water without needing any fancy engineering, and you can shape your creation easily with scissors. The fly has a weighted shank to help it sink.

Cam Sigler, Sr.

I was born in South Louisiana and began fishing with my father and brother at about age five. My father worked on hydroelectric and coal power plants and we moved every couple of years, so I had the opportunity to fish in many different places, both salt and fresh water, from East Coast to West and North to South.

We moved to Virginia when I was in my teens. When I was seventeen, I went to work in a local sporting goods store part time and met my friend and mentor, Joe Brooks. Joe was the one who sparked my interest in fly fishing and fly tying, and I started to tie bass bugs and saltwater streamers. At this time I also met Bill Gallasch, who tied the Blonde and Skipping Bug series that Joe had developed for the store.

During college and a stint in the Coast Guard, I continued fishing. After the service I went back to work full time in the sporting goods store, but because I was spending more time with Joe, I was drawn to the Florida Keys. I worked in the evening as a bellhop and had all day to fish. This was a period when I learned a great deal about saltwater fishing techniques and equipment.

In 1968 I moved to Seattle to manage an outdoor store for a major Seattle company. After a few years I went into product development and was responsible for all its fishing and hunting equipment. I needed to learn all I could about all types of fishing.

Buying flies for the local store, I was introduced to tube flies, which are very popular for salmon in the Northwest. My friend Bill Knox, of Vashon Island, showed me how to tie them for fresh and salt water. I have been hooked ever since.

I have always been interested in big-game fishing, and have been a mate on charter boats in Virginia, North Carolina, and Florida.

I remember the story that Dr. Webster Robinson told Joe Brooks about catching the first sailfish on a fly, and I had always dreamed about throwing a fly to a billfish. When my friend Jack Samson invited me to accompany him and a group of fishermen to Mazatlán, I jumped at the chance. I took my first sailfish on a tandem-hooked fly that Jack had given me, on a four-piece 12-weight with a single-action reel. The skipper and my fishing companions, all experienced offshore fishermen, believed it to be a world record for a 16-pound tippet. I released the fish, so we will never know.

During subsequent trips to Panama and Mexico we used the same style of flies, tandem hooks with foam cylinder popper heads. If the fish bit down on the head, it didn't collapse, and the fly would explode out of the fish's mouth on the strike. I had one crazy sailfish in Panama take the fly eight times before it was hooked.

Trying to solve the popper head problem, I began to work on the development of the tandem tube flies. When I came home from Panama, I turned down the back part of the cylinder, making a smaller diameter. I still needed the full diameter on the front in order for the head to pop. I noted that many of the teasers we used had holes in the head to make bubbles, so I decided to put holes in the popper end of the tapered popper, hence the name Bubble Head.

At this time I started to look at the flies we were using. I am not the most organized person when it comes to caring for my tackle and I noticed that the hooks on the tandem flies were tarnished, and some of the feathers were ragged. This gave me an idea: If I used tubes like I did for local salmon, I could change hooks, taking them apart once used. If I used two tubes I could make a single streamer or, rigged in tandem, a double streamer. I would then have a fly or set of flies that I could use as a single or double streamer or popper by adding the bubble head. By turning the head around, so the small end was facing forward, I could have a slider. It was then that I realized the beginnings of the Big Game Fly.

When I started to develop the Big Game patterns, I used the same process that I use to tie small tubes. To hold the tube in the vise I have a couple of nails, because I seem to misplace one every now and then or it gets lost in the materials box, but I know I'll find it again someday. I take a small nail a little larger than the diameter of the tubing I am using and taper the end with a grinding wheel or file, so the tube will slide up on the shaft about an inch. The taper is very important if you're using a nail. If you tie the fly tightly and get into the soft tube, you can actually tie the fly to the nail. The taper will allow you to wiggle the tube enough to slide the fly loose. To put the nail in the jaws of the vise, I just flatten the nail head with a hammer.

The Big Game Tubes are easy to tie. I start with a 1/8-inch OD high-pressure tube and superglue, then glue a 1/8-inch OD soft tube to that. Slide the soft tube onto the tapered nail and push until the hard end inside is also on the taper. This stabilizes the tube so you can tie on it. I lay a base wrap of thread beginning at the base of the hard tube. I use size D rod-winding thread, usually white, because I will color it later. If you are used to tying small flies, the rod-winding thread will feel like rope. Once my base wrap is on, I start building the fly by adding marabou to the bottom and top. Make it as heavy and thick as you prefer. Once the marabou is on, add saddles, the longest you can find. I use 6- to 8-inch saddles, usually four per color on each side. I also have a couple of patterns in which I use yellow in the center. I put two yellow saddles between the top and bottom colors. Once the saddles are in place, I put four strands of Witchhair tape on each side, wrap these down, and tie them off.

Once they are tied off, I am ready to finish the head. If I tie two of the same tubes I put eyes on one and leave them off the second. I color the heads with Magic Marker. Then I am ready to set the eyes. I like

---

Big Game Tube Fly—Pink Squid

Hook	Rigged tandem tube flies: Owner SSW #5/0 and 6/0
Thread	White
Tube	1/8-inch OD Nylaflow high-pressure tubing; 1/8-inch ID PVC tubing glued to hard tubing
Tail	Marabou: white, pink; hackle: white, pink; Witchcraft Witchhair mini-fish: silver
Head	Five-minute epoxy; pink top
Foam Head	Edgewater white foam; silver glitter line; top painted pink
Eyes	Rear, 15-millimeter oval doll eyes, black on white; front, plastic black on amber

1. Start with 2 inches of Nylaflow 1/8-inch OD tubing, and glue on 1/2 inch of 1/8-inch ID clear PVC tubing so that it extends 1/4 inch past the hard tube.

2. Using large-gauge white thread, tie in ten to twelve 7-inch white hackles on the underside of the tube just forward of the PVC tube. Tie in the same number of hot pink hackles on the top side of the tube. Tie in the same colors of marabou feathers on top and bottom, four each.

3. Cover the head with thread and whip-finish. Color the top of the head with a pink felt pen.

4. Apply 15-millimeter doll eyes to the head, then five-minute epoxy.

5. For the front tube, repeat all steps except the addition of the eyes. Slide a popper head over the hard tubing and you are ready to rig.

---

big eyes, so I use a 15-millimeter oval eye. I set one on each side of the head using a dab of superglue. Once they're set I mix five-minute epoxy and fill the space between the eyes. You will need to rotate the tube until the epoxy flows evenly around the head. I also epoxy the head of the tube with no eyes.

No finesse here, just gobs of feathers, small rope, gooey glue, and Big Eyes for big fish. What makes these flies fun is being creative with materials, and the idea is to have fun with them. I believe if you tease the fish properly and he is excited, he'll eat your shoe if you cast it to him. I know they also like cigars.

I encourage those who have the chance to fish for billfish with a fly to do so. It is very exciting to have an eight-foot fish jumping at the end of your fly rod.

1, 2	**The Halloween Machine**
Hook	Not rigged; tandem tube flies
Thread	White
Tube	$\frac{1}{8}$-inch OD Nylaflow high-pressure tubing; $\frac{1}{8}$-inch ID PVC tubing glued to hard tubing
Tail	Marabou: orange, black; hackle: orange, black; Witchcraft Witchhair mini-fish: orange
Head	Five-minute epoxy; black top, orange bottom
Foam Head	Edgewater white foam; silver glitter line; painted black top, orange bottom

3, 4	**Pink & Purple**
Hook	Not rigged; tandem tube flies
Thread	White
Tube	$\frac{1}{8}$-inch OD Nylaflow high-pressure tubing; $\frac{1}{8}$-inch ID PVC tubing glued to hard tubing
Tail	Marabou: pink, purple; hackle: pink, yellow, purple; Witchcraft Witchhair mini-fish: purple
Head	Five-minute epoxy; pink bottom, purple top
Foam Head	Edgewater white foam; silver glitter line; top painted purple, bottom painted pink
Eyes	Rear, 15-millimeter oval doll eyes, black on white; front, plastic black on amber

5, 6	**Chartreuse & White**
Hook	Not rigged; tandem tube flies
Thread	White
Tube	$\frac{1}{8}$-inch OD Nylaflow high-pressure tubing; $\frac{1}{8}$-inch ID PVC tubing glued to hard tubing
Tail	Marabou: chartreuse, white; hackle: chartreuse, white; Witchcraft Witchhair mini-fish: green
Head	Five-minute epoxy; white bottom, green top
Foam Head	Edgewater white foam; silver glitter line; painted green
Eyes	Rear, 15-millimeter oval doll eyes, black on white; front, plastic black on amber

1	2
3	4
5	6

Cam Sigler, Jr.

Lucky is what most people would say about me. I was born in Richmond, Virginia, and at the age of four my family relocated to the Pacific Northwest, where my father took a job with a major outdoor retailer. Home from that time on was a beach house on an island surrounded by salt water. Very fortunate for a kid who liked to fish.

By the age of ten I was following after my father and his friends with a fly rod in my hand. I learned from him and also from a number of so-called uncles I still have the pleasure of spending days afield with.

Most of my jobs have been in the sporting goods industry, other than a sabbatical of a couple of years with several ballet companies. (Not conducive to finding time to fish, but I did find a wife.) That career ended and two weeks later I was on a plane to the Alaskan bush with the title of fishing guide.

I will be the first to admit that full-bodied silicone flies may stretch the limits of the word *fly*. I initially came up with the concept to solve a problem I was having with bucktail streamers. In all the years I spent guiding Alaska coasts and wandering the beaches of Puget Sound, there were few days without wind. And on these days I was frustrated by the streamer's tail wrapping. Sitting at the vise one day I covered the whole fly with head cement. I fished this pattern with success but it soon broke down and tail wrapped again. Then in conversation one day a fellow tier mentioned silicone.

I had silicone everywhere in my workshop, because I had replaced natural materials with synthetics. After tying a few flies, I was off to the beach. Even though these flies were crude, they worked. They did not tail wrap, swim erratically, or tumble when let fall. So it was back to the vise for a little more flash and a couple of colors.

Initially I developed these flies for the anadromous salmon and cutthroats in the salt water near home, but soon many found their way into fresh waters, taking large brown trout, cutthroats, and small- and largemouth bass. From there they found their way into the brackish waters of the South and the mouths of speckled trout and redfish.

These flies are very durable, and the softness of the silicone has the fish believing that he has real bait in his mouth. He won't let go. I also tie these silicones on a wide-gapped worm hook that I pinch the barb on. Once I push the fine wire into the bend, just keeping it tight will keep it on. One thing I have learned wielding a fly rod for two-thirds of my life is, Once you think you have it all figured out, nature will soon humble you.

I have spent the last year working with my father in his business. We design and supply outdoor products—waders, flies, and many others too numerous to mention. In my spare time I also supply saltwater leaders, six to seven thousand fifty-turn Bimini twists a year. I live on Vashon Island in Washington State with my wife, Katrina, daughter, Teal, and hunting dogs of various sizes and types.

Silicone Candlefish

1. Start with your favorite long-shanked saltwater hook; I prefer the Owner spinnerbait. Start wrapping clear mono thread behind the hook eye; wrap back $1/4$ inch. Tie in twenty to thirty white Super Hair fibers $2^{1}/_2$ inches long under the hook.

2. Starting on the top side of the hook, tie in equal amounts of crystal white Sparkle Flash, white Super Hair, gold Super Hair, green pearl Sparkle Flash, and olive Super Hair. Build up a bullet-head shape with mono thread.

3. Apply a #2 stick-on eye to each side and over-wrap with mono thread. Cement the head.

4. Trim the fibers at a 45-degree angle, from behind the hook bend back and up.

5. Using clear silicone or Softex, coat the fly completely, forming it into a tapered bullet shape. You can also coat just to the hook bend.

6. A rattle may be pushed up into the fly and siliconed in after the initial drying.

Silicone Series

Hook	Owner spinnerbait
Wing	White FisHair, silver Flashabou
Top	Blue FisHair; blue Flashabou
Bottom	White FisHair
Eyes	Black on silver
Hook	Owner spinnerbait
Wing	White and olive FisHair; pearl Flashabou
Top	Blue and green Flashabou
Bottom	White FisHair
Eyes	Black on silver
Hook	Owner spinnerbait
Wing	White, light green, dark green FisHair; pearl Flashabou
Bottom	White FisHair
Eyes	Black on silver
Hook	Owner spinnerbait
Wing	Light green and peacock Tiewell
Bottom	White FisHair
Eyes	Black on silver
Hook	Owner spinnerbait
Wing	Green FisHair; green Flashabou
Bottom	White FisHair
Eyes	Black on silver
Hook	Owner spinnerbait
Wing	Red FisHair; red Flashabou
Bottom	Yellow FisHair
Eyes	Black on silver

SILICONE SERIES
BAITFISH

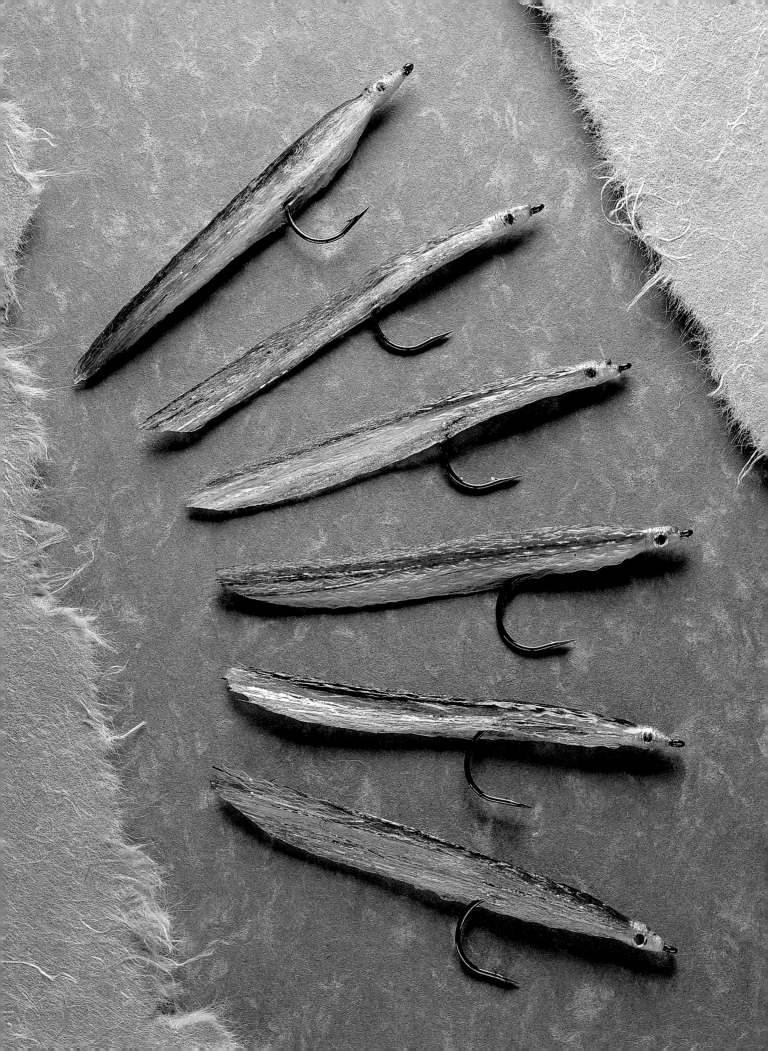

David Skok

I used to fish for trout. That's not to say that I don't enjoy trout fishing anymore, because I do. It's just that I've found something that's a little easier to see, a little closer to home, and a lot more compelling.

I wasn't quite as fond of fly rodding in the salt when I started as I am today. I was frustrated by fish constantly on the move. How the hell was I supposed to know where the fish were gonna be that night? I liked trout, whether or not I could catch them, because at least I knew they were there. Saltwater fish were different, and I spent more time driving around looking for them than I did actually fishing. Not until I figured out I had to stop the car, turn off the engine, get in the water, and stand there for a couple of hours did I get it.

Finding the fish was the hard part; catching them was easy. Clouser, Deceiver, slider! Clouser, Deceiver, slider! Why fish anything else? That's all you need! At least that's what I thought. Catching striped bass on a fly rod was beginning to seem like glorified bluegill fishing.

One night, while fishing a local tidal creek, things happened a little differently. Fish were popping with amazing consistency and a long cast quartering upstream with a Clouser was sure to provide a strike. But I followed my fly downstream and across current all the way to the swing without even a bump. Hmm. That was strange. I cast again with the same result. I cast again, and again, and again. Nothing! If not the Clouser, maybe the Deceiver, or a slider. . . . I must have cast a million times that night. The final tally was one twelve-incher lost on a jump. Probably one of those stupid shad. I fished till dawn, drove home, and crawled into bed feeling fortunate there'd been no witnesses.

Two P.M. rolled around and I rolled out of bed. Not understanding the behavior of last night's stripers, I consulted an experienced salty fly rodder at the local fly shop. After I recounted the night's events, he smiled and said one word: "Shrimp." Aaah! I should have known. I fished again that night, but with a brand-new box stuffed full of shrimp patterns, and things turned out a little different this time.

That was the turning point in my fly-fishing career. If it weren't for those shrimp, I'd probably still be spending my June nights on the Beaverkill instead of Lobsterville Beach. I found out that stripers can act like trout if they want to, and can be just as difficult to catch. Tying saltwater flies took on a new importance. Flies suddenly began to matter, and they were a lot more interesting than any variation of the Gold-Ribbed Hare's Ear. I began to tie strange-looking flies. Variations, hybrids, and mutants of standard saltwater fare. A few flies succeeded; most did not.

The flies I tie today range in style from Abrames to Popovics. When I tie a fly, I keep several important criteria in mind: It should catch fish; it shouldn't foul; it should be realistic looking; and it should emulate life. If I can meet these objectives with a fly that is easy to tie, great! If not, I don't mind spending a little longer on a better fly. Flies should not be taken for what they are but rather for what they should be. I am thankful to tiers like Bob Popovics, Jack Gartside, and Eric Peterson for pushing saltwater fly tying to its newest standard. Fish can be caught on a simple white bucktail, but that wouldn't be nearly as much fun, would it?

4   Skok's Baby Bunker

Hook	Eagle Claw 254SS, #3/0
Thread	White monocord, #3/0, and Dyneema or GSP thread for head
Belly	Polar-pearl Lite Brite dubbed on the bend, and also tied to the length of the finished fly
Wing	Two bunches of white bucktail separated by pearl Krystal Flash
Head	White deer belly, spun and trimmed to shape
Collar	Flash along the sides, color to suit; sparse white Streamer Hair on the bottom and sides; olive Streamer Hair on top
Eyes	Prismatic, #4.5EY
Dots	Pupils of prismatic eyes cut out with a small hole puncher

1. Start 3/0 monocord at the midway point of the hook shank and wrap half-way down the bend. Dub polar-pearl Lite Brite up to the point on the shank just above the barb. Tie in long, trailing strands of Lite Brite to the finished length of the fly. Tie in two bunches of white bucktail and pearl Krystal Flash the same length as the Lite Brite, encircling the hook shank. Tie off the 3/0 thread. Apply deep-penetrating superglue to all exposed thread wraps.

2. Start Dyneema or GSP thread at the tie-off point. Using several bunches of white deer belly hair, ceate a flared collar that encircles the hook shank 360 degrees. Use slightly longer bunches on the top and bottom, and be sure to leave the tapered tips of the deer hair intact. Spin white deer belly hair around the rest of the hook shank, taking care to leave an eye length bare for the head.

3. Using a tea kettle, steam the deer hair head of the fly. This will make trimming the deer hair a lot easier. Using either a double-edged razor blade or serrated scissors, trim the head to a slab-sided shape. Begin shaping the bottom of the fly first to ensure an adequate hook gap. Shave the sides next and fine-tune by trimming the head to a slope.

4. Restart the thread at the space directly behind the hook eye. Tie several strands of Flashabou-style pearlescent flash on each side, outside of which, tie in sparse amounts of white Streamer Hair on either side and under the belly. Tie in olive Streamer Hair over the back. Whip-finish and coat the head with deep-penetrating superglue.

5. Prepare prismatic eyes and back spots by peeling them off the backing. Apply GE Clear Household Sealant to the fly using your index finger. Start at the hook eye and work your way back to the point just above the end of the bend, but no farther. Care must be taken to push the silicone into the Streamer Hair and deer hair as deeply as possible. A simple surface coat of silicone will leave you with a one-fish fly. The eyes and dots are then applied with a second coat of silicone. The final step is to smooth out the second coat of silicone with Fotoflo 200. Let dry at least 24 hours before fishing.

1   Surf Candy Bay Anchovy

Bob Popovics

Hook	Eagle Claw 254SS, #2
Thread	Ultrafine clear monofilament
Body	Pearl Krystal Flash
Collar	Polar white Fly Fur on the bottom and sides; light blue and rust Fly Fur on top
Stripe	Silver Glimmer
Belly	Pearl holographic glitter applied when the first coat of epoxy is still tacky
Eyes	Prismatic, #2EY
Gills	Red and black Sharpie permanent markers

2   Bonito Deceiver

Lefty Kreh

Hook	Daiichi 25446 or Tiemco 811S, #2
Thread	White monocord, #3/0
Tail	Two thin white saddle hackles supported and flanked by short, sparse bunches of fine white bucktail or calf tail
Body	Pearl Krystal Flash
Wing	Sparse pearl Krystal Flash just longer than the hook shank
Collar	Sparse white bucktail on the bottom and sides, blue or green bucktail on top
Eyes	Prismatic, #1.5EY, covered with epoxy

In 1994 this fly landed one tier a world record 10.45-pound Atlantic bonito while fishing with Captain Steve Burnett at Watch Hill, Rhode Island.

3   Softbody Squid

Hook	Eagle Claw 254SS, #3/0
Thread	White monocord, #3/0
Body	White Mystic Bay Softbody Slider, colored ginger with black spots, threaded on the hook backward and glued in place over thread wraps
Tail	Ginger ostrich, ginger Flexi-Floss, two long thin ginger saddles, and purple Flashabou whipped together with thread and inserted and glued into a hole in the slider body
Fins	Orange mottled marabou spun in a dubbing loop and palmered over purple Estaz
Eyes	7.5-millimeter yellow animal eyes

Other good colors are white and red, white and chartreuse, white and orange, fluorescent pink, orange and chartreuse, and claret.

Ken VanDerlaske

In 1975 weakfish returned in great numbers to the Great South Bay on Long Island. With a rubber shrimp jig on a spinning rod, I drifted the deep channels, running my small boat from Babylon to Bayshore, and then south to Ocean Beach on Fire Island. My best discovery occurred under the Robert Moses Bridge.

The bridge linked the mainland to the barrier beaches and Jones Beach, and spanned the waters to the western end of Fire Island. Late one summer night, alone in the small skiff, I found myself hanging around the pilings of the bridge that runs through the flats of the bay then rises over the channel, allowing pleasure craft to glide under it. My attention was drawn to the section of the bridge descending low to the water. Along this stretch, overhead lights, strung a hundred yards apart, illuminated the water around the pilings. The glow of the lights revealed small baitfish and grass shrimp lurking beneath the surface. As I slowly motored along the footings of the bridge, I'd noticed random weakfish waiting in the current, using the structure to evade the tide and feed leisurely on the abundant bait drawn to the light source.

One evening, after much thought, I decided to try my eight-foot fiberglass 6-weight fly rod. I tied on a small freshwater streamer. On my second cast a weakfish drifted up and took the fly. Revelation!

Over the next decade I found I could cast a fly at saltwater game fish and succeed. My fly rod became my companion. Although I've owned a number of boats, I prefer to fish the surf. Born and raised on Long Island, I felt invariably drawn to Montauk Point and every fall since 1965 I've spent my weekends surf casting for stripers. I am a Montauk regular. Fishing keeps me at the water's edge from dusk to dawn.

Night fishing has always thrilled me, in particular the quest for the perfect spot. Fish swarm at the front of Montauk Point, but the site is accessible to everyone. Serious fishermen foraged the surrounding shores, searching for spots less popular with anglers. I'm elated when I find fish in places I've never tried now that I'm able to seek and catch stripers, bluefish, and weakfish. At times I come up empty handed, but learning the tides and developing a sense of timing I catch fish more often than not.

The return of the weakfish has been a godsend. For a few years the waters teemed with them, and they were relatively easy to catch on a fly.

In 1979 the striper population reached a low point. I recall surf casting hard for seven weekends at Montauk without landing a single fish. The regulars huddled on the beach at night were wondering what was happening to the fishery. As fall slid into November, many of us grew discouraged. A couple of friends departed to try their luck on Martha's Vineyard, seven miles off the coast of Massachusetts. I was skeptical. Fish are migratory and should have distributed themselves along the entire coast of the Northeast rather than congregating in one or two places. I was wrong. Maybe the sizes of the schools were reduced, but the reports I received from my friends Howard Gaber and Ron Hall let me know they'd encountered excellent results surf casting on the Vineyard.

It was too late to plan a trip in the fall of 1979; the season was over. I marked my calendar to travel to the island in 1980, and the following September I arrived to try my luck both surf casting and fly fishing. I rented a small cabin in picturesque Chilmark and set out to see what all the fuss was about.

Many times I heard whispered the names of great fishing spots: Wasque, Menemsha, Lobsterville, Mink Meadows, and, most of all, Squibnocket. My first foray yielded a couple of small bluefish. Still relying on surf casting, I was disappointed when I failed to reel a striper from Vineyard waters. Yet one of my friends, Ed Rodell, pulled a twenty-five-pound bass from the rocks at Squibnocket. That was all I needed: Ed's success inspired a second trip.

Ed and I returned in early November and Lady Luck slipped me a wild card. My first striper on the Vineyard weighed in at sixty pounds! This enormous catch shimmering on the midnight sands marked a turning point in my life. I forfeited my weekend trips to Montauk and instead made regular sojourns to the Vineyard.

It was a heady time, when twenty-pound fish were common and a fisherman would be hard put to find one smaller. One October day, at dawn on Chappaquiddick, I landed my first twenty-five-pound striper on a fly. I can still recall the thrill of standing waist deep in water, fly rod arced to the max, with the glow of first light spreading pink over the eastern horizon. Once again I was seized with the significance of the moment. In those days fishing with a fly rod was still a relatively unconventional way to pursue the sport. Yet on the Vineyard, I got to know a handful of aficionados: Kib Bramhall, Cooper Gilkes, Bruce Pratt, Arnold Spofford, and Roberto Germani. I found myself leaning in their direction.

The following fall brought more surprises. A Long Island buddy, Paul Sharpe, and I arrived on the Vineyard for a three-night weekend. (*Night* is the operative word here—days were reserved for sleeping.) Paul had been my constant fishing partner at Montauk. His ability as a fisherman was bolstered by his never-say-die attitude and his eternal belief in one last cast. Like me, Paul still fished with both surf and fly rods. During that same mid-October weekend, Howard Gaber and Ron Hall joined our ranks, both accomplished fishermen equally at home with surf and fly rods.

Come Saturday, reports of fish were dismal. That night, Paul, with surf stick in hand, ventured off to Squibnocket in search of a big bass. I wandered the open beach near Gay Head, and it was there that I bumped into Howard. We chatted about our prospects for finding fish that weekend, and he told me he was en route to a sandbar that had proved productive the week before. We parted ways, Howard to his sandbar, I to ramble along the edge of the water. The surf was tranquil as it glittered in the moonlight, and I contented myself with stopping every thirty yards to make a cast or two or three.

Along the lip of the beach I saw something. A fish? I had my doubts. I dumped my surf bag and surf rod on the beach. Gripping my fly rod, I strolled back to the spot, stopping just six feet short of it. I saw a weakfish. Could it be sick or injured? It sat there parallel to the beach, right-side up in ten inches of water. It was too absurdly close to shore to cast to it. I slowly reached out with my fly rod and touched the tail of the fish. In a flash it spooked, shimmering off into the sea. I stood alone in the fog. Were there more? I made a cast. Nothing. I cast again and again. Zero! Reluctant to leave, I tried a different approach. I cast out the line and chose not to retrieve it. I waited until I felt that the black Deceiver may have settled to the bottom. I began to strip and *bang!*—I was on to an eight- or nine-pound weakfish.

After the fish made its initial long run it gave up, and I slid it onto the beach. I took some moments to admire it as I removed the fly and slipped the fish back into the wash. I wondered if this was the same fish I had glimpsed before.

For the next cast I followed the new method: Count to ten, start to strip, then *bang!* on again. I caught five more before Howard returned from the sandbar to see what was up. He made a cast with his surf rod and hooked up immediately. He lamented the fact that he hadn't brought along his fly rod.

The next afternoon Paul and I sat in the cottage and hatched a plan for the evening. We were serious fishermen, both of the same mind-set. October meant striped bass. If you looked for them, you found them. We knew what we had to do: Leaving our spinning rods at home, we would return to my spot in Gay Head, fly rods at the ready.

After dark we headed out in search of Howard's sandbar. The trek runs a little over a mile, not a bad walk if you fish along the way. Our plan was to head directly to the bar, then slowly wend our way back.

A light northwest breeze flattened the water. With the wind at our backs, we waded out to the bar and fished the edges. We worked it thoroughly for a couple of hours without a touch, a sign of bait, or any activity whatsoever. We meandered down the beach experimenting with a spot here, a spot there, then moving on to the next bump—a bump being the smallest point of sand before an outcropping of rocks. We came finally to a small cove where the tide moved strongly to the west. Perfectly contained, it resembled a salmon pool.

Paul hooked up first. I reeled in and approached him to watch. He backed up out of the wash, fly rod doubled over and pulsing with the first long run of the fish. At last the fish tired and Paul started retrieving line or, should I say, backing line, lots of it! We both believed we had found the weakfish from the night before. As the fish neared the beach, I shined a light out about fifteen feet. A striper of twenty-five or thirty pounds slithered toward the shore.

As I turned to congratulate Paul, the fish wandered off! It wasn't Paul's fish, but instead one of who knows how many that were currently feeding on the pencil-size sand eels along that cove. Paul's fish finally emerged: a twenty-seven-pound bass.

We hooted, howled, and slapped each other on the back. In those days we killed the fish, at least the larger ones, so now we dispatched it and buried it in the sand. Moments later a jeep bounced by, and we were glad the fish was out of sight. Again we cast, hoping for one more great fish. I hooked up next. It didn't feel like much. The fish had picked up my black Deceiver close to the beach. I stood, rod bent, line tight to the fish. Aside from a little head thrashing, the creature barely stirred. Whatever it was it was small, had to be.

Paul and I conferred, and we decided that I should apply pressure to the fish to see what it might do. It responded with its first long run. I felt comfortable with a 12-pound-test leader and a 30-pound shock tippet. This fish had no trouble running up the tide. After ten minutes or so I could feel the first impulse of weakening. When the fish spilled into the wash, Paul gaffed it and slid it up onto the dry sand. It weighed over forty-three pounds.

I was jubilant! After more hollers and pounds on the back, we returned to casting into the dark. We tried to reproduce what we had done before. Once again Paul succeeded, hooking and landing a twenty-five-pound fish.

That night, everything I had learned about surf casting died and was reborn as fly fishing.

I took stock of my life. At that time in the early 1980s other partners and I owned and operated a large wallpaper manufacturing company. Divorced, in my early forties, I was passionate for fishing, and I fished a lot. I decided to invest even more energy in what I truly loved. My business allowed me to take time off and, accordingly, for two months every fall I rented a cottage on Martha's Vineyard. Island life and island fishing reeled me in. Thanks to tips from Howard and Ron, I caught my first bonito on a fly. A year later I hauled in my first false albacore. At that time I knew of no other place where these great fish could be caught from the shore.

In the fall of 1985, a great school of bluefish moved into the Lobsterville Beach area. It was phenomenal. The school stretched from Menemsha to the Gay Head Lighthouse, a distance of several miles. Their movements were languorous. Rather than race around and crash bait, they lay low and picked off the millions of sand eels to be found that year along the shore.

For five weekends in a row, I caught bluefish weighing in at anywhere from ten to twenty pounds. On a good day it was not uncommon to land a couple of seventeen-pound-or-larger fish. On the first day of that incredible run of fish, I met Roberto Germani.

Roberto was a great fisherman and a flamboyant individual. He fished bonito from his small canoe. He had a fly he tied for bonito called the Mary Magdalene. A still more successful tie he dubbed Mary Magdalene with Make-Up. I wanted a Mary Magdalene of my own. In 1992 Roberto died, leaving behind a legacy of catch-and-release, a program he had helped to make popular.

I was still living on Long Island when I met Lori. It was almost irrelevant that she happened to be beautiful, blond hair halfway down her back, because, on the evening we met, we found we had fishing in common. She told me that, in the company of her father and grandfather, she had fished from her childhood to the present day. Our first dates, more often than not, turned into fishing excursions.

One evening in June we traveled up to the north shore of the Long Island Sound. Lori, in waders, held a one-handed spinning rod with a small floating Rebel lure. I stood nearby and watched. The sun sank beneath the horizon, streaking the sky with brilliant red and orange. Slowly darkness crept in, and so did the stripers. Fish surrounded us. Although I'd enjoyed this experience before, it was new to Lori. She felt a few tugs and grabs at her line, but she wasn't hooking up. It didn't matter. She was mesmerized by the fish swimming so close to us.

We had discovered the fish and now we tried to fool them. At last a small fish grabbed the lure. After a few runs, Lori landed her first striped bass. Charged with excitement, she pulled in fish after fish. With each solid hookup she let out a scream. At the end of the evening she turned to me and said, "I don't care if we ever go to dinner, or a movie, or any other social event, just as long as we can fish together."

I had found the girl of my dreams.

For the next two seasons I fished the fly rod and Lori fished the spinning rod. I found it unusual that she showed no curiosity about the fly rod, but instead kept on fishing her own tried-and-true way.

One fall at Lobsterville Beach, a huge school of bluefish invaded the shallows, turning the water black with their presence. I handed Lori my fly rod. She protested that it was too complicated. I assured her that all she needed to do was have the fly hit the water. On her first cast, twenty fish turned for the fly; one strip and she was on. She landed and released that fish, then cast again. Another fish on, and so it went. Lori was a fly fisher.

The year 1989 was pivotal for me. I left my business and married Lori, two events that had nothing to do with one another, and yet coincided in a way that was to further change our lives. For the next 3½ years we stayed purposefully unemployed, living in my home in Sayville, Long Island, fly-fishing both shores. We took extended trips to Florida and Martha's Vineyard.

Lori's newfound enchantment with fly fishing combined with her uncanny ability to locate fish. On many occasions she surprised me with a technique that would dupe a fish into taking her fly. Often she wandered to a spot that I might have overlooked, and before I could spirit her farther down the beach, without warning she would land a fish. Before long she became her own angler. Effortlessly she could read the water, present the fly, then reel in and release the fish. Frequently on the Vineyard she would suit up and wander off alone to work the beach under the stars. She had honed her senses—sight, sound, and feel—to locate stripers at night.

In her quest to catch her first bonito or false albacore, Lori sought help from the great Roberto Germani and Red Herter. These two men had the ingenuity and persistence to develop their own methods for hooking great fish, Roberto from his tiny green canoe, and Red roll-casting from the Lobsterville jetty. These fishermen inspired Lori who finally, after two seasons, landed her first false albacore from the shore.

Every time Lori and I left the island, we found we couldn't wait to get back. More and more it seemed like a wonderful place to live. In 1992, we caved in to the inevitable and bought a house on the Vineyard.

The fishing season on Martha's Vineyard spans a full six months. Our move to the island put fishing at the top of our priority list. When in mid-May the fishing starts, we gravitate to the water. Wind and tides inform our daily conversation. As the water slowly warms, one fishing event breaks after the next. Schools of baitfish crowd the shoreline. Stripers appear, followed by large schools of bluefish. Over the past decade, the bluefish run has proved extremely predictable. Mid-June marks a striper invasion that makes for world-class fishing, inspiring scores of fly fishermen to congregate at night on the water's edge. Fabled Lobsterville Beach is the scene of blitzes that can last for six hours or more.

Nighttime anglers listen for the sound of stripers slowly sipping sand eels. Catching and releasing twenty fish a night is not unusual. On one unforgettable evening, Lori landed and delivered back into the sea ten stripers over three feet long. These are nights to dream about through the long chilly winters.

The heat of summer brings schools of bonito close enough to shore to make it feasible to seek them there, though by and large most of them are still caught by fly fishermen casting from a boat. The Vineyard's bonito run is variable. Water temperature and the amount of bait in the area both come into play, determining whether the bonito run will be great or merely fair.

Cool September breezes coincide with the exodus of tourists. This is the time we watch for the advent of the first false albacore, aka little tunny. For a fly fisherman in the Northeast, this could be the most exciting game fish. An albie over ten pounds is capable of a 250-yard run. These fish are true testers of tackle.

The late fall brings with it the return of schools of bass and bluefish. Trophy fish cruise the shoreline. The season's largest stripers and bluefish are generally caught at this time. Last October, Lori, led by a vision that came to her in a dream, sallied off on her own to a quiet, favorite spot, a spot she'd mentioned to me on numerous occasions. Alone in the night she hooked and landed an eighteen-plus-pound bluefish. The fish qualified for a new fly-rod record on 20-pound test.

We're both grateful we made the decision to move here. To fish in the place where we live seems to us one of life's miracles. Our wish is that this bliss continues.

We'll see you when you get here!

---

2   The Natural—Double Wing

Hook	Mustad 34007, #4
Thread	Olive unwaxed, #3/0
Tail	Four natural badger saddle hackles, each 3 to 3½ inches; gold Flashabou
Body	Gold mylar tinsel (braided)
Wing	¼-inch clumps of natural brown bucktail, ½ inch long
Throat	Red calf tail
Eyes	Enamel paint, black on yellow

1. Wind the thread from ⅛ inch behind the eye of the hook to a point above the end of the barb.

2. Secure the four tail feathers Deceiver-style. Add three or four strands of gold Flashabou.

3. Attach gold mylar body material by starting at the rear of the hook and winding forward. Cover the rear one-third of the hook and stop. Tie in the first wing (natural bucktail), then continue winding until two-thirds of the hook is covered with gold mylar. Add the second wing, then continue winding gold mylar to ⅛ inch from the eye of the hook.

4. Add a small bunch (1/16 inch) of red calf tail for the throat.

5. Tie off the head, paint the eyes, and apply clear-coat.

---

1   Calftail Deceiver

Hook	Tiemco 800S, #4
Tail	Four white hackles; four to six strands of pearl Krystal Flash
Body	Gold tinsel
Wing	White calf tail or white bucktail
Throat	White and red calf tail
Eyes	Mylar silver with black pupils. Coat the head with cement or epoxy

This pattern is simply a small, slim white Deceiver. It can be deadly on false albacore.

---

3   Worm Fly

Hook	Mustad Salmon, #4
Tail	Four red hackles 1½ inches long; four strands of red Krystal Flash
Body	Red saddle hackle. Tie it in at the base of the tail, with the tip of the feather trailing off the rear of the fly. Tie in red chenille and wrap from the rear to ¼ inch from the eye. Tie off. Palmer the red hackle forward and tie off. Add in front of this three wraps of olive chenille. Tie off neatly. Cement the head.

I like using a salmon iron on this fly because of its strength.

	1
	2
	3

At the bottom of the color plate of Ken VanDerlaske's flies is one of his hand-painted striped bass pins.

Bob Veverka

My life has been centered on fishing as long as I can remember. I have had good days fishing, great days fishing, and days I don't care to remember. I'm thankful for it all. I have made some of my living tying flies and giving fly-tying classes since 1980.

I have tried all types of fishing and fly fishing gives me the greatest pleasure. I remember the first fly rodder I ever saw. It was on the Little Beaverkill in upstate New York. Several years later I caught my first trout in that same spot—as clear in my mind as if it happened yesterday, it happened thirty years ago. I like to think that some young fly fisher is getting his or her start in the same spot that brought me to where I am today.

I remember when I first fished in salt water. I was a young boy, not even in my teens. My aunts had summer houses (bungalows) on the Jersey Shore. It was on Raritan Bay just inside Sandy Hook, a popular spot to fish. I had a spinning outfit with a Mitchell 300 reel and a fishing survival kit given to me by a relative. The kit was made of canvas that folded up and had sections for various fishing items: knife, ruler, line, hooks, sinkers, and a few metal-headed tuna feathers all hooked up to steel leaders. It is one of those things that you wish you still had today. I used to fish with two buddies, Billy and Gregory, who had eight-foot prams with small outboards. We would travel a mile out to a set of nets used to catch bunker and there we would troll our lures, me with my feathers and they with their surgical tubes. I had better luck than they did and caught bluefish in the two- to five-pound range. The blues put up quite a fight on that light tackle. I did very well until all my feather lures were busted off on fish. I didn't understand drag settings at the time. When I returned home from summer vacation my reel did not work the same. I removed the side plate of my Mitchell 300 and the gears looked like I'd turned them down with a grinder.

No gears left at all! That started my fishing for bluefish, striped bass, and weakfish on light spinning gear.

I began to fly-fish in salt water thirty years ago on Shinnecock Canal on eastern Long Island. In a time filled with long nights of fishing for weakfish, bluefish, and striped bass, our main target was the weakfish, which had returned after many years of a down cycle. Actually the first time we caught one we were not even sure what we had; we'd never seen them before. Each year we fished them they grew a pound or two until they were up to thirteen pounds. I desperately tried to get them on my fly rod while my friends attacked them with light spinning rods and a rubber shrimp called the Salty Dog. I averaged one fish to their twelve. More than once I heard, "Why are you wasting your time with that fly rod?" It was a time of excess, with fish everywhere, and in my mind a time to experiment. My fly at the time was a tuft of orange marabou tied to a hook. I wish I had the flies back then that I have today. I know I would have been much more productive. There are times I feel that a fly can outfish conventional gear. You can match small baitfish, spearing, sand eels, and bunker much better with a fly.

During the late 1970s the saltwater fishing where I lived on Long Island was at an all-time low. It was time to find some new fishing grounds. In 1980 I had the urge to move to the mountains where I spent countless hours perfecting flies of all types—trout, landlocked salmon streamers, steelhead Speys and Atlantic salmon, and occasionally some saltwater flies. (With seven months of winter, you have plenty of time to tie flies.) At that time I fished for trout, Atlantic salmon, and steelhead during the summer, with trips to Canada, the Pacific Northwest, and many places in between. I enjoyed all types of fishing, but my mind always returned to those long summer nights of fishing in the salt. I yearned for those times to return. During the late 1980s, I saw some new patterns being developed for saltwater fly fishing, and the fishing on the coast was starting to come back.

Almost all my fishing now takes place somewhere in salt water—striped bass fly fishing from the coast of Maine to the Chesapeake Bay in Maryland, flats and offshore fishing in the Florida Keys, and bluewater fly fishing in Baja, Mexico.

There are many things that draw me to salt water. The fish tend to be bigger, more powerful, faster, wilder, and meaner, and all have the ability to take you well into your backing and beyond. I have many memories and images etched in my mind. I love the sunrises and the anticipation of what the day will bring and what I'll encounter out on the water. There is always the chance that it will be something we have not experienced before. Like the first experience with a species of fish I have not caught before. Or the sudden jolt at the end of the line, then the snap of the leader that leaves me with the thought, What the hell was that, and how big? Or the sight of a large flash with a washtub boil behind my fly for a split second, never to return. Or the anticipation of finding out what is on the end of my line after a long, powerful battle where the fish doesn't show until you get it to the beach or boat.

Then there are the spectacular sunsets, which for some is the beginning of their fishing. There's the nervous anticipation waiting for the fish to show that only come out at night. I have seen many things on the salt water that I would never have seen anywhere else. I've watched in awe as the baitfish on the south shore of Long Island's surf were jumping out of the water onto the beach to get away from the marauding bluefish that had them pinned against the shore. Bluewater fly fishing in the Florida Keys, I had my first blackfin tuna bit in half by a large barracuda while I was reeling it in. As we brought the tuna aboard, I watched the 'cuda follow it up with its menacing eyes searching, then slowly head for the depths. It was an awesome sight. Watching a school of tarpon coming across a flat in three to four feet of gin-clear water, or seeing a billfish all lit up, its tail churning, fin-up out of the water with its bill slashing at your fly, or watching a large school of flying fish lift off the water with greyhounding dorado in hot pursuit will burn an image in your mind that will last a lifetime. These are some of the many things that keep me going down to the sea in search of entertainment. So fish hard, have fun, and release most of your catch to fight another day.

Flies

Most of the flies I tie for saltwater fly fishing are baitfish imitations. When you're tying flies to represent baitfish, everything should be tied on in a way to keep the fly balanced, and a lot of thought must be put into how the fly will swim in the water. When a fly is balanced, it should track in the water. Reacting to the slightest touch of the rod, your fly should naturally flow when you turn it in any direction. I like my fly to carry most of its weight up front so it takes a natural dive on a slack line.

I put a lot of thought about size, shape, color, action, durability, and castability into my patterns. I feel size is the most critical element. I have seen fish refuse flies that were an inch longer than the baitfish they were feeding on. I try to make my flies the same size as the natural I am trying to represent.

I also try to shape my flies to resemble the naturals I'm trying to imitate. Some baitfish have wide profiles, and I feel that if you can incorporate this shape into your fly, all the better. I add epoxy to the front of my flies and arrange the materials into the shape I want as the epoxy sets.

Most of my baitfish patterns are tied in very subdued colors. I try to match the natural. Most baitfish have light-colored sides with a darker-colored back. Blues, greens, olives, and some almost black on top. Their sides usually have slight hues of pink and purple, which can be added to a pattern. My patterns contain some white on the sides and bottom, with darker backs. I use silver and pearl Fire Fly (Flashabou) to add some flash to my flies. I don't add a lot of flash to my patterns. A little goes a long way; I add just enough to catch their attention. Most of the areas I fish have crystal-clear water and at times too much flash can be negative—it just doesn't look natural.

I like both natural and most synthetics for tying saltwater flies, although I prefer to use natural materials, because I feel they have a superior action to synthetics. Natural materials are not as durable but except for the real toothy fish, such as barracudas, bluefish, and the mackerel family, most hold up fairly well. Still, some of the new synthetics are great. You can make all kinds of attractive, precise flies using them. One of my favorites is craft fur, which I use on small baitfish patterns and bonefish flies. When wet, it is translucent, a quality I look for in materials.

Bucktail is one of the most important materials used in tying baitfish patterns. Its natural color white can be dyed any color. Today many use synthetics in place of bucktail—FisHair, Big Fly Fiber, and so on. They are very durable and come in a wide array of colors, but they lack the natural taper that bucktail has, a quality that I like in my baitfish patterns.

For larger baitfish patterns or billfish flies, I like to use Yak hair, as you can get it in lengths up to 16 inches. It has translucent fibers that can be dyed any color or can be tinted with marking pens.

I like to use materials that breathe in the water and have lots of action. Marabou fits this category. Many flies use marabou, which is plentiful and can be dyed any color you desire. Used on baitfish patterns in the wing and tail, nothing else pulsates like it. When a fly is tied with marabou the slightest current will put it into action and it looks alive.

Rabbit fur is another material that has incredible action in the water. It's as close to marabou as you can get, and some of its natural colors match the grays, tans, and browns we need. Many bonefish patterns use rabbit fur in strips on the hide or tied in in bunches, and streamer flies incorporate it in the wing and tail. The only drawback is when it is used in large flies: When wet, it can be very heavy to cast.

Saltwater flies should be built as durable as possible. Some saltwater fish have wicked teeth, and long continuous casting can beat flies to death. The saltwater environment itself is harsh with its rocks, coral, and barnacles. There is nothing more annoying than flies that come apart. I tie my flies to be durable but not to the point where they lose their action. It's a trade-off, but I will put up with a less durable fly if it has the action I want.

A fly that tail wraps when cast can be very frustrating. I have never had a fish take a fly that was tail wrapped and not swimming true. I try to tie most of the action in my flies at the tail, and I always tie these materials in at the back of the hook. The shape I want is the front of the fly shielding the tail and helping avoid tail wrapping.

I always add eyes to my baitfish patterns. I feel, as many do, that game fish target that area of the fly. Eyes on flies are an attractor in themselves.

I always tie my flies to the leader with some type of loop knot; it tends to give the fly more action. Almost all my patterns are tied to represent the baitfish that the game fish I'm after are feeding on. My striped bass flies are tied to match sand eels, silversides, bunker, herring, and squid. My flats flies are tied to match shrimp and crabs, and my offshore patterns are tied to match sardines, flying-fish, and mackerel.

My flies are continually evolving and I make additions to patterns as I feel they are needed.

14	Marabou Sand Eel
Hook	Tiemco 811S, #2
Thread	Monofilament
Tail	White bucktail; silver and pearl Fire Fly; tuft of marabou
Body	Pearl braid, epoxied and tinted on top with an olive marking pen
Eyes	Witchcraft stick-on eyes, #2

1. Start the tying thread just behind the eye of the hook and wind it to the back of the hook, just above the point.

2. Tie in small bunch of white bucktail the same length as the hook shank. Tie in four strands of silver Fire Fly and four strands of pearl Fire Fly. Finally, tie in a tuft of olive marabou. White, chartreuse, or any other color marabou can also be used.

3. Tie down the butt ends of all materials and glue.

4. With the thread (mono) at the back of the hook, just above the point, slide on the pearl body braid cut to size, then wind the mono forward over the braid and tie off at the head of the fly.

5. Place on the eyes.

6. Epoxy the entire fly body and place it in a rotary until dry.

7. Tint the top of the body with an olive marking pen.

1	Braid Bay Anchovy—1
Hook	Tiemco 800S, #2
Thread	Monofilament
Tail	Pearl and copper Krystal Flash
Body	Pearl E-Z Bodi-Braid
Eyes	Witchcraft, black on silver. #2
Head	Epoxy

2	Braid Bay Anchovy—2
Hook	Tiemco 800S, #1
Tail	Tuft of marabou
Body	White ½-inch Corsair, stretched; doubled holographic foil, slid inside body material
Eyes	Witchcraft, black on silver, #2
Head	Epoxy

3	Braid Craft Fur Sand Eel
Hook	Tiemco 800S, #1 or 2
Thread	Monofilament
Tail	Gold craft fur; pearl Fire Fly; olive craft fur on top
Body	¼-inch pearl E-Z Bodi-Braid. This must extend past the hook bend
Eye	Witchcraft, black on silver, #2
Head	Epoxy

4	Braid Silverside
Hook	Tiemco 800S, #1 or 1/0
Tail	Olive Flashabou
Body	Pearl E-Z Bodi-Braid
Belly	Silver foil
Eyes	Witchcraft, black on silver, #2
Head	Epoxy

5	Braid Ballyhoo
Hook	Tiemco 800S, #4/0
Tail	Hackle with the tip of the stem cut out, or a tuft of gray marabou
Body	½-inch white Corsair tubing; silver holographic foil
Eye	Witchcraft, silver on black, #4
Head	Epoxy

Color the top of this fly blue-black; the beak, red.

6	Braid Sardine
Hook	Tiemco 800S, #2/0 to 3/0
Tail	Hackle with the tip of the stem cut out, or a tuft of gray marabou
Body	½-inch white Corsair; silver holographic foil
Eyes	Witchcraft, silver on black, #4
Head	Epoxy

When tying Braid Flies I use Corsair or E-Z Bodi-Braid material for the body, then add to it. I preshape the braid material to the general shape of the baitfish I wish to duplicate. Size and length are very important.

I taper both ends of the braid to make it easier to tie in. Then I feed the hook through the braid and set the hook in the vise. Now is the time to feed your body colors. I use various colors of Flashabou to accent the colors of baitfish I wish to duplicate: silver, pearl, and various shades of olive. Then I tie off the head and tail to lock in the body colors. The fly is done except for shading the top with marking pens, and adding eyes and an epoxy head.

7	Braid Sand Eel
Hook	Tiemco 800S, #2
Tail	Silver Fire Fly
Body	¼-inch clear Corsair
Eyes	Witchcraft, black on silver, #2
Head	Epoxy

Tint the top of this fly with an olive marking pen.

```
          8
          9
   11        10
   13        12
          14
```

8	Ballyhoo
Hook	Mustad 34007, #4/0
Tail/Wing	Long white goat hair;, holographic tinsel; two 6-inch-long white marabou plumes
Topping	Long olive Icelandic goat hair shaded on top with a purple waterproof marking pen
Cheeks	Pearlescent dubbing
Eyes	Green with black pupils

I use this fly when trolling from one spot to another, and also when I need a larger pattern than my sardine.

9	Mackerel
Hook	Tiemco 811S, #2/0 to 8/0
Tail	White bucktail, pearl Fire Fly, two white hackles, two green hackles, two purple hackles
Throat	White goat hair
Front wing	Two green hackles, two blue hackles, two purple hackles
Sides	Two grizzly hackles
Eyes	Black on silver Witchcraft

10	Baby Bunker
Hook	Tiemco 811S, #1
Tail	Pink and white bucktail with silver holographic tinsel; white marabou; pearlescent Fire Fly
Body	Opalescent braid
Throat	White goat hair
Wing	Blue bucktail with black goat hair on top
Sides	Pintail
Eyes	Silver with black pupils

I use this fly when I'm fishing for striped bass in the Northeast. At times large schools of juvenile bunker invade the Northeast, and striped bass and other game fish feed heavily on them. Such fish can be very selective; you need a fly that matches the naturals as closely as possible, especially in size.

11	Capt. Crabby
Hook	Mustad 34007, #4
Thread	Tan
Tail	Pearl flash; small tuft of marabou
Claws	Brown variant hackles, splayed
Body	Corsair tubing
Legs	Rubber hackle
Eyes	Burned monofilament
Weight	Dumbbell eyes

12	East Cape Anchovy
Hook	Mustad 34007, #1/0
Tail	White bucktail; white marabou; pearl Fire Fly
Body	Opalescent braid
Throat	White bucktail
Top	Olive bucktail topped by gray bucktail darkened on top with a blue waterproof pen
Sides	Baitfish side ribbing
Eyes	Silver with black pupils
Head	Epoxy sides and head

13	Ginger Squid
Hook	Tiemco 811S, #1/0 to 3/0
Thread	Tan
Tail	Long, narrow grizzly hackles; brown ear pheasant hackle wound as a collar, tan or gray, very webby; tuft of tan marabou
Eyes	Glass taxidermist eyes
Body	Ginger-tan dubbing

Lani Waller

The guy who really got me excited about salt water is a friend and expert named Frank Bertaina. At one time, we worked together selling worldwide fishing trips from an office in Santa Rosa that he ran with his partner, Bob Nauheim, another well-known and well-traveled angler. It was here in the early 1980s that Frank persuaded me to take a break from steelhead fishing and give the salt a try.

In 1983 the two of us took a trip to the Bahamas for bonefish. It was my first trip and I fell in love with the salt and its special beauty. I realized it was, in many ways, the most challenging casting and angling I could ever hope for.

I learned from Frank what it meant to be prepared and to always be ready for anything. Amazing things can and do happen fast. If you are not ready, you'll miss what will never be repeated. Frank is an expert at being prepared and can launch a cast faster than anyone I have ever fished with.

In the years since then, I have focused my inshore angling on the waters of Belize, which have some of the greatest permit, bonefish, and tarpon fishing in the world, and the only real classic sight-fishing possibilities for tarpon outside of the Florida Keys. The bonefish there are very large despite rumors to the contrary, and the permit fishing cannot be surpassed.

This fishing has become very popular now with my customers and clients. Many of them accompany me each year to the flats of Belize and the Yucatán Peninsula. We fish there for all the major inshore species—permit, tarpon, bonefish, barracuda, snapper, and so on.

I began offshore fly fishing in 1985, on trips to the Baja Peninsula. Like most other anglers I started with dorado, then eventually went on to tuna and bonito, and finally to sailfish and marlin. I lead many groups there, even providing all their fly-fishing tackle and equipment, and it is still one of my most popular destinations.

I have always been interested in floating lines and surface fishing, and in 1984 I first saw one of George "Chappie" Chapman's beautiful handmade cork poppers, featuring an amazing overlay of pearlescent mylar tubing laminated to the body. George's flies are so beautiful I won't fish them, and I still have some of the originals.

I felt that Chappie had found the perfect finish and appearance for a surface fly, but I decided to try to improve upon it—to simplify the construction to save time and effort without sacrificing effectiveness.

At the same time, another friend, Tom Eggler of the Gaines Popper Company, was making superbly painted poppers with carefully air-brushed, two-tone finishes. One day, as a lark, I slid some mylar tubing over one of Tom's blue-and-white poppers and saturated it with five-minute epoxy. The effect was incredible.

Suddenly I had a popper body that shimmered as effectively as the real thing, with all the multicolored, scalelike effects of a baitfish. I experimented with other factory colors from Gaines and eventually settled on two favored combinations: blue over white and black over yellow. I kept the discovery to myself and a few close friends and began fishing these poppers everywhere I went in the salt. Since then I have added other colors.

Any popper can fool a fish if you keep it moving, because the surface disturbance covers any defects in the fly and makes it impossible for a feeding game fish to really get a good look. The moment of truth comes when your fly pauses between strips, or when it is at rest. At those moments it is very vulnerable, and its flaws are obvious.

The mylar-covered poppers remained relatively effective even during these times and I found myself with a fly that dorado, tuna, sailfish, tarpon, barracudas, trevally, striped bass, and snappers would slam even when it was barely moving or when it was sitting still between strips.

I remember one day in Baja when a friend had cast to a trio of big bull dorado we had chummed close to the boat. All three of the fish followed his streamer as he worked it all the way back to the side of the panga, but none would take the fly.

All three fish just sat there, four feet from the side of the skiff, lit up and flashing neon colors of blue, green, and gold. My friend didn't have time to change flies and was giving the fish a look that I thought should have killed them anyway. I didn't know what to do, but simply flopped my mylar popper over the side of the boat, suspended on a five-foot leader.

I didn't have enough line or leader to retrieve the popper and it just sat there in front of the three dorado, with the pearlescent mylar tail quivering in the blue water and the shimmering body looking like a baitfish.

All three dorado rushed the motionless popper at once, throwing a bomblike explosion of water into the boat and scaring the hell out of the panga captain, who thought this was the work of the Devil himself.

Later that week George Cook, who was working at Kaufmann's at the time, came down as I was leaving and I gave him a few of my new mylar poppers. He used one to take a very large bull dorado, and continued to hook many fish on that trip with the green-and-yellow version.

On another occasion I was using the popper for sailfish, trying to find out if they would take the Gaines 3-inch, #2/0 popper with the mylar overlay. From out of nowhere, four sails came in at once, two from port and two from starboard, slashing at the teasers and ripping

the prop wash into a boiling cauldron of foamy whitewater. Everyone on the boat was screaming and jumping up and down in a well-intentioned display of frenzy that ended with the captain holding the fly rod and popper, as my companion and I tried to clear three teaser lines at once.

Never having held a fly rod in his hands before, yet recognizing the need for instant action of some kind, the captain threw the popper and ten feet of fly line at one of the sailfish that had decided to stick around for the madness. The popper landed in the middle of the spaghettilike coils of orange fly line, and the sailfish tried to spear the green-and-yellow floating pattern through the floating coils of line.

At that point my friend and I began fighting the captain for the rod. He was so mesmerized or confused that he could not, or would not, let go. I lost the battle for the fly rod. The sailfish stuck around for another second or two before leaving in a brilliant display of flashing colors that remained in my memory even after a six-pack of ice-cold Mexican beer, five enchiladas, and three margaritas.

I fished the popper for another five years, to make sure it was not a fluke. In 1988 or 1989, I slipped one to Lefty Kreh at Bob Marriott's fly-fishing fair in Los Angeles. Lefty flipped when he saw it and insisted I write about it before someone else picked up on the pattern. At the time it didn't matter to me and I just kept fishing it.

Two years later Ken Menard of Umpqua Feather Merchants saw a sample of the popper, and we signed an agreement to have them tie and distribute it. Umpqua now makes these poppers available at various fly shops across the country.

In 1989 or 1990, I took Trey Combs to my marlin haunts along the East Cape of Baja. He was working on his new, offshore saltwater fly-fishing book and we wanted to give the billfish there a whack at his poppers and techniques—including some teasing strategies Trey had picked up in Costa Rica.

On one trip we must have raised fifteen to eighteen billfish and ten to twelve blue marlin of around 200 to 230 pounds. We hooked about six of these, as I recall, and lost them all to the inevitable snapped leaders, pulled-out hooks, and so on. The thing I found most exciting was the way Trey's poppers pulled the fish from the teasers to the fly. I had never seen another pattern so effective. They even worked on blue marlin.

They were so effective I started making my own versions of them and now lend them to clients and friends. We take these poppers to the East Cape of Baja each season for striped and blue marlin and sailfish. Combining them with the smaller #2/0 mylar poppers, we take care of all our topwater fishing with two basic fly types.

My traditional streamer flies are usually simple blue, green, gray, or tan over white, and I add flash according to how I will fish them. If they are to be used with teasers or chummed bait, I add more flash, because a "hot" fish attacking a teaser or an excited fish coming in for the chum is less cautious than a fish that I cast to without teasing or chumming.

For example, my favorite dorado streamer has a tan-over-white Lefty's Deceiver type of dressing with just a few touches of flash. In my experience cautious dorado and tuna often shy away from a fly that has too much glitter or flash, unless they are teased or chummed into a frenzy. The tan back imitates the color of the baitfish we use as chum, a small fish called *sardinias.* In my opinion tan with a bright blue or green back is a much overlooked combination.

I believe that nature is not capricious or whimsical. Everything happens for a reason. I also believe that natural events are part of a pattern of survival that is universal. If you learn something in one part of the world, you may be sure it has a good chance of working in other parts of the world as well.

When a fish comes to a fly, no matter the species or location, it does so because the fly triggers part of its natural process: the desire to feed, to survive, or to compete against other predators. Even a curious non-feeding fish, rising out of instinct or habit, is behaving according to its nature.

After twenty years in the international fly-fishing travel business, I have seen many, many examples of this. In my travels I have often observed fish, all kinds of them, as they are feeding, or attacking, or both. There is nothing accidental or whimsical about it. After careful observation, you'll begin to see patterns you can count on, no matter where you are fishing.

I therefore always pay attention to how my fly fishes and what I think the fish perceives when it sees or hears the fly. I judge patterns by their size, shape,

---

4, 5	**Mylar Poppers**
Hook	Popper hook
Body	Edgewater popper colored green on the top and yellow on the bottom, overlaid with pearl Flashabou tubing left long, which forms a skirt, then epoxied
Eyes	7-millimeter doll eyes, black on white
Variation	Green, blue, and white

1. Cut a 5-inch length of large-diameter mylar piping and remove the core. Slip this over the popper from the hook end, until the piping is slightly past the head.

2. Using a toothpick, apply a small amount of five-minute epoxy around the head.

3. When the epoxy has hardened, pull the mylar piping back so that it is flush against the popper body.

4. Apply five-minute epoxy to the entire body—in effect extending the body.

5. Trim the mylar so that is extends about one body length past the body. Trim flush to the head.

6. Using five-minute epoxy, secure 7-millimeter doll eyes to each side.

Large and powerful game fish can straighten the long-shanked #2/0 hook used in these poppers.

---

light-absorbing or -reflecting properties, translucency, and action (including noise) in the water.

It matters little to me what the pattern or the fly materials. If the fly imitates life, or suggests life realistically, then it is a good fly. Issues of craftsmanship and traditional concepts of beauty are secondary. The issue to me is fish appeal.

1	**Sardinia**
Hook	Tiemco 800S, #2/0
Thread	Tan
Tail	White bucktail; four white saddle hackles; pearl Flashabou
Wing	White bucktail; two olive saddle hackles; olive bucktail
Sides	Pearl Flashabou and tinsel flash
Eyes	7-millimeter doll eyes, black on white

2	**Billfish Popper**
Hook	Mustad 9255S, #5/0 to 7/0, tied tandem
Body	Styrofoam popper head skirted with white bucktail, white saddle hackle, pearl Flashabou, and holographic Flashabou
Eyes	Doll eyes, black on white

3	**Billfish Fly**
Hook	Mustad 92553S, #5/0 to 7/0, tied tandem
Thread	White
Wing	Tied heavily with white bucktail, pearl Fire Fly, pearl Krystal Flash, white saddle hackles, white FisHair, green FisHair, green Krystal Flash, and holographic Flashabou
Belly	White bucktail and pearl Krystal Flash
Sides	Short, very fine chartreuse and red FisHair
Eyes	7-millimeter doll eyes, black on white

1 2
3
4
5

Bob Warren

For fly fishing, New England is the best place in the world. From the lakes and salmon streams of Maine to the quiet brook trout meadows of Massachusetts and the coastal fishery for stripers, blues, and sea-run trout, New England has a lifetime's worth of fly fishing. My first flies were bucktails and streamers for northern New England trout and landlocked salmon. From that beginning in the 1950s I have spent time at the vise searching for productive patterns for trout, bass, Atlantic salmon, and, most recently, the saltwater species found in New England coastal waters.

The varied coastal fishery from Connecticut to Maine, and especially Cape Cod and the Islands, has placed fly fishing the salt high on my list. I've done much of this fishing with minimal expense for equipment. Wading can be very productive. So can casting from a boat. I've had good fishing from all types, from canoes to fifty-foot sportfisherman craft.

My first encounters with striped bass and bluefish did not involve the fly rod, but like any other fishing, the challenge for the fly fisherman was there, and to meet it I needed fruitful imitations for the salt. The natural approach for me was to look back at the flies I used in fresh water and try to convert them for stripers and blues. My first attempts were not unlike bucktail jigs with no lead. From there the flies began to show the influence of proven freshwater patterns.

This type of fly has its roots in New England. Carrie Stevens tied a bucktail streamer for salt water using the so-called reverse-tied bucktail method—a style of tying in which the hair of choice is attached to the hook heading forward, then folded back and tied down.

The head is then saturated with cement. In the 1960s Keith Fulsner carried the style farther with his Thunder Creek series. Today his twenty-one patterns of baitfish use new materials such as mylar tubing for bodies and epoxy heads. The evolution of duplicating saltwater baitfish using new and different materials continues.

Material for saltwater flies should be, most of all, durable. Many synthetics meet this requirement, but I still prefer natural hair and feathers for their look and action in the water. I prefer Icelandic sheep hair to bucktail and many of the synthetics for creating the large silhouette sometimes needed to fool stripers. Most of my flies are winged with some combination of bucktail, polar bear, Icelandic sheep, marabou, and saddle hackle, with a small amount of synthetic for flash— Krystal Flash, Lite Brite, or FisHair. Eyes have come a long way from jungle cock and paint-ons. I've used glass, plastic, and prismatic stick-ons.

Saltwater species may not be as selective as trout but many times I have seen the fly make a difference. Size, shape, and color are important, probably in that order. I never underestimate the value of eyes on a baitfish imitation, because most fish will take larger bait head first.

Be careful selecting hooks. They should be strong enough to hold a large fish and sharp enough for good penetration. They may require barb and point sharpening to improve performance.

My favorite flies are variations of the bucktail. They have good action in the water and cast well with no fouling. I've found a green color combination to work best.

1	**Brown Shrimp**
Hook	Stainless, #1
Thread	White
Eyes	Monofilament, melted and dipped in epoxy
Antennae	Gray Ultra Hair; copper Krystal Flash; tan craft fur
Body	Dubbed tan craft fur
Legs	Brown-dyed palmered grizzly hackle
Back/Head	European brown squirrel tied over the body and epoxied along the back

1. Attach thread to a stainless hook and wind back to a point above the hook barb.

2. Select antenna material about twice the hook length and tie in each bunch, one over the other.

3. Attach the eyes along the top of the hook shank.

4. Tie in body hackle at the rear of the hook. Begin dubbing at the hackle and wind forward up the body. Palmer the hackle feather over the body.

5. Tie in squirrel tail over the top of the hook. Trim to form a tail, and whip-finish the head.

6. Epoxy the hair down along the top of the hook, taking care to keep the hackle pulled down and out of epoxy.

The best fishing results seem to come when this pattern is dressed quite sparsely.

2	**Broadsider**
Hook	Stainless, #4/0
Thread	White
Underwing	White bucktail and pearl Krystal Flash tied in at the back of the hook
Body	Pearl Axxel
Wing	White and gray Streamer Hair; green Fire Fly; fluorescent green and dark green Streamer Hair
Cheeks	Pintail flank
Eyes	Prismatic eyes coated with epoxy

3	**Generic Baitfish**
Hook	Stainless, #2
Thread	White
Underwing	White bucktail and pearl Krystal Flash tied in at the back of the hook
Body	Pearl Axxel with wing material over, epoxied
Wing	Fluorescent green Streamer Hair and Fire Fly; green Streamer Hair reverse-tied
Eyes	Prismatic eyes coated with epoxy

Of the many color combinations I have fished, this has been a consistent producer for bass and blues.

1
2
3

Mark Waslick

Fishing has always been a part of my life. Growing up, it seemed as though my father and I were constantly slipping away to go fishing somewhere, either to the neighborhood bluegill pond for a few hours or to a remote lake in Canada for a couple of weeks. While the fishing trips themselves were always great, whether we caught a lot or not, the times leading up to the trip were often just as exciting. I'd spend hours readying tackle, practicing casting, and reading everything I could about the spots we were going.

Back then, we used spinning gear almost exclusively. I really didn't know much about fly fishing at the time, but soon, that all changed. Going through my father's tackle box for yet another time in anticipation of an upcoming trip, I came across a small plastic box containing two trout dry flies. I was only in grade school but to this day, I remember finding those flies as clearly as if it happened yesterday. The moment I saw them, I knew that I had to learn to tie flies and, ultimately, to fly-fish.

Since I knew no one who tied flies or fly-fished, books and magazines were my teachers. I struggled for a long time, but eventually my tying and casting improved enough so that I could catch the trout and bass near home. I began feeling more comfortable with leaving the spinning gear at home, taking only my fly rod and flies.

And I anticipated the next trip. If I was planning a first trip to a new location, I would read all I could find about the water, techniques, and flies. I'd talk with anyone who claimed to know anything about the spot, whether he had been there or not. If this was to be a repeat visit, I'd try to improve on the flies I had used in previous trips. In either case, I'd arrive with many more flies than I could possibly use.

To this day, I carry enough flies for an army of anglers and very few are the same. Even across one size

of one pattern, each fly is a bit different, either in material, hook type, weight, or proportion. I'm constantly trying new ideas. If a fly doesn't work, I want to know why it doesn't work. If a fly catches fish, I want to know why it catches fish. In both cases, I'll probably change the flies a little, trying to improve them. I'm more intrigued with which flies will work when than I am with catching fish after fish. If I am catching fish on a certain fly, I'll change to something a little different, or maybe entirely different, just to see if it will work.

Living in Vermont, I don't fish in the salt frequently. Therefore, when I do make a trip to the salt, I bring many different flies and fly types with me so I can experiment. Many of my saltwater flies have evolved; they begin as ideas I want to try and over time and a number of trips they become more and more refined. The Sea Bait, Sea Popper, and Sea Slider flies developed this way.

A few years ago, I planned on making a trip to Loreto, Baja California, primarily to fish for the schools of dorado beneath the floating sargasso weed in the Sea of Cortez. Never having fished for dorado in the West, I contacted some friends who had, and read about fishing the Sea of Cortez. I learned that the successful flies imitated various baitfish, including flying fish, and that the guides who operated the open pangas often attracted schools of dorado by tossing live *sardinias* into the water. Although we would be fishing in the deeper blue water, the dorado were seldom far down in the water, preferring to gather near the surface close to the floating weeds. I was warned that my flies would take a beating because of the numbers of fish and their prominent teeth. Some people I had talked to avoided having their flies destroyed by constructing tube flies that slide up the leader and out of harm's way when a fish is hooked.

Among the many flies I brought with me on that trip to the Sea of Cortez were tube fly streamers, sliders, and poppers. During the ten days I spent there I was happy with the tube flies, catching dorado, tuna, and a twenty-five-pound roosterfish. When I returned home I continued to fine-tune, making them more lifelike and more durable. In their present form, the Sea Bait, Sea Slider, and Sea Popper have gone along on many more trips, and have taken a variety of species including stripers, bluefish, dorado, roosterfish, mackerel, record-size tuna, and billfish.

In the water, the Sea Baits do not look like most conventional flies tied on hooks. Because they are tied on tubes they are essentially hollow, trapping air and releasing bubbles throughout the retrieve. And while conventional flies appear opaque, the Sea Baits look more translucent, because light can pass into and through the fly, reflecting off the FisHair and Krystal Flash. To me, and I hope the fish, these flies look alive.

A variation of the Sea Bait that has worked well with beaked forage fish is the Sea Bait—Ballyhoo. During the winter months in the Florida Keys, ballyhoo show up in great numbers, with schools of game fish close behind. These are big baitfish, anywhere from seven inches to well over a foot in length. By tying imitations on tubes, I can create enough bulk and profile to accurately simulate the schooling ballyhoo while keeping the weight to a minimum, making casting a little easier and a lot less hazardous.

The Sea Sliders have proved to be the most versatile flies of the group. With a floating line they can be fished so they skip and jump like fleeing flying fish or, when fished more deliberately, leave a wake and distinct bubble trail similar to an injured baitfish. By switching to an intermediate or slow-sinking line, the Sliders can be made to dive beneath the surface and then rise during a pause in the retrieve. This effect can be varied by adjusting the leader length: Long leaders

allow the Slider to rise to the surface, and shorter leaders keep the fly suspended.

When a conspicuous bait is called for, the Sea Poppers are my favorite. Not subtle flies, these throw a lot of water and have a lot of flash—perfect for fishing the surf or in the wake of a boat pulling hookless teasers. In the right circumstances, they attract attention and draw aggressive strikes.

The flats of the Florida Keys and in Florida Bay are special places for fly fishermen. Each spring and summer, anglers from all over the world migrate here in hope of finding another migrant, the tarpon. Nowhere else are tarpon as accessible in the transparent water of the flats as they are here. Pure sight fishing for one-hundred-plus-pound tarpon on clear flats, when it's right, it's like nothing else.

Although the fish are enormous, the flies are tiny in comparison; 3 or 4 inches seems to be the standard. Unlike the more realistic flies used for the other two players in the flats Grand Slam, bonefish and permit, tarpon flies don't necessarily look like food. Bait fishermen take tarpon on live crabs, small fish, and shrimp, but there are few flies used with regularity on the flats that closely resemble any of these. Tarpon on the flats can be temperamental. A fly that can't make it back to the boat without drawing a strike one day will consistently draw nothing more than a shun the next. Often, there doesn't appear to be any reason for the change. Rather than concentrating on imitating the food of the tarpon, many fly fishermen come prepared with flies in three color types: light, neutral, and dark. If one color is refused a couple of times, a different color is given a chance.

The Tarpon Tricolor is my light tarpon fly. I try to build in as much color as I can by using three hot colors—yellow, orange, and red. At the rear of the fly, I add a couple of turns of plastic chenille and Krystal Flash to catch and reflect light. At the front I stagger dyed Polar Hair in yellow, orange, and red. No natural material can duplicate Polar Hair. Each individual hair is like a tiny splinter of stained glass reflecting colored light in every direction. If the tarpon are in an aggressive mood, there is not a more conspicuous fly I can throw.

My neutral fly, The King's Shrimp, is more suggestive of food than any of my other tarpon flies. I wanted a pattern that I could use for tarpon when they were in a passive mood, as they often are in Florida Bay. These fish aren't really moving anywhere or doing anything. At times they can be exasperating, refusing every fly thrown at them. The King's Shrimp, with its natural coloration and resemblance to a shrimp, will often draw a strike when nothing else has worked, especially in a smaller size.

The Reluctant Peacock is one of my most reliable dark flies. I wanted a dark fly with enough color and reflected light to keep it interesting—if not to the tarpon, at least to me. I wanted to avoid an all-black, heavy-looking fly. I combined dyed grizzly hackles at the rear and a wound black hackle collar to provide a strong silhouette. If you limit the synthetics to a few strands of Krystal Flash at the rear and use naturally iridescent materials from the peacock, the reflected light is subtle but apparent. The result is a darker fly with a strong profile that still maintains a lifelike quality.

During the rest of the year, when the larger, migratory tarpon are elsewhere, the waters around the Keys continue to furnish fly-fishing opportunities. Closer to the Everglades and mainland Florida, on the flats and along the mangrove islands of Florida Bay referred to as the backcountry, resident tarpon can always be found. These young tarpon, up to thirty pounds or so, respond well to a fly dropped in front of them on a flat or tucked into a shoreline pocket. In addition, snook and redfish cruise these same waters. It is not uncommon to have many shots at all three species in the course of a day, and catching one of each in a day, a "backcountry slam," is a real possibility. With the addition of the ever-present speckled trout, you can never be sure which of the four will show up.

Because it is impossible to know in advance to which species I'll be casting, I wanted a fly that I could use to take all four of these fish. In addition the fly had to have a few special characteristics. First, because of the heavy grass flats and mangrove shorelines, it had to be weedless. Second, it had to have a lot of built-in action; I didn't want to depend on manipulating the fly to give it lifelike action. When cast against a mangrove shoreline, it had to look alive immediately; snook and tarpon won't chase a fly far from the protection of the mangroves. On the flats, redfish often have their heads buried in the grass, and the water is sometimes discolored. As a result, they often have trouble seeing a fly as it is retrieved past them. The fly had to look alive with a minimal retrieve, even when sitting motionless on the

9	Backcountry Slammer
Tail	White rabbit, marked with a green Sharpie; three or four strands of Krystal Flash on each side
Collar	White and red soft saddle hackles
Head	Pearl Estaz and nontoxic red eyes
Weed Guard	20-pound Ande

1. With the thread just above the hook point, tie in a tail of a white rabbit Zonker strip that has been barred with a green Sharpie marking pen. Add three or four strands of Krystal Flash on each side of the tail.

2. Just in front of the tail wrap white, then red, soft hackle as a collar.

3. Wrap the entire body with pearl Estaz.

4. Place the red nontoxic eyes.

5. Add the weed guard.

bottom, giving the redfish time to find the fly. Third, it had to sink, either to the level of the fish on the flats or vertically against an undercut mangrove shore.

The result, the Backcountry Slammer, does all these things. The double-mono weed guards resist snagging even when the fly is punched into a mangrove pocket a couple of feet too far. The Slammer can be crawled out of the branches, slipping into the water just inches from the shore. The rabbit tail and soft collar breathe in response to the slightest retrieve or water current. In fact, this fly looks so good in the water that a tarpon once picked it up off the bottom, where it lay motionless, while I worked on a tangle in my fly line. (The ensuing fight, while short lived, was memorable.) And by using differently weighted eyes, the sink rate is easily varied for different water depths. I'm confident that the Slammer will work on most fish in the backcountry. There is seldom reason to change flies, except to see if something else will work as well.

The Mangrove Skipper is a companion to the Slammer. I wanted a fly that had a profile a little more like the broad forage fish on which game fish like to feed—pinfish in Florida Bay and talapi farther up in the Everglades, where the water sweetens. The Skipper has many of the same characteristics as the Slammer—it's weedless, has a lot of action, and sinks readily. I usually use the chartreuse variation to imitate pinfish and an orange version for talapi. In addition to snook and redfish, it takes the largemouth bass that begin to show up the farther you go into the Everglades.

1   Sea Popper—Blue Mackerel

Tails	Pearl and silver Flashabou on each side; two white, two light blue, two medium blue, one dark blue grizzly saddle. The two sides meet at the top to form a tent shape
Head	$^3/_4$ inch of $^5/_8$-inch Live Body, covered with bluetone Minnow Body. Mylar is left long and frayed to form a skirt. Apply stick-on eyes and epoxy to finish

2   Sea Slider—Flying Fish

Tails	Pearl Flashabou on each side; then two white, two chartreuse, one light blue, one dark blue. The two sides are assembled so that they meet at the top to form a tent shape. Tie in a tuft of red marabou at the throat
Head	$^3/_4$ inch of $^5/_8$-inch Live Body, formed into a slider shape, covered with pearl Minnow Body, and frayed to form a skirt. Apply stick-on eyes and epoxy to finish

3   Sea Bait—Blue Ballyhoo

Bottom Half	Polar bear FisHair; pearl Krystal Flash
Top Half	Chartreuse Krystal Flash; light blue FisHair; smolt blue Krystal Flash; a small amount of medium blue FisHair over the top
Head/Back	Pearl mylar piping over the tie-in point of FisHair and over the extended narrow tube. Finish the beak with hot orange tying thread. Apply stick-on eyes and epoxy to finish

4   Sea Bait—Gray Grizz

Bottom Half	White polar bear FisHair; lavender Krystal Flash
Top Half	Light blue FisHair; smolt blue Krystal Flash; olive FisHair; gray FisHair; black FisHair
Sides	Slender grizzly saddle on each side
Head	Pearl mylar braid and stick-on eyes, finished with epoxy

5   Reluctant Peacock

Tails	Six to eight strands of pearl Krystal Flash; chartreuse, blue, green grizzly
Gill Patch	On each side, a short male peacock feather
Collar	Black hackle, followed by a male peacock blue breast feather
Head	Black with green eyes

6   The King's Shrimp

Aft	Three turns of pearl Estaz; six strands of light yellow Krystal Flash; a short tuft of orange marabou; a short tuft of apricot marabou
Tails	Three pairs of light cree neck hackles
Eyes	Epoxy over burned 80-pound monofilament
Collar	Light cree hackle
Body	Dubbed arctic fox tail; copper-tinted Lite Brite
Legs	Wound cree hackle
Dorsal Surface	Holographic piping, tinted copper, pulled over the collar and body, and tied down

7   Tarpon Tricolor

Aft	Bloodred Estaz; yellow Krystal Flash
Tail	Red, yellow, and orange grizzly on each side
Collars	Yellow, orange, and red Polar Hair, staggered
Head	Black with red eyes

8   Mangrove Skipper

Tail	Chartreuse rabbit with a chartreuse grizzly neck hackle on each side; three strands of chartreuse Krystal Flash
Collar	White, chartreuse, and dark green marabou, over which are ten to twelve peacock herls
Head	White, chartreuse, and light green Flashabou dubbing, mixed and wound through glass taxidermy eyes
Weed Guard	20-pound Ande

1	2
3	
	4
5	
	6
7	
8	9

Chris Windram

One of my earliest memories is of my grandfather's cabin in the mountains of Pennsylvania near Seven Springs. I think it was on my fourth birthday, my family took me fishing on the pond near the cabin. In the very center of the pond was a windmill, which pumped the water into the pond. I don't remember casting into the pond, but I remember watching a little bobber as it floated by the leg of the windmill. And I remember seeing the bobber go down and reeling in a fish.

I was very excited. I wanted to know all about it; what kind of fish it was. My paternal grandfather, George Windram, told me that it was a sunfish. I turned my face to the sky to feel the warmth of that midsummer sun. The name of the fish took on a power for me and the experience was illuminating. Until that time, I had many questions, one of which was, Why are we here? I felt as if I had the answer.

I remember being fascinated with fish from that time on, though as a young boy I didn't get to fish very often. When my family moved to eastern Pennsylvania, I found myself surrounded by farm ponds filled with sunfish and largemouth bass. It was here that I came to understand the habits of those species. I spent hours fishing.

When I was in my teens, I began to fish for trout in a small nearby stream. It was also about this time that my maternal grandfather, Francis Prunier, told me captivating stories of the great striped bass he had caught. Although I didn't realize it at the time, the stream where I fished for trout flowed into the Chesapeake Bay. I wouldn't catch a striped bass for another ten years, but at that time I was probably only half an hour away from stripers in the upper Chesapeake.

Although I fly-fished sporadically, I was far from being proficient at it. I didn't develop any real fly-fishing skills until my early twenties. Attending college in Boston, I began to make frequent trips to Walden Pond, that body of water lovingly described by Henry David Thoreau in *Walden.*

Later I vacationed in the Berkshire Mountains of western Massachusetts, and it was here that I began to fly-fish seriously for trout. It was also here that I tied my first trout fly, from the feathers of songbirds scrounged from streamside brush. I caught my first brook trout on a wet fly made from robin feathers lashed to a hook with sewing thread. Soon after, I moved to southern Berkshire County.

I never had any formal training in fly tying. But I was so fascinated that within two or three years, I was tying flies to sell to Lake Buel General Store in Monterey, Massachusetts.

I gained a thorough education in fly fishing for trout on the streams and rivers of western Massachusetts. My understanding of the way fish relate to structure and current in fresh water translated well into helping me understand fly fishing in salt water.

It was about this time that I read a book about surf fishing—*Reading the Water,* by Robert Post. The book's description of striped bass fishing in New England triggered memories of my grandfather's stories. Within a couple of weeks, I started striped bass fishing on the Hudson River near Croton, New York, where a friend of mine lived.

This was not fly fishing. We fished bait on the bottom. But it was an important event for me to catch my first striper.

Soon after, I began to take trips to Martha's Vineyard, and here I took my first striper on a fly. I also caught my first bluefish, bonito, and false albacore.

Around this time I stopped selling flies for fresh water and began tying saltwater flies professionally. The diversity of the saltwater environment, the pelagic nature of the game fish, and the possibility of catching large fish on a fly were huge draws to a lifelong fishing fanatic.

I've always had dreams about fishing. If you were to put my dreams about fishing into a book, it might be called Fly Fishing on Other Planets. These dreams include fantastic visions of fishing in otherworldly settings, of fish that swim through liquid atmospheres.

I have two dreams about what I'd like to do in fly fishing. The lesser dream is to go quietly into the past with a fly rod. The greater is to go boldly into the future with a fly rod.

A local filmmaker here in Berkshire County did a very short film, a parody of fishing, in which the main character proclaims his philosophy about fishing. He says, "The number of fish that a man will catch on any given day is already predetermined by the manner in which he approaches the trout stream. Inner attitude is everything. It determines the length, it determines the limit, and it determines the number over the limit that he might want to bring home."

Apart from the humorous comment on human nature at the end of that statement, I believe that attitude *is* everything. The fly fisher has no more important tool than him- or herself—a healthy mind and body. For me, fly fishing is an endless journey, a pathway toward learning and enjoying life. If we are here to live joyously, for me there is no more joyous expression of living than fly fishing.

My challenge has become not to catch fish, but to assist others in the fulfillment of their fly-fishing dreams. I have taken to guiding on the Housatonic River and find that helping others catch fish is at least as satisfying as catching fish myself. I also assist others in their angling through my work as a saltwater fly tier.

I have a vision for what I do in fly tying. I try to incorporate the traditional with the modern. I have a fondness for flies that are finished with polish and flair. Each tier develops his or her own personal style; I like my own flies to have an aesthetic element as well as utility as fishing lures. Flies made by people who fish have magic in them, an expression of the connection between fly tying and fly fishing.

Anytime we sit down to tie flies, we borrow from the creativity of those tiers who have come before us. My earliest influences in saltwater tying came from Lefty Kreh and Stu Apte. I enjoy tying and fishing the

5	**Epoxy Marabou**
Hook	Mustad 34007, #1
Thread	Chartreuse
Tail	Marabou plume over white bucktail; pearl Krystal Flash
Body	Epoxy over pearl mylar tubing
Eyes	1/8-inch prismatic eyes

1. Start the thread just behind the hook eye and wrap to the back of the hook, just above the hook barb.

2. Tie in sparse white bucktail for a tail. At the same spot, tie in pearl Krystal Flash. Finally, tie in a chartreuse marabou plume.

3. For the body, tie in pearl mylar tubing.

4. Place the eyes.

5. Paint on red gill slits.

6. Epoxy the entire body.

This is my favorite fly for bonito. I fished this the first time I made a boat trip for bonito with Captain Jon "Moe" Flaherty of Vineyard Haven, Massachusetts. I remember that Moe was fishing a new 7-weight rod, which had been given to him. Using his well-developed fish sense, Moe placed us in the path of a school of hot-running bonito. When the school erupted around the boat, Moe placed a cast into the middle of the fray. A big bonito followed and then boiled on the fly. Moe kept his cool and continued to retrieve, slowing down the fly, his face contorting into a grimace. It was a moment I'll never forget when the bonito took the hook and the rod exploded at the butt!

Deceiver and rabbit strip styles of fly. Later, I was influenced by the more modern styles of Page Rogers, Bob Popovics, and Glen Mikkelson. These tiers, with others, began a tradition of imitation here in the Northeast for generations of tiers to come.

Saltwater patterns of the past were frequently impressionistic flies designed to take fish, but not necessarily to imitate them. Following the tradition of imitation known to freshwater tiers, New England tiers are leading the way in creating specific prey imitations for salt water.

If I have a hope for the future, it is to see anglers convert to fly fishing. Becoming a fly fisher leads you to learn more about the fish and its environment. It is important to encourage this attitude of learning, because it is this kind of understanding that will help preserve our fisheries for the future.

It would be incorrect to say that what I have learned about fishing has come entirely from my own efforts. I would not be where I am today without the generous help of others: my family, friends, and many others along the way.

Thanks to the efforts of people like Bob Veverka, we can witness the creativity of those who tie flies for salt water.

1	**Sand Eel Special**
Hook	Mustad 34011, #1
Thread	Light olive
Tail	Fly Fur or craft fur, olive over white; pearl Krystal Flash
Body	E-Z Shape Sparkle Body; use pearl tinsel for the lateral line
Eyes	Painted, black on yellow

New England fly fishers should never be without a sand eel imitation.

2	**Deep Sea Serpent**
Hook	Mustad 34007, #1
Thread	Chartreuse
Tail	Chartreuse rabbit fur strip, 2 to 3 inches long
Body	Rabbit fur strip, palmered
Hackle	Two white hackle collars, one behind and one in front of the eyes
Eyes	1/24-inch lead eyes, painted black on white

This is one of the most useful and most popular flies that I produce. It's a big favorite among anglers on Nantucket Island.

3	**Windram's Worm Fly**
Hook	Mustad 34007, #1
Thread	Black
Tail	Pink rabbit fur
Body	E-Z Shape Sparkle Body
Head	Dimensional craft paint

I tie this fly in pinks, reds, and oranges to imitate swarming cinder worms and palolo worms.

4	**Chris' Squid**
Hook	Mustad 34011, #1/0
Thread	Pink
Tail	Tan, white, and grizzly saddle hackles; Flashabou and Krystal Flash accents over white bucktail
Body	E-Z Shape Sparkle Body
Eyes	7-millimeter doll eyes
Head	Tan rabbit fur collar; grizzly hackle collar

I think it was John Gierach who said that freshwater fly tiers are in constant competition to see who can create the cutest mouse. Every saltwater tier has his or her own pet squid imitation; this is mine. Captain Karen Kukolich showed me a squid fly with a rabbit fur collar. I incorporated this design into my own fly.

6	**Chartreuse Bucktail**
Hook	Mustad 34007, #1
Thread	Black
Tail	Chartreuse bucktail
Wing	White bucktail; chartreuse bucktail; olive and silver Krystal Flash
Eyes	1/8-inch prismatic eyes

This style of fly is my own variation on a Joe Brooks's Blonde. It is very popular among New England tiers. I use it to imitate sand eels and silversides.

7	**March Hare**
Hook	Mustad 34007, #1
Thread	Light olive
Tail	Light olive rabbit fur strip over white calf tail
Body	Epoxy over pearl mylar tubing
Eyes	1/8-inch prismatic eyes

Originally, the March Hare was made with a mottled gray rabbit fur strip to imitate the markings of mummichogs. This fly produces well in estuaries for small bass. In various colors, it works well in many different situations.

8	**Lefty's Deceiver—Menhaden**
Hook	Mustad 34007, #5/0
Thread	White
Tail	Six to eight white saddle hackles; pearl Flashabou
Wing	White bucktail; pale chartreuse saddles; olive bucktail; Krystal Flash accents; peacock herl topping
Eyes	5/16-inch prismatic eyes under epoxy

Influences on this big fly came from tiers such as Mark Sedotti and Bill Peabody. Freshwater tiers delight in learning to tie the tiniest flies; saltwater tiers delight in trying to make the biggest.

9	**American Eel**
Hook	Mustad 34007, #3/0
Thread	Olive
Tail	Olive rabbit fur strip, cut wide, over white bucktail
Body	Olive wool, spun and trimmed
Eyes	1/24-inch lead eyes, painted black on red

I tied this fly to imitate the small eels that stripers love to feed on. Although I have never used live eels as bait for stripers, I used to fish for eels in Big Elk Creek near my home in New London, Pennsylvania. A full mono weed guard keeps this fly from snagging while fishing among the rocks, and keeps the long rabbit fur tail from fouling on the hook during the cast.

10	**Lefty's Deceiver—Tinker Mackerel**
Hook	Mustad 34007, #3/0
Thread	Chartreuse
Tail	Four to six white saddle hackles
Body	Pearlescent mylar tinsel
Wing	White and chartreuse bucktail; blue-green Flashabou; Krystal Flash accents; peacock herl topping
Eyes	1/4-inch prismatic eyes, coated with epoxy

Glen Mikkleson showed me a fly like this several years ago, and I loved it so much I had to make one of my own. I never miss an opportunity to fish this fly if game fish are feeding on mackerel, and I never miss an opportunity to catch a mackerel in order to look at it. What a beautiful fish!

8
9
10

Index

Lily Cay Flats by Chet Reneson